Microsoft® Outlook™ For Dummies

COMPUTER BOOK SERIES FROM IDG

Cheat Sheet

W9-CMD-340

Outlook Toolbars

Clicking an icon in the Toolbar is a super-speedy way to open any item in Outlook. Some tools disappear when not needed, so don't be surprised if your toolbars look different from these at times.

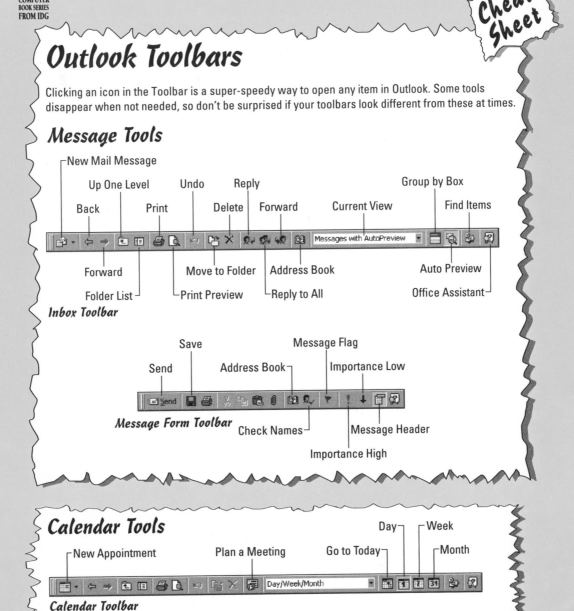

Message Tools

Inbox Toolbar — New Mail Message, Up One Level, Back, Print, Undo, Delete, Reply, Forward, Current View, Group by Box, Find Items, Forward, Move to Folder, Folder List, Print Preview, Address Book, Reply to All, Auto Preview, Office Assistant

Messages with AutoPreview

Message Form Toolbar — Send, Save, Address Book, Message Flag, Importance Low, Check Names, Importance High, Message Header

Calendar Tools

Calendar Toolbar — New Appointment, Plan a Meeting, Go to Today, Day, Week, Month

Day/Week/Month

Appointment Form Toolbar — Save and Close, Invite Attendees, Recurrence, Insert File, Previous Item, Next Item

Microsoft® Outlook™ For Dummies®

COMPUTER BOOK SERIES FROM IDG

Cheat Sheet

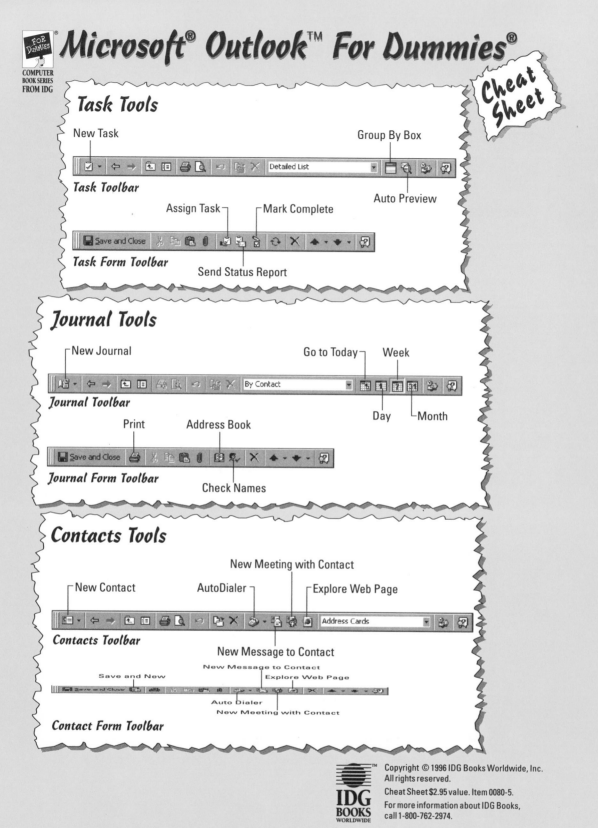

Task Tools

New Task

Group By Box

Detailed List

Task Toolbar

Auto Preview

Assign Task — Mark Complete

Save and Close

Task Form Toolbar

Send Status Report

Journal Tools

New Journal

Go to Today — Week

By Contact

Journal Toolbar

Day — Month

Print — Address Book

Save and Close

Journal Form Toolbar

Check Names

Contacts Tools

New Meeting with Contact

New Contact — AutoDialer — Explore Web Page

Address Cards

Contacts Toolbar

New Message to Contact

Save and New — New Message to Contact — Explore Web Page

Save and Close

Contact Form Toolbar

Auto Dialer — New Meeting with Contact

...For Dummies: #1 Computer Book Series for Beginners

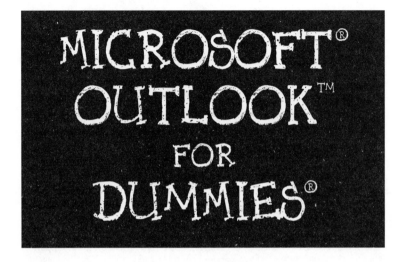

by Bill Dyszel

IDG
BOOKS
WORLDWIDE

IDG Books Worldwide, Inc.
An International Data Group Company

Foster City, CA ♦ Chicago, IL ♦ Indianapolis, IN ♦ New York, NY

Microsoft® Outlook™ For Dummies®

Published by
IDG Books Worldwide, Inc.
An International Data Group Company
919 E. Hillsdale Blvd.
Suite 400
Foster City, CA 94404
www.idgbooks.com (IDG Books Worldwide Web site)
www.dummies.com (Dummies Press Web site)

Library of Congress Catalog Card No.: 96-80190

ISBN: 0-7645-0080-5

Printed in the United States of America

10 9 8 7 6 5 4

1DD/TQ/QW/ZY/IN

Distributed in the United States by IDG Books Worldwide, Inc.

Distributed by Macmillan Canada for Canada; by Transworld Publishers Limited in the United Kingdom; by IDG Norge Books for Norway; by IDG Sweden Books for Sweden; by Woodslane Pty. Ltd. for Australia; by Woodslane Enterprises Ltd. for New Zealand; by Longman Singapore Publishers Ltd. for Singapore, Malaysia, Thailand, and Indonesia; by Simron Pty. Ltd. for South Africa; by Toppan Company Ltd. for Japan; by Distribuidora Cuspide for Argentina; by Livraria Cultura for Brazil; by Ediciencia S.A. for Ecuador; by Addison-Wesley Publishing Company for Korea; by Ediciones ZETA S.C.R. Ltda. for Peru; by WS Computer Publishing Corporation, Inc., for the Philippines; by Unalis Corporation for Taiwan; by Contemporanea de Ediciones for Venezuela; by Computer Book & Magazine Store for Puerto Rico; by Express Computer Distributors for the Caribbean and West Indies. Authorized Sales Agent: Anthony Rudkin Associates for the Middle East and North Africa.

For general information on IDG Books Worldwide's books in the U.S., please call our Consumer Customer Service department at 800-762-2974. For reseller information, including discounts and premium sales, please call our Reseller Customer Service department at 800-434-3422.

For information on where to purchase IDG Books Worldwide's books outside the U.S., please contact our International Sales department at 650-655-3200 or fax 650-655-3297.

For information on foreign language translations, please contact our Foreign & Subsidiary Rights department at 650-655-3021 or fax 650-655-3281.

For sales inquiries and special prices for bulk quantities, please contact our Sales department at 650-655-3200 or write to the address above.

For information on using IDG Books Worldwide's books in the classroom or for ordering examination copies, please contact our Educational Sales department at 800-434-2086 or fax 317-596-5499.

For press review copies, author interviews, or other publicity information, please contact our Public Relations department at 650-655-3000 or fax 650-655-3299.

For authorization to photocopy items for corporate, personal, or educational use, please contact Copyright Clearance Center, 222 Rosewood Drive, Danvers, MA 01923, or fax 978-750-4470.

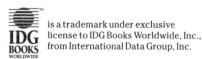 is a trademark under exclusive license to IDG Books Worldwide, Inc., from International Data Group, Inc.

About the Author

Bill Dyszel likes to make complicated things seem simple. He writes frequently for leading computer magazines, including *PC Magazine, Windows Sources,* and *Computer Shopper,* while also working as a consultant to many of the leading firms in the securities, advertising, and publishing industries. His consulting practice, PC Studio (`www.pcstudio.com`), focuses on providing business solutions and training to users of office automation programs such as Microsoft Office 97.

The world of high technology has led Bill to grapple with such subjects as Multimedia (or how to make your $2,000 computer do the work of a $20 radio), Personal Information Managers (how to make your $3,000 laptop computer do the work of a $3.00 date book), and graphics programs (how to make your $5,000 package of computers and peripheral devices do the work of a 50-cent box of crayons). All joking aside, he has found that once you figure out the process, most of this stuff can be useful, helpful, and, yes, even cool. He'll gladly send you his periodic e-mail newsletter about the things he finds useful; just drop a note to his e-mail address (`BillDyszel@pcstudio.com`).

Like many public figures with skeletons in their closets, this author has a secret past. Before entering the computer industry, Bill sang with the New York City Opera and worked regularly on the New York stage as a singer, actor, and writer in a number of plays, musicals, and operas. He even turns up in the movie *Big* for about one second (watch closely). His opera spoof — *99% ARTFREE!* — won critical praise from *The New York Times,* New York *Daily News,* and the *Associated Press* when he performed the show Off-Broadway. The success of *99% ARTFREE!* has often prompted the author to consider creating a similar musical spoof on high technology, but so far he feels that high technology looks ridiculous enough without his help. He lives in New York City.

ABOUT IDG BOOKS WORLDWIDE

Welcome to the world of IDG Books Worldwide.

IDG Books Worldwide, Inc., is a subsidiary of International Data Group, the world's largest publisher of computer-related information and the leading global provider of information services on information technology. IDG was founded more than 25 years ago and now employs more than 8,500 people worldwide. IDG publishes more than 275 computer publications in over 75 countries (see listing below). More than 90 million people read one or more IDG publications each month.

Launched in 1990, IDG Books Worldwide is today the #1 publisher of best-selling computer books in the United States. We are proud to have received eight awards from the Computer Press Association in recognition of editorial excellence and three from *Computer Currents'* First Annual Readers' Choice Awards. Our best-selling *...For Dummies®* series has more than 50 million copies in print with translations in 38 languages. IDG Books Worldwide, through a joint venture with IDG's Hi-Tech Beijing, became the first U.S. publisher to publish a computer book in the People's Republic of China. In record time, IDG Books Worldwide has become the first choice for millions of readers around the world who want to learn how to better manage their businesses.

Our mission is simple: Every one of our books is designed to bring extra value and skill-building instructions to the reader. Our books are written by experts who understand and care about our readers. The knowledge base of our editorial staff comes from years of experience in publishing, education, and journalism — experience we use to produce books for the '90s. In short, we care about books, so we attract the best people. We devote special attention to details such as audience, interior design, use of icons, and illustrations. And because we use an efficient process of authoring, editing, and desktop publishing our books electronically, we can spend more time ensuring superior content and spend less time on the technicalities of making books.

You can count on our commitment to deliver high-quality books at competitive prices on topics you want to read about. At IDG Books Worldwide, we continue in the IDG tradition of delivering quality for more than 25 years. You'll find no better book on a subject than one from IDG Books Worldwide.

John Kilcullen
CEO
IDG Books Worldwide, Inc.

Steven Berkowitz
President and Publisher
IDG Books Worldwide, Inc.

Eighth Annual Computer Press Awards 1992

Ninth Annual Computer Press Awards 1993

Tenth Annual Computer Press Awards 1994

Eleventh Annual Computer Press Awards 1995

Author's Acknowledgments

A book like this is not the product of one person's effort — it's a collaboration. I'd like to thank all the wonderful people from IDG Books who helped me make this book entertaining and useful to the reader, especially Kathy Cox, the tireless but ever-cheerful Project Editor of this book, and Acquisitions Editor Gareth Hancock, who gave me the chance to write my first ...*For Dummies* book. I'm grateful for the help and support of everyone I've encountered at IDG, especially Mary Bednarek, Diane Steele, Judi Taylor, Seta Frantz, Gwenette Gaddis, Debbie Stailey, and Darlene Wong, as well as dozens of other people I haven't yet had the pleasure of meeting.

Special thanks also goes to my friend Mike Zulich for an unfailingly thorough and accurate technical review. Thanks to my friends, editors, and colleagues at *Windows Sources* magazine, especially Gayle Ehrenman, Kathleen Caster, and Patrick Norton; the good folks at *Computer Shopper* magazine, especially Francesca Boseckar and Brooke Wurst; and the people at *PC Magazine*. Thanks also to the people at Waggener Edstrom, especially Jeanne Bolduc and Kevin Murphy, for helping pry information out of Microsoft that I couldn't pry myself and to the people at Microsoft who also helped me figure things out, including Scott Gode, Lani Ota, and Dale Maynard.

My personal cheering section has also been a big help, including Jack Walters, Gloria Norris, Bob Aspland, and the whole "Back-to-back" gang at the YMCA, Shelley Reciniello at the Ritz, as well as the Westside M&M club, including Simone, Elissa, Jim, and Bill, and my improv comedy companions who helped me keep it light. Last but not least, thanks to my sweetheart Leigh Williams, who put up with my long hours and sometimes grumpy moods while writing this book.

Publisher's Acknowledgments

We're proud of this book; please register your comments through our IDG Books Worldwide Online Registration Form located at: http://my2cents.dummies.com.

Some of the people who helped bring this book to market include the following:

Acquisitions, Development, and Editorial

Project Editor: Kathleen M. Cox

Senior Acquisitions Editor: Jill Pisoni

Acquisitions Editor: Gareth Hancock

Product Development Director: Mary Bednarek

Media Development Manager: Joyce Pepple

Copy Editor: Kathy Simpson

Technical Editor: Michael Zulich

Editorial Manager: Mary C. Corder

Editorial Assistant: Michael D. Sullivan

Production

Project Coordinator: Debbie Stailey

Layout and Graphics: E. Shawn Aylsworth, J. Tyler Connor, Elizabeth Cárdenas-Nelson, Maridee V. Ennis, Angela F. Hunckler, Todd Klemme, Drew R. Moore, Brent Savage, Kate Snell

Proofreaders: Melissa D. Buddendeck, Kelli Botta, Rachel Garvey, Nancy Price, Dwight Ramsey, Robert Springer, Carrie Voorhis

Indexer: Sherry Massey

Special Help
Mary Goodwin, Project Editor

General and Administrative

IDG Books Worldwide, Inc.: John Kilcullen, CEO; Steven Berkowitz, President and Publisher

IDG Books Technology Publishing: Brenda McLaughlin, Senior Vice President and Group Publisher

Dummies Technology Press and Dummies Editorial: Diane Graves Steele, Vice President and Associate Publisher; Mary Bednarek, Director of Acquisitions and Product Development; Kristin A. Cocks, Editorial Director

Dummies Trade Press: Kathleen A. Welton, Vice President and Publisher; Kevin Thornton, Acquisitions Manager

IDG Books Production for Dummies Press: Michael R. Britton, Vice President of Production; Beth Jenkins Roberts, Production Director; Cindy L. Phipps, Manager of Project Coordination, Production Proofreading, and Indexing; Kathie S. Schutte, Supervisor of Page Layout; Shelley Lea, Supervisor of Graphics and Design; Debbie J. Gates, Production Systems Specialist; Robert Springer, Supervisor of Proofreading; Debbie Stailey, Special Projects Coordinator; Tony Augsburger, Supervisor of Reprints and Bluelines

Dummies Packaging and Book Design: Robin Seaman, Creative Director; Jocelyn Kelaita, Product Packaging Coordinator; Kavish + Kavish, Cover Design

♦

The publisher would like to give special thanks to Patrick J. McGovern, without whom this book would not have been possible.

♦

Contents at a Glance

Cartoons at a Glance

By Rich Tennant

page 9

page 191

page 297

page 95

page 130

Fax: 978-546-7747 • E-mail: the5wave@tiac.net

Table of Contents

· ·

Introduction

• •

*U*p until now, every time you added a handy new function to your computer, you had to get a whole new computer program, which usually confronted you with a new look, menus, tools, and directions. Worst of all, you were supposed to pore through tons of boring documentation to get any benefit from this new whatchamacallit. That was great for the folks who make a living translating all that gobbledygook into plain English but lousy for normal people who just need to get their work done.

Microsoft has been studying how actual people — not geeks — use software. (Now that Microsoft has most of the money in the world, it has time for things like that.) The company has designed the current line of Office 97 products to work more like you do, rather than forcing you to work more like the computer.

Outlook is one of the results of the Microsoft studies. The program pulls together the jobs that most people use most of the time, such as finding addresses, sending e-mail, or making appointments. Outlook puts several functions in one screen and makes a bunch of different functions speak the same language and follow the same directions (pretty much). Although Outlook is one of several programs in the Office 97 suite, you can take advantage of Outlook's communicative skills in any Office 97 program.

You still use your word processing and spreadsheet programs for the same highfalutin stuff that you always did, but you use Outlook to deal with all those itsy-bitsy details that fill your life, such as

- ✔ Finding the customer's phone number
- ✔ Remembering that important meeting
- ✔ Planning your tasks for the day and checking them off when you're done
- ✔ Recording all the work you do so that you can find what you did and when you did it

Outlook is a Personal Information Manager (Microsoft calls it a Desktop Information Manager) that can act as your assistant in dealing with the flurry of small but important details that stand between you and the work you do. You can just as easily keep track of personal information that isn't business related and keep both business and personal information in the same convenient location.

Who Should Buy This Book

Outlook is a completely new product. As you read this book and work with Outlook, you'll discover how useful Outlook is, as well as new ways to make it more useful for the things you do most. If you fit any of these categories, this book is meant for you:

- ✔ You're planning to purchase Office 97 or Outlook and want to know what you can do with Outlook and how to do it.

- ✔ You've already purchased Office 97 or Outlook and want to get up to speed quickly.

- ✔ You've used versions of Microsoft Office sold before 1997 and want to see how much easier Outlook can make your work.

- ✔ You want an easier, more efficient tool for managing tasks, schedules, e-mail, and other details in your working life.

Even if you don't fall into one of these groups, this book is aimed to give you a simple, clear guided tour of what you can get from Outlook. It's hard to imagine any computer user who wouldn't benefit from the features that Outlook offers.

How This Book Is Organized

To make it easier to find out how to do what you want to do, this book is divided into parts. Each part covers a different aspect of using Outlook. Because you can use similar methods to do many different jobs with Outlook, the first parts of the book focus on how to use Outlook. The later parts concentrate on what you can use Outlook to do.

Part I: The Outlook Lookout

I learn best by doing, so the first chapter is a fanciful, but not entirely fictional story about the things you can do with Outlook on a typical day. You'll see how easy it is to use Outlook for routine tasks like messages, phone calls, and appointments. You can get quite a lot of mileage out of Outlook even if you only do the things our fictional detective does in the first chapter.

Because Outlook allows you to use similar methods to do many things, I go on to show you the things that stay pretty much the same throughout the program: how to create new items from old ones by using drag and drop, ways to view items that make your information easy to understand at a glance, as well as the features Outlook offers to make it easier to move, copy, and organize your files.

Part II: E-Mail and Contacts: Not Just Playing Post Office

E-mail is now the most popular function of computers; tens of millions of people are hooked up to the Internet, an office network, or to one of the popular online services, such as the Microsoft Network and CompuServe.

The problem is that e-mail can still be a little too complicated. Outlook makes it easier. Computers are notoriously finicky about the exact spelling of addresses, correctly hooking up to the actual mail service, and making sure that the text and formatting of the message fit the software you're using. Outlook keeps track of the details involved in getting your message to its destination.

Outlook also allows you to receive e-mail from a variety of sources and manage the messages in one place. You can slice and dice your list of incoming and outgoing e-mail messages to help you keep track of what you send, to whom you send it, and the day and time you send it. Some folks even use their e-mail as primitive to-do lists; Outlook allows you to flag each message to make it easier to use your collection of e-mail messages any way you want.

Part III: Taking Care of Business

Outlook takes advantage of its special relationship with your computer and your office applications (*Microsoft* Outlook with *Microsoft* Office and *Microsoft* Windows — notice a pattern emerging here?) to tie your office tasks together more cleanly than other such programs and make it easier for you to deal with all the stuff that you have to do and when you have to do it.

Beyond planning and scheduling, you probably spend a great deal of your working time with other people, and you need to coordinate your schedule with theirs (unless you make your living doing something strange and antisocial, such as digging graves or writing computer books). Outlook allows you to share schedule and task information with other people (if you're on the same network) and synchronize with them. You can also assign tasks to other people if you don't want to do them yourself (now *there's* a time-saver). Be careful, though; other people can assign those tasks right back to you.

If you've got yellow sticky notes covering your monitor, refrigerator, desktop, or bathroom door, you'll get a great deal of mileage out of the Notes feature of Outlook. Notes are little yellow (or blue, or green) squares that look just like those handy paper sticky notes that we stick everywhere as reminders and then lose. About the only thing that you can't do is set your coffee cup on one and mess up what you wrote.

Sometimes, the "find-the-sticky-note" game takes a dark turn; you don't remember *what* you jotted down, you don't remember *where* you put the note, but you do remember *when* you wrote it. That's when Outlook's automatic Journal feature comes in handy. The Journal keeps track of every document that you create, edit, or print; it remembers when you sent e-mail to anyone and when you scheduled that important appointment. You can also make a Journal entry to remember any task you scheduled or any conversation you had with anyone. If it sounds too Big Brother-ish to have a computer recording everything you do, I'll tell you how to turn the Journal off.

Part IV: The Part of Tens

Why ten? Why not! If you must have a reason, ten is the highest number you can count to without taking off your shoes. A program as broad as Outlook leaves a great deal of flotsam and jetsam that doesn't quite fit into any category, so I sum up the best of that material in groups of ten.

Conventions Used in This Book

If all you want is a quick guided tour of Outlook, you can skim this book; it covers everything that you need to start with. Getting a handle on most of the major features of Outlook is fairly easy; that's how the program is designed. You can also keep the book handy as a reference for the tricks that you might not need every day.

The first part gives you enough information to make sense of the whole. Because Outlook is intended to be simple and consistent throughout, when you've got the big picture, the details are fairly simple (usually).

Don't be fooled by Outlook's friendliness, though — you'll find a great deal of power in it if you want to dig deeply enough. Outlook links up with your Microsoft Office applications, and it's fully programmable by anyone who wants to tackle a little Visual Basic script writing (I don't get into that in this book). You may not want to do the programming yourself, but finding people who can do that for you isn't hard; just ask around.

How much do you need to know?

I'm assuming that you know how to turn on your computer and how to use a mouse and keyboard. If you need a brushup on Windows 95 or Windows NT 4.0 or later, I'll throw in reminders as we go along. If Windows 95 and Microsoft Office are strange to you, picking up *Windows 95 For Dummies* or *Microsoft Office 97 For Windows For Dummies,* both from IDG Books Worldwide, Inc., will be a big help.

If all you have is a copy of this book and a computer running Outlook, you'll
certainly be able to do basic useful things right away, as well as a few fun ones.
After a time, you'll be able to do many fun and useful things; just follow along.

Some helpful terms

To reduce confusion, here are a few things you need to understand.

- ✔ As you move your mouse around, notice that the mouse pointer moves,
  too. If you move the pointer to different areas of the screen, you'll notice
  that it changes shapes, depending on what it's hovering over. Sometimes,
  the pointer is an I-beam; sometimes, it's an arrow; sometimes, it's another
  shape. The shape of the mouse pointer tells you something about what will
  happen if you click the mouse at that spot.

- ✔ *Clicking* means pressing the left mouse button once quickly and letting it
  go. Most of the time, clicking is the way to activate menus and tools.

- ✔ *Right-clicking* means pressing the right mouse button once. It's possible to
  set your mouse to reverse the mouse buttons, if you're left-handed. If
  you've reversed the buttons, when I say *right-click,* do the opposite and
  left-click.

- ✔ *Double-clicking* means clicking the left mouse button twice, quickly, in the
  same place. Some commands are activated by double-clicking.

- ✔ *Dragging* means holding the left mouse button down while moving the
  mouse. You'll do a great deal of dragging in Outlook because dragging's an
  easy way to create new contacts, tasks, and messages. Dragging isn't such
  a drag; it's really easy.

You'll often tell Outlook what to do by choosing from menus at the top of the
screen. Each menu command has one letter underlined; File, Edit, Help, which
means that you can hold the Alt key while pressing the underlined letter to
open the menu; press Alt+F to open the File menu, Alt+E to see the Edit menu,
or Alt+H to see the Help menu.

One Outlook menu changes its name depending on which Outlook module
you're using. The second-to-last menu, just to the left of the Help menu, says
Calendar when you're using the Calendar, Tasks when you're using the Tasks
module, and so on. When you're using the Inbox, Outbox, or any other Outlook
module that has to do with e-mail, however, this menu is called Compose. (If
you think Compose is a confusing name, I agree; the name Mail would make
more sense to me; I expect a Compose command to write me a symphony or at
least a short rock opera.) Fortunately, the Compose menu choices are fairly
straightforward, and the things you need to do with e-mail are quick and easy to
do without using the menu.

Dialog boxes

Even if you're not new to Windows, you deal with dialog boxes more in Outlook than you do in many other Microsoft Office programs because so many items in Outlook are created with dialog boxes, which may also be called forms. E-mail message forms, appointments, name and address forms, and plenty of other common functions in Outlook use dialog boxes to ask you what you want to do. The essential parts of a dialog box are

- ✔ **Title bar.** The title bar tells you the name of the dialog box.

- ✔ **Text boxes.** Text boxes are blank spaces where you type information. When you click a text box, you see a blinking I-beam pointer, which means that you can type text there.

- ✔ **Control buttons.** In the upper-right corner are three control buttons. The *close button* looks like an X and makes the dialog box disappear. The *size button* toggles between maximizing the dialog box (making it take up the entire screen) and resizing it (making it take up less than the entire screen). The *minimize button* makes the dialog box seem to go away but really just hides it in the taskbar at the bottom of your screen until you click the taskbar to make the dialog box come back.

- ✔ **Tabs.** Tabs look like little file-folder tabs. If you click one, you see a new page of the dialog box. Tabs are just like the divider tabs in a ring binder; click one to change sections.

The easiest way to move around a dialog box is to click the part that you want to use. If you're a real whiz on the keyboard, you may prefer to press the Tab key to move around the dialog box; this method is much faster if you're a touch typist. Otherwise, you're fine just mousing around.

Keyboard shortcuts

Normally, you can choose any Windows command in at least three ways (and sometimes more). You can

- ✔ Choose a menu command or click a toolbar button.

- ✔ Press a keyboard combination such as Ctrl+B, which means holding down the Ctrl key and pressing the letter B to make text bold.

- ✔ Press the F10 key or the space bar to pull down a menu, press an arrow key to choose a command, and press Enter (way too much trouble, but possible for those who love a challenge).

I normally simplify menu commands by saying something like Yeah➪Sure, which means "Choose the Yeah menu; then choose the Sure command."

Icons used in this book

Sometimes the fastest way to go through a book is to look at the pictures — in this case, icons that draw your attention to specific types of information that's useful to know. Here are the icons in this book:

The Remember icon points out helpful information. (Everything in this book is helpful, but this stuff is even *more* helpful.)

A hint or trick for saving time and effort, or something that makes Outlook easier to understand.

The Warning icon points to something that you might want to be careful about to prevent problems.

The Technical Stuff icon marks background information that you can skip, although it might make good conversation at a really dull party.

The Time Saver icon points out a trick that can save you time in places where you might not even know there are places.

The Network icon points out information that applies primarily to people using Outlook on a computer network at the office.

The Internet icon points out a feature of Outlook that helps connect you to the Internet or use the Internet more effectively.

Getting Started

A wise person once said, "The best way to start is by starting." Okay, that's not all that wise, but why quibble? Plunge in!

Part I
The Outlook Lookout

The 5th Wave   By Rich Tennant

"ALL THIS STUFF? IT'S PART OF A SUITE OF INTEGRATED SOFTWARE PACKAGES DESIGNED TO HELP UNCLUTTER YOUR LIFE."

In this part . . .

Outlook is an all-in-one information management system that lets you organize and manage your appointments, activities, e-mail, and office life with a few clicks of the mouse. In this part, I give you a basic vision of how Outlook works to improve the way you manage your days.

Chapter 1

This Is Your Life with Outlook

● ●

In This Chapter

▶ Enjoying an out-of-box experience

▶ Reading e-mail

▶ Creating a contact from a message

▶ Creating an appointment from a contact

▶ Creating a task from an appointment

▶ Creating a phone message from a contact

▶ Taking notes

▶ Using AutoDialing

▶ E-mailing a file

● ●

*O*utlook is an information manager. That means that Outlook doesn't just help you deal with your computer; it also helps you deal with people. We're not just talking about documents or databases here. Dealing with other people and the things we do in connection with other people is much more important than what kind of documents we produce.

I leave Outlook running on my computer constantly. Why? Because I'm never sure when an idea will hit me or when I'll remember a new task I have to complete. I find it handy to just have Outlook going so that I can deal with whatever comes up at the spur of the moment.

You can use the same methods to do many different things in Outlook; click an icon to do something, view something, or complete something. Drag an item from one Outlook module to the icon for another module to create an item that represents something else you have to do. (I explain things like icons and modules as I go along.)

The pictures I show you in this book and the instructions that I give you assume that you're using Outlook the way it comes out of the box from Microsoft. If you don't like the way the program looks or what things are named when you install Outlook, you can change nearly everything. If you change many things, how-ever, some of the instructions and examples I give you won't make sense because the parts of the program I talk about may have names that you gave them, rather than the ones that Microsoft originally assigned. The Microsoft people generally did a good job of making Outlook easy to use. I suggest leaving the general arrangement alone until you're comfortable with Outlook.

An Out-of-Box Experience

Warning — the story that you are about to read could be true, with a few small changes. Just change the names to those of the people you need to meet, call, and work with. The actual work you do may differ, but all the things that Outlook does in the story are true.

The story starts in the offices of your successful business, Dot Company. You sell dots. You have a Web site (www.dotcom.com). You're a dot dealer. Everybody knows that you've got dots (megadots, baby!). It's your job to keep those dots moving and make sure that they get to their destinations by 10 a.m. on the dot.

Read e-mail

You start your computer and double-click the Outlook icon on the desktop. There's a message waiting for you. Before you open it, you know that this message means the start of another busy day. The title of the message tells you that it's from Stan Spotman, the dotmaster of Megacorp. That outfit needs lots of dots. Something about the message tells you that Stan's got trouble and needs your help fast. It's not just your keen instincts that give you the clue: The message is new, so it's in AutoPreview (see Figure 1-1). You can see the first three lines: (Because my page isn't as wide as a computer screen, this message takes more than three lines on this page.)

```
Subj: Dot supplies
We've had a sudden drop in our dot supply at Megacorp. We
don't know yet whether there's a leak or some kind of me-
chanical difficulty, but our dot supply is down to less than
48-hours worth. We're willing to pay
```

Pay — the magic word! What is the massive but miserly Megacorp ready to shell out for your premium dots?

Here's how to see the entire message:

1. **Click Inbox in the Outlook Bar.**

   You instinctively click the Inbox icon. You don't need this step if you can already see the messages, but it doesn't hurt.

Inbox icon

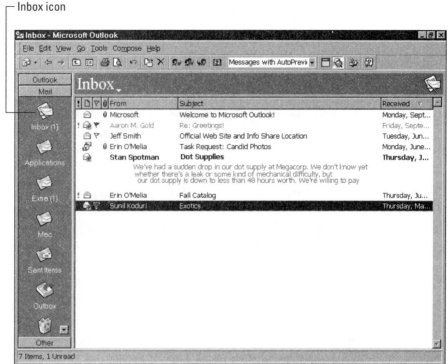

Figure 1-1:
A message
in
AutoPreview
mode.

2. Double-click the title of the message.

Now you can see the entire message, which reads as follows:

```
Subj: Dot supplies
We've had a sudden drop in our dot supply at Megacorp. We
don't know yet whether there's a leak or some kind of me-
chanical difficulty, but our dot supply is down to less than
48-hours worth. We're willing to pay up to 5 cents per dot
for top-quality dots that last more than 48 hours.  We've
contacted you and Dot's Dots for immediate supplies. Contact
me ASAP.
Stan Spotman
Megacorp, Inc.,
555 Grand Avenue
Chicago, IL 60632
312 555-9730
```

3. Press Escape.

You close the message and swing into action. There's no time to lose.

Create a contact

You need to keep Stan's vital statistics handy for messages, phone calls, deliveries, and (most important) the bill.

Here's how you save stats on Stan:

1. **Hold down the mouse button and drag the mail message to the Contacts icon.**

   The Contact form opens, with Stan's name and e-mail address already filled in. You think back to the old days, when you had to waste time entering e-mail addresses again and again. You always figured that computers should know how to do that; that's what they're for. The text of Stan's e-mail message is in the box at the bottom of the Contact form (see Figure 1-2).

   To save time, swipe your mouse over the part of the message where Stan put his phone number and drag it up to the Business Phone block of the Contact form. Then do the same with his mailing address. You've got the goods on Stan.

2. **Click the Save and Close button (or press Alt+S).**

You click the Contacts icon again to see whether Stan's stats wound up in the Contact list. You know Outlook has never let you down, but you like to be sure.

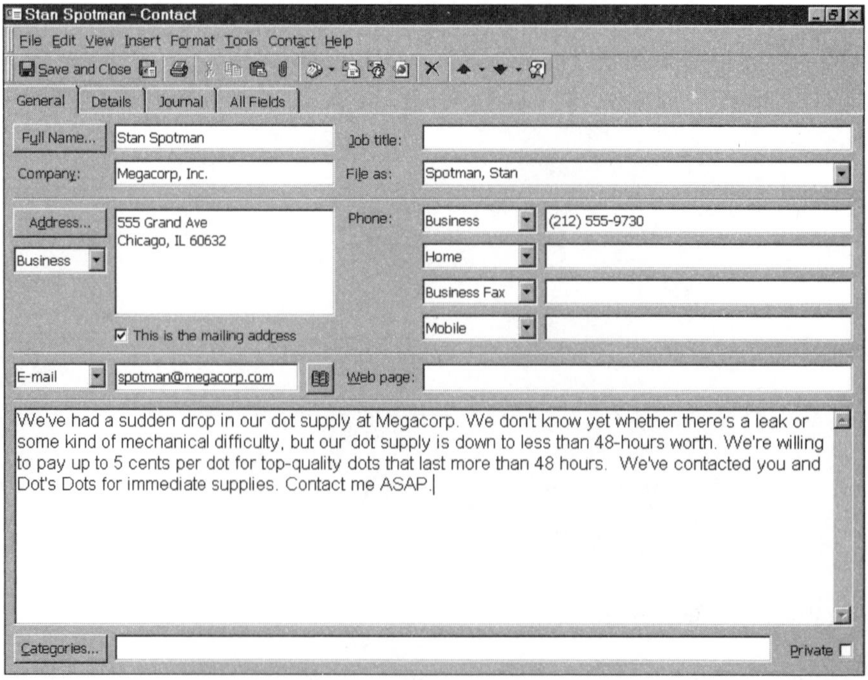

Figure 1-2:
The Contact
form.

Make an appointment

Your finely tuned business instincts tell you that you need to meet a client in person when he's in a really tough spot. Also, something fishy about this sudden dot loss makes you want to see Stan face to face. You decide to invite Stan to lunch tomorrow.

Here's how you enter an appointment in your calendar:

1. **Click the Contacts icon.**

   You see Stan's record in the Contact list.

2. **Drag the icon next to the name on the Contact list to the Calendar icon.**

   The Meeting form appears (see Figure 1-3). Stan's name is already in that form, with an underline — Outlook's way of telling you that it will handle the e-mail, leaving you to handle Stan.

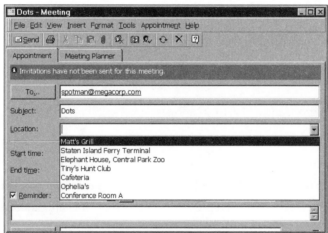

Figure 1-3:
New
Meeting
form.

3. **Type a subject in the Subject box.**

   Your subject — **Dots** — gets right to the point.

4. **Open the Location menu and choose one of your favorite haunts as a meeting location.**

   You can type any place you want, but for people in the dot game, Matt's Grill is the spot. You go there often, so Outlook automatically stores it in your location list.

5. **Click the Start Date box and type** Tomorrow.

   What's tomorrow's date? That's not your concern; Outlook takes care of it.

6. **Click the Start time box and type** Noon.

You know a lot, but whether noon is 12 a.m. or 12 p.m. is still confusing. Leave the problem to Outlook; you've got better things to do.

7. **Click the Reminder box and choose 30 minutes in the adjacent box.**

You like to have Outlook remind you to leave early enough to get your regular seat at Matt's Grill.

8. **Type a message in the text box at the bottom of the form.**

Your message might say something like "Let's have lunch tomorrow. Matt's at noon? Call to confirm." You know that Stan's a regular at Matt's Grill, so lunch won't be a problem.

9. **Click the Save button (or press Alt+S).**

Saving steps is the name of the game, and you just saved three: You simultaneously suggested a meeting with Stan, entered the meeting in your calendar, and set a reminder for yourself.

Create a task

Before you make a deal with Stan, you'll have to check the dot market. If you're meeting him at noon, you should check the market in the morning.

Here's how you add a task to your Tasks list:

1. **Click the Calendar icon.**

The appointment that you entered for Stan is already in your calendar.

2. **Drag the icon for the appointment that you made to the Tasks icon.**

The new task borrowed the subject from your Dots appointment and borrowed the date.

3. **Change the subject to** Check dot market.

This message is just for you — now you have a task to do!

4. **Click the Reminder check box.**

The reminder is already set for 8 a.m. Because you don't get to the office until 9, a reminder message will pop up at 8 a.m. and remain on your screen until you postpone or dismiss the message. You could change the reminder to later if you want, but it's best to get to your top task first thing.

5. **Click Save and Close (or press Alt+S).**

The Task form closes and your task is entered on the Tasks list.

Take a phone message

No sooner do you send your message to Stan than the phone rings. Stan sounds worried. "I have to do this dot deal today," he stammers. "Dot's Dots is out of dots; you're my only shot for dots."

"For only a nickel a dot?" you shoot back, knowing that he'll get your point.

"OK," he says. "Eight cents."

Without a pause, you respond, "I'll have to check my sources." You know that you've got him on the spot.

"Ten cents. Period," he replies.

You have some fast work to do. You tell Stan you'll get back to him.

First, you need to get a record of this conversation in the Journal in case Stan "forgets" what he offered.

Here's how you create a Journal entry to keep a record of a phone conversation:

1. **Click the Contacts icon.**

   Stan's record is there on-screen.

2. **Drag the contact record to the Journal icon.**

   The Journal form opens, with Stan's name and the current time filled in. At the bottom of the form is an icon, which is a shortcut to Stan's contact record, in case you need to refer to it. Below that icon is a blinking bar that indicates where text will appear when you start typing (see Figure 1-4).

3. **Type** Ten Cents a Dot.

4. **Click the Save and Close button (or press Alt+S).**

Now you have a record of exactly when Stan called and what you need to remember about the call.

Take notes

The fact that your competitor, Dot's Dots, is totally out of stock is curious. You don't have much time to check out the situation, but you want to make a note of it for later reference.

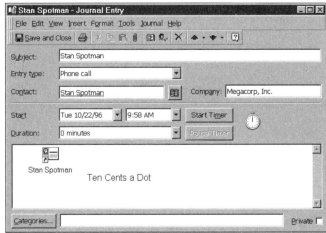

Figure 1-4:
Journal
entry for
recording a
phone call.

Here's how you can take a quick note:

1. **Open the New items menu from the New tool at the left end of the toolbar and choose Note.**

   A yellow square pops up on-screen; it looks like a yellow paper sticky note (see Figure 1-5).

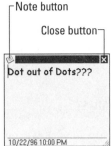

Figure 1-5:
A Note.

2. **Type the note that you want to remember (in this case,** Dot out of Dots???).

   That note will be enough to jog your memory later. The note automatically includes the date and time when you wrote it, just for your records.

3. **Click the Close button in the upper-right corner of the note (or press Alt+F4).**

This note is just for your own use; you won't be reminded. Sometime later, though, you may want to search for the phrase *out of dots,* and you'll have a note of exactly when it happened.

Return a phone call

You've checked your own dot supply, and you've decided to do the dime-a-dot deal with Stan. You don't need to look up his number to call him back because your modem is set up to dial for you.

Here's how you use the AutoDialer to make a call:

1. **Click the Contacts icon.**

   Stan's record is on-screen.

2. **Click Stan's name in the contact screen.**

   Stan's record is highlighted to show that he's the one you want to call (see Figure 1-6). You see Stan's name and address in a little box that looks like an address card, because you're using the Address Card view of the Contact list.

3. **Click the AutoDialer button in the toolbar.**

   The New Call dialog box pops up with Stan's name and phone number already filled in (see Figure 1-7).

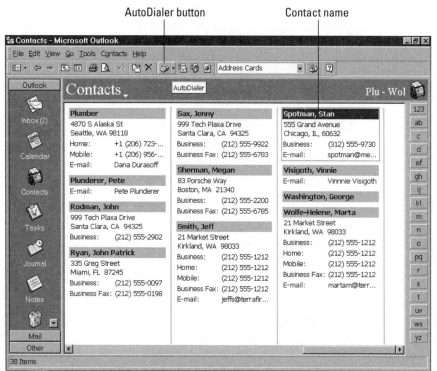

Figure 1-6:
The AutoDialer button is on the toolbar.

Figure 1-7:
The New
Call dialog
box shows
you the
name of the
person
you're
dialing.

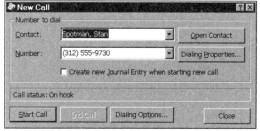

4. **Pick up the phone and click the Start Call button in the New Call dialog box.**

The Call Status dialog box opens (see Figure 1-8).

Figure 1-8:
The Call
Status dialog
box tells you
whether
your call is
going
through.

5. **Click Talk to begin talking.**

You reach Stan and tell him that dimes for dots is a done deal. He recalls offering eight cents. You refresh his memory and tell him that you're sending a contract by e-mail. He agrees, grudgingly.

6. **Click the Hang Up button.**

You're back in the New Call dialog box.

7. **Click the Close button in the New Call dialog box.**

You're done with the call, but you're not done with Stan just yet.

Send a file

The file for your standard contract for dots is stored in your My Documents folder; it's called DotCom Standard Contract. You can mail Stan this contract file without using the Post Office — just your computer.

Here's how you send a file by e-mail:

1. **Click the word *Other* in the lowest gray bar in the Outlook Bar.**

   The My Computer icon appears.

2. **Click the My Computer icon.**

   A list of your disk drives appears (see Figure 1-9).

3. **Double-click the (C:) icon.**

   A list of the folders on your C drive appears.

4. **Double-click the My Documents folder icon.**

   A list of the files in your My Documents folder appears; DotCom Standard Contract is among them.

5. **Click the word *Outlook* in the highest gray bar in the Outlook Bar.**

   The list of Outlook icons appears — Inbox, Contacts, Calendar, and so on — but the main part of the screen still shows the files in your My Documents folder.

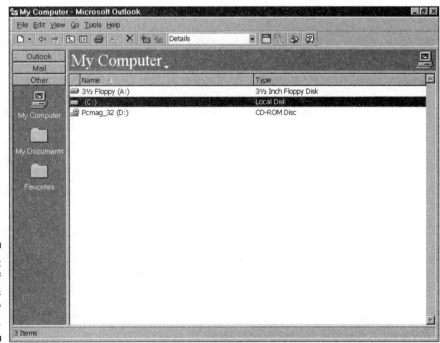

Figure 1-9:
The list of disk drives under My Computer.

6. **Click the name of a file and drag it to the Inbox icon.**

   In this case, you'd drag DotCom Standard Contract to the Inbox icon. The Message form appears, with an icon in the bottom box titled DotCom Standard Contract. That icon represents the file that you're sending to Stan (the contract). The title of the message is the same as the name of the file (DotCom Standard Contract).

7. **Click the To box and type the name of the person to whom you're sending the file.**

   Because you've already entered Stan in your Contact list, all you have to do is type **Stan Spotman**. Outlook figures out what to do about sending the message.

8. **Click Send (or press Alt+S).**

Your contract is on the way to Stan, and you're ready to return to business as usual.

The Bottom Line

Your daily working life may not run like a detective story, but a well-organized desktop information manager such as Outlook can help you out. If you use Outlook only for the few things I mention in this chapter, you'll save time. But Outlook has more — lots more.

Later in the book, I show you other ways to use Outlook to save steps and combine tasks automatically. Some tasks, such as keeping track of your files, make more sense when you handle them through Outlook than if you use the Windows Explorer that comes with Windows 95. You can also kill two or more birds with one stone by using the drag-and-drop method of creating new Outlook items from old items so that you don't have to keep retyping the same information over and over. I get into more ways to save time and effort with drag-and-drop techniques in Chapter 3.

You can install Outlook in a variety of ways that can make a difference in how you do things. I'm assuming that, if you're on a corporate network, a computer staff deals with setup and configuration. Corporate users may have different names for the folders and icons that I'm describing because of the way that their computer departments set things up. I'm using the names that Office 97 gives to commonly used files and folders in which most documents are stored, such as the My Documents folder. Where names may differ wildly, I try to make a note of that fact so that you know.

Chapter 2

Inside Outlook: Mixing, Matching, and Managing Information

• •

In This Chapter

▶ Bellying up to the Outlook Bar

▶ Choosing menus: one from column A, one from column B

▶ Using the tools of the trade

▶ Taking the shortcut: speedier keystrokes

▶ Getting the big picture from the Information Viewer

▶ Fine-tuning with the Folder List

• •

*C*omputer companies love new stuff. Every so often, they beef up their products with new names and new features, which usually pop up just before I've figured out how to use the old ones. It's kind of confusing, but I can't deny that many of these newfangled features make my life easier once I get a handle on them.

In the old days BC (Before Computers), every task in an office required a different machine. You'd type letters on a typewriter, calculate on an adding machine, file names and addresses in a card file, and keep your appointments in a datebook. It would be very difficult to add up your monthly sales on the typewriter and even harder to type a letter on the calculator.

When computers started creeping in, each of those functions was taken over, one by one, by the computer. Each machine was replaced by a different program. First, the word-processing program eliminated the typewriter; next, the spreadsheet replaced the calculator. After a brief flirtation with the giant record-keeping database, the frequent job of keeping track of names, addresses, and dates slowly (but not completely) gave way to a program called the Personal Information Manager (PIM). Microsoft claims to take the information manager concept one step farther with Outlook.

Outlook is the centerpiece of a set of programs called Microsoft Office 97. It's taken years for the people who write computer programs to make their products make sense to each other, and more important, to make their programs make sense to the folks who use them. Nothing about computers makes perfect sense just yet, but Outlook and Office 97 take a big step in that direction.

Outlook Express?

The folks at Microsoft were mighty proud after they released Outlook — so proud, in fact, that they gave the name Outlook to a second, totally different product a few weeks later. *Outlook Express* is a program that used to be called Internet Mail and News before going big-time and getting a new name. I'm sure Microsofties find the new names perfectly sensible, but I get very confused when I have to deal with two different products that go by the same name.

Like regular Outlook (Outlook Local?), Outlook Express can exchange e-mail, but it can't do many of the fancy tricks with your mail that you can do with regular Outlook. For example, you can't drag an e-mail message to the Contacts folder to create a new Contact record or flag messages to remind you to take action.

Outlook Express can also do tricks that regular Outlook hasn't learned yet, however, such as reading Internet newsgroups. Newsgroups are places on the Internet where people can read each other's messages and post replies to any message. The Public Discussion Folders that I discuss in Chapter 17 are very similar to newsgroups, except that newsgroups are available to anyone on the Internet, while Public Discussion Folders can only be used by people you work with.

Microsoft has hinted strongly that someday regular Outlook (which you have to pay for) will be able to read Internet newsgroups just like Outlook Express (which is free). Don't worry if this is confusing to you, it's confusing to everybody.

Office 97 and Outlook

Office 97 is an Office *suite,* which means it's a collection of programs that includes everything you need to complete most office tasks. Ideally, the programs in a suite work together and let you create documents that you couldn't create as easily with any of the individual programs. For example, you can add a copy of a chart from a spreadsheet and paste it into a sales letter you're creating in your word processor. You could also keep a list of mailing addresses in a spreadsheet or database and use the list as a mailing list for form letters (see Chapter 18). Microsoft Office 97 includes five programs that cost less to buy together than you would pay to buy them separately. The concept is a little like buying an encyclopedia; it's cheaper to buy the entire set than it is to buy one book at a time. Besides, who wants just one volume of an encyclopedia (unless you're only interested in aardvarks)?

If you own Office 97 (or if Office 97 is the program you use at work), Outlook is the Big New Thing that's been added since Microsoft's last model, Office 95. What happened to Office 96? Good question. For people who love numbers so much, these computer geeks sure can't count.

A bit about Office suites

Office suites can be confusing because, although the five parts do different business tasks, each part looks so similar to the others that you can't tell at first glance what it is ready to do for you. Even worse, the suite gives you no clear, obvious way to manage the kinds of information that you need to know most of the time — all that who, what, where, and when business that takes up most of your day.

Earlier versions of Microsoft Office tried to pull all the common office tasks together to act like members of the same team, but there were limits.

- ✓ Word is the English major — great with text, spelling, and grammar, but throw in a calculation and forget it. Word is still just a typewriter at heart.

- ✓ Excel's job is to calculate, graph, sort, and the like, but don't try to use it to type a letter.

Excel's grandpa, the adding machine, didn't type letters, so don't ask.

- ✓ Word and Excel are friendly, but they come from different worlds and do different things.

- ✓ PowerPoint is the performing artist of the group, but like many performers it's only concerned about appearances and not equipped to deal with text and numbers.

When it comes to trying to make sense of the daily activities of normal people, however, neither Word nor Excel has much interest or experience. They're a bit like may Holleywood marriages. Fortunately, Word and Excel are still hanging out together, and they've lots of friends like Outlook interested in making sure they work well together.

Enter the PIM

When it comes to the basic work of managing names, addresses, appointments, and e-mail, the word-processing and spreadsheet programs just don't get it. If you're planning a meeting, you need to know whom you're meeting, what the other person's phone number is, and when you can find time to meet.

Several small software companies recognized the problem of managing addresses and appointments long ago and offered Personal Information Managers (PIMs) to fill in the gap. PIMs such as Lotus Organizer, SideKick, and Act! specialized in names, addresses, dates, and tasks, leaving the word processing and number crunching to brawnier business applications such as Microsoft Word and Excel.

The problem with PIMs before Outlook has been that they must communicate with the word processors of the world, but they often can't. If you have a person's name and address stored in a PIM like SideKick, and you want to write a letter to that person in Microsoft Word, you have to copy and paste the address from the PIM into your letter, assuming both programs allow you to do that. Even if they do allow that, however, the address is likely to be sliced up in the PIM in a way that doesn't work in Word. So the PIM that was supposed to make your life easier in fact doubled your workload.

PIMs of the past

Microsoft Office 95 provided an earlier pair of programs for personal-information management: Schedule+ and Exchange. Schedule+ is designed to store names, addresses, tasks, and calendar items while Exchange can send and receive e-mail. Although both programs are fairly efficient at their appointed jobs, they weren't designed to be easy to use. They acknowledge each other and even exchange some information if you push them into it. But the two programs were something of an afterthought for Microsoft; the company never really took PIMs seriously until Outlook.

Other manufacturers of PIMs talk about making everything work with your word processor, but you still have to start the PIM and the word processor separately and then beat them both over the head to get them to talk to each other politely. Even then, the things that you enter into the PIM aren't always easy to use when you're doing something simple, like writing a letter.

With Outlook, you can access any of Microsoft's other Office 97 programs with the click of a mouse, making information management much more manageable.

In designing Outlook, Microsoft took advantage of the fact that most people use Microsoft products for most of the work that they do. The company created a PIM that speaks a common language with Microsoft Word, Excel, and the rest of the Office 97 suite. Microsoft also studied what kind of information people use most often and tried to make sure that Outlook can handle most of it. The company also added the capability to move, copy, rename, and manage your files, using the same simple drag-and-drop techniques that you use for managing e-mail, tasks, appointments, and the like. There's also enough customizability (what a tongue-twister — it just means you can set it up however you need once you know what you're doing) that Microsoft doesn't even call Outlook a PIM, but a Desktop Information Manager. Yeah, that's right — it's a DIM. Microsoft doesn't always come up with the swiftest names for things.

Above all, Outlook is easy to understand and hard to mess up. If you've used any version of Windows, you can just look at the screen and click a few icons to see what Outlook does. There's nothing to break. If you get lost, going back to where you came from is easy. Even if you have no experience with Windows, Outlook is fairly straightforward to use.

There's No Place Like Home: Outlook's Main Screen

Outlook's appearance is very different from the other Microsoft Office applications. Instead of confronting you with a blank screen and a few menus and toolbars, Outlook begins by offering you large icons with simple names and a screen with information that's easy to use and understand.

It's nice to feel at home when you work. (Sometimes when I'm at work, I'd rather be at home, but that's something else entirely.) Outlook makes a home for all your different types of information: names, addresses, schedules, to-do lists, reminders, and even a list of all the files on your computer. You can customize the main screen as easily as you rearrange your home furnishings — although, to make it easier to find your way around at first, I recommend that you wait until you feel entirely at home with Outlook before you start rearranging the screen.

The Outlook main screen has all the usual parts of a Windows screen (see the Introduction if you're not used to the Windows screen), with a few important additions. At the left side of the screen, you see the Outlook Bar. Next to the Outlook Bar are the parts of the screen that take up most of the space: the Information Viewer and the Folder List (see Figure 2-1).

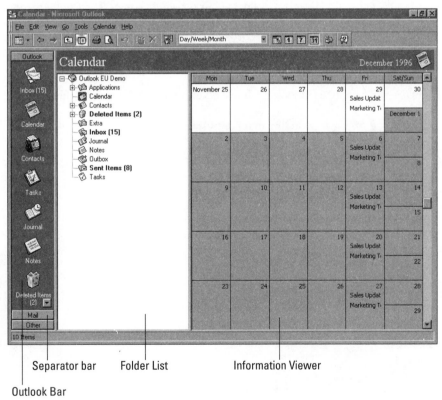

Figure 2-1:
The Outlook
main
screen.

Separator bar   Folder List   Information Viewer

Outlook Bar

Outlook modules

All the work you do in Outlook is organized into modules, or sections. Each module performs a specific job for you; the Calendar stores and manages your schedule, the Tasks module stores and manages your to-do list, and so on. Outlook is always showing you one of its modules in the main screen or Information Viewer. Whenever you're running Outlook you're always using a module even if there's no information in the module, the same way your television is always tuned to a channel, even if there's nothing showing on that channel. The name of the module you're currently using is displayed in large type at the top of the Information Viewer part of the screen, so you can easily tell what module is showing.

Each module has an *icon* (picture) in the Outlook Bar portion of the screen. Clicking the module's icon is a shortcut that takes you to a different module of Outlook. The Inbox collects your incoming e-mail. The Contacts module stores names and addresses for you. The Tasks module keeps track of all the work that you do. The Journal records all your activities, and the Notes module allows you to keep track of random tidbits of information that don't quite fit anywhere else.

To change Outlook modules, do either of the following things:

✔ Click <u>G</u>o in the menu bar to display the menu shown in Figure 2-2; then choose the module you want.

✔ For faster action, simply click the module's icon in the Outlook Bar.

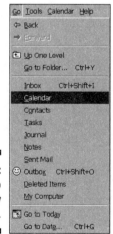

Figure 2-2:
Click <u>G</u>o to
get a new
module.

If you're using Outlook on your company network, your network's system administrator may have created a different set of icons for you to work with. You may have a few more or a few less than you see in this book, but the icons should work the same way.

After you're comfortable with Outlook, you may want to customize it to suit your taste. For example, you may want to add an icon for your floppy drive to make it easier to move or copy files onto a floppy disk. In Chapter 6, where I show you how to create custom forms, you see how to create a new Outlook folder, which acts like a separate module. You can customize it beyond recognition, if you want. What the hey — have it your way.

Beware, however; your local computer guru may get cranky if you keep deleting an icon installed expressly for you to use on your company's system.

Belly up to the Outlook Bar

Although you don't get purple drinks with umbrellas at the Outlook Bar, it's still where the action is in Outlook. When you use Outlook, you see a column on the left side of the screen containing some icons (pictures) with names such as Calendar, Contacts, Tasks, Journal, and Notes — the basic Outlook modules. I explain these modules later, but the names alone already tell you the story.

Just click an icon, any icon, and you'll see what it sets in motion. Clicking the icon changes the stuff on the main screen to fit what the icon describes. Click the Calendar icon, and a Calendar screen shows up. Click Contacts, and you get a screen for names and addresses. The process is like changing the channels on the TV set. If you switch to a channel that you don't want, switch to another; no problem.

Although it's handy to have the items that you use most often in the Outlook Bar, if you add too many things to that little bar, finding them can be hard. That's why the Outlook Bar is divided into groups. Each group is like a drawer in your file cabinet. You put different sorts of things in different file drawers so that you know right where to look when you want to find something. If you threw everything in one big box, finding anything would be harder. Outlook groups work the same way.

At the top and bottom of the Outlook Bar, you see little gray *separator bars* with names such as Outlook, Mail, and Other. Click each of these separator bars, and you see the column slide up or down to reveal a different group of icons representing different things you can do with Outlook. The technical term for one of these groups is . . . *group.* That's easy. Again, if you don't like the group that you chose, choose a different one.

To change Outlook groups, click the separator bar that has the name of the group you want, such as Outlook, Mail, or Other. You see the little bars slide up or down to reveal the group that you select. If nothing happens, the group that you selected was already selected.

Adding items to the Outlook Bar

The Outlook Bar comes set up with the icons that Microsoft thinks you'll use most often. You can add or remove icons if you don't like the ones that Microsoft gave you. You can also add or remove the separator bars that separate groups in the Outlook Bar, which I discuss in the next section about Outlook groups.

You can add nearly anything to the Outlook Bar — folders, documents, network drives, and even icons that launch other programs.

To add an item to the Outlook Bar, follow these steps:

1. **Choose File➪Add to Outlook Bar from the menu bar.**

   The Add to Outlook Bar dialog box appears. Your list of folders is displayed in the box at the bottom of the Add to Outlook Bar dialog box.

2. **Click the folder or drive that you want to add to the Outlook Bar.**

   The name of the folder or drive you clicked is highlighted.

3. **Click OK.**

   You see a new icon for the folder or drive you selected in the Outlook Bar. That icon comes in handy when you want to copy files between folders or drives that you use frequently. I get into that in Chapter 4 when I talk about file management.

The Look in box lets you choose between the two different types of folder you can add to the Outlook bar; Outlook folders that only contain Outlook items or Windows file system folders that contain all the other types of files you create in Windows as well as disk drives. For more about the two types of folders you can use in Outlook, see "Navigating the Folder List," later in this chapter.

Adding Outlook groups

Wouldn't it be nice if you could divide your filing cabinet into an unlimited number of file drawers? You can create as many Outlook groups as you want and name them whatever will make it easier for you to find things — on your computer, at least. Finding that one lost sock in your dresser drawer is still a problem.

To add a group to the Outlook Bar, follow these steps:

1. **Right-click any group name in the Outlook Bar.**

   A menu appears with choices that pertain to items in the Outlook Bar.

2. **Choose <u>A</u>dd New Group.**

   A new group divider, called New Group, appears at the bottom of the Outlook Bar, highlighted in blue.

3. **Type the name that you want to use for your new group (something like** Special Group**).**

4. **Press Enter.**

No matter what you do, the new group winds up at the bottom of the list. Sorry about that.

You can also change the name of any icon or group. You could rename the three original groups Larry, Curly, and Moe, for example, after the Three Stooges. Renaming the sections that way might make Outlook more fun but harder to explain.

You can do most of your work in one Outlook group; that's okay. The main reason for having groups is to be able to keep all your icons visible on-screen. You could just as easily have a list of icons scrolling way below the screen; the icons would just be harder to use. You could also add icons for folders that pertain to different functions you perform or areas of interest. For example, you might have a group of icons that relate to sales matters, others for production, and others for human resources.

Admittedly, it's confusing that Microsoft named Outlook's main group Outlook. (You wouldn't name your kid Johnson Johnson, but Microsoft is funny that way.) The company gives its programs strange secret-agent-style names, such as Blackbird and Cairo, when the programs are being written. Then, when Microsoft releases the products to market, it uses the same couple of names — Windows XX or the XX Explorer, for example. The point is that the group named Outlook in Outlook contains icons that lead you to tasks that Outlook does best — the Outlook of Outlooks. You can change the group's name to anything you want to use but I think it's best to leave it alone and let the Outlook group contain just the icons for the six basic Outlook modules: Inbox, Calendar, Contacts, Tasks, Journal, and Notes.

The name of the group that's open appears in the separator bar at the top of the icons. If you click the name of the group that's already open, nothing happens. Don't worry — that's normal. You have to click a different group to see a change.

The Information Viewer: Outlook's hotspot

The Information Viewer is where most of the action happens in Outlook. If the Outlook Bar is like the channel selector on your TV set, the Information Viewer is like the TV screen. When you're reading e-mail, you look in the Information Viewer to read your messages; if you're adding or searching for contacts, you see contact names here. The Information Viewer is also where you can do all sorts of fancy sorting tricks that each module in Outlook lets you perform. (I talk about sorting Contacts, Tasks, and so forth in the chapters that apply to those modules.)

Because you can store more information in Outlook than you want to see at any one time, the Information Viewer shows you only a slice of the information available. The Calendar, for example, can store dates as far back as 1600 and as far forward as 4500. (Got any plans on Saturday night 2,500 years from now?) That's a lot of time, but Outlook breaks it down and shows it to you in manageable slices in the Information Viewer. The smallest Calendar slice you can look at is one day, and the largest slice is a month.

The Information Viewer organizes the items it shows you into units called views. You can use the views that are included with Outlook when you install it, or you can create your own views and save them. I go into more details about views in Chapter 5.

You can navigate between the slices of information that Outlook shows you by clicking different parts of the Information Viewer. Some people use the word *browsing* for the process of moving around the Information Viewer; it's a little like thumbing through the pages of your pocket datebook (that is, if you have a million-page datebook).

To see an example of how to use the Information Viewer, look at the Calendar module in Figure 2-3.

Figure 2-3:
You see a calendar in the Information Viewer.

To browse the Calendar data in the Information Viewer, follow these steps:

1. **Choose Go➪Calendar.**

   The Calendar appears.

2. **Choose View➪Current View➪Day/Week/Month.**

   The information in the Calendar appears in a form that looks like a conventional calendar.

3. **Choose View➪Week.**

The weekly view of the Calendar appears, showing a small calendar in the upper-right corner of the Information Viewer and a larger calendar on the left half of the screen. Try these tricks to see how the Information Viewer behaves:

- ✔ Click a date in the small calendar in the upper-right corner. Notice that the large calendar changes to a one-day view.

- ✔ Click the *S* for *Saturday* or *Sunday* at the top of one of the small calendars. Notice that the large calendar changes to a monthly view.

You can change the appearance of the Information Viewer an infinite number of ways to make the work that you do in Outlook make sense to you. For example, you may only need to see appointments for a single day or items that you've assigned a certain category; views can help you get a quick look at exactly the slice of information you need.

Navigating the Folder List

If you want to navigate Outlook in a more detailed way than you can with the Outlook Bar, you can use the Folder List. If you think of the Outlook Bar as being like the buttons of your car radio, which you use to pick your favorite stations, then the Folder List is like the fine-tuning button, which you use to tune in any of the stations between your favorite ones. The Folder List simply shows you your folders — Your Windows folders or your Outlook folders — which are where your files and Outlook items are stored.

A tale of two folders

Folders can seem more confusing than they need to be because, once again, Microsoft gave two different things the same name. Just as two kinds of Explorer (Windows and Internet) exist and more than two kinds of Windows (3.1, 95, and NT), you run across two kinds of folders in Outlook, and each behaves differently.

You may be used to folders in Windows 95, which are the things you look in to organize files. You can copy, move, and delete files to and from folders on your disk drive. When you're using Outlook for file management, as I describe in Chapter 4, those are the kinds of folders you're dealing with.

In addition, Outlook has its own kind of folders for storing items that you create in the various Outlook modules: calendar items, contact names, tasks, and so forth. Each module has its own folder that you can see in the Folder List.

If you're looking at an Outlook module such as the Inbox, for example, and you turn on the Folder List by choosing View➪Folder List, you see a list of folders that represent the other standard Outlook modules, like the Tasks list, Contacts, Calendar, and so on.

If you go to the My Computer folder by choosing Go➪My Computer, you see an entirely different set of folders that represent your disk drives and the folders in them in the Folder List. Don't be alarmed; there's nothing wrong with either you or your screen. That's just how Outlook works.

Because the two types of folders are different animals, the Folder List won't show you both types at the same time. You see either all of one type or all of the other. Make sense? I didn't think so.

Using the Folder List

It's quite possible that you'll never use the Folder List at all. The Outlook Bar includes the folder choices that most people use most of the time. You may never need to get a different one. Fortunately, you can leave the Folder List turned off except when you really want it, if at all.

The only times you must use the Folder List are when you want to add a new icon to the Outlook Bar or create a new folder for a separate type of item (such as a special Contact list or for filing e-mail). Using the Folder List is also a faster way to move, copy, or delete files when using Outlook.

When you're using the Outlook group, the Folder List does many of the same things that the Outlook Bar does, except it takes up more room.

You can change Outlook groups to see the Folder List do other jobs. Follow these steps:

1. **Click the Other group in the Outlook Bar.**

2. **Click My Computer.**

   That's right — the very same My Computer that you see on the Windows 95 Desktop. If you've used the My Computer icon to explore your computer or if you've used the Windows Explorer, what you see next will look familiar; if not, it's useful stuff (see Figure 2-4).

Figure 2-4:
My
Computer on
the Outlook
screen.

> **3. Click the plus sign next to My Computer.**
>
> You see the names of your drives.
>
> **4. Click the (C:) drive icon.**
>
> **5. Click any folder icon.**
>
> You see the names of all your files in the Information Viewer. This way, you can view, copy, and move files without ever leaving Outlook.

You can also take advantage of the slick Outlook viewing tricks that you never could do with Windows Explorer, the file manager that comes with Windows 95. (Don't worry if you've never used Windows Explorer; hardly anybody does.) I get into the file-management tricks that Outlook can do in Chapter 4.

Clicking Once: The Outlook Toolbar

Tools are those little boxes with pictures in them that are all lined up in a row just below the menu bar. Together, they're called the *toolbar,* and they're even more popular than menus when it comes to running Windows programs. One little click on a little picture, and voilà — your wish is granted and you're off to lunch.

Viewing ToolTips

Like menus, tools in Office 97 programs get a little drop shadow when you hover the mouse pointer over them. The shadow tells you that if you click there, the tool will do what it's there to do: paste, save, launch missiles, whatever.

Another slick thing about tools is that when you rest the mouse pointer on them for a second or so, a little tag pops up to tell you what the tool's name is (see Figure 2-5). Tags of this sort, called *ToolTips*, are very handy for deciphering the hieroglyphics on those tool buttons.

To view a ToolTip, follow these steps:

1. **Place the mouse pointer on the word File in the menu bar.**

2. **Slide the mouse pointer straight down until it rests on the icon just below the word File.**

   After about half a second, you see a little yellow tab that says "New Office Document" or "New *Something-or-Other.*" (The text changes, depending on what section of Outlook you're in.)

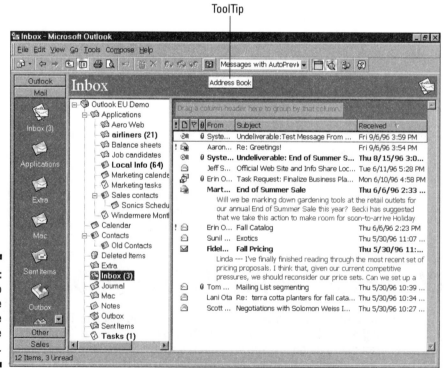

Figure 2-5:
A ToolTip tells you the name of the tool you're using.

Scrolling around with IntelliMouse

If you think the computer mouse is the greatest thing since the invention of the wheel, you'll be glad to know that Microsoft's new IntelliMouse even has a wheel. The new mouse is a tricky little gadget because the wheel that sits between the mouse buttons rolls like a wheel and clicks like a mouse button. The wheel doesn't do a lot in Outlook; it's designed primarily for making it easier to scroll through lengthy Web pages on the Internet as well as for scrolling up and down your Word documents and zooming both Word and Excel pages to make the type look larger or smaller. My favorite IntelliMouse trick is to click the wheel on the scroll bar of any long document and let the document scroll slowly up the screen like credits for a movie. Why do I like that? I guess I'm still just a sucker for show business.

Some tools have a little down-pointing triangle to their right. This triangle means that the tool has a pull-down menu. The very first tool at the left end of any Outlook toolbar is the New tool. Click the triangle to pull down its menu, and you see all the new things that you can create — a new appointment, a new e-mail message, or even a new Office document.

Using the New tool

You can use the New tool, which is available in any module of Outlook, to create an item in any other module. Perhaps you're entering the name and address of a new customer who is also mentioned in an interesting article in today's paper, and you want to remember the article, but it doesn't belong in the customer's address record. While you're still in the Contacts module (see Figure 2-6), you can pull down the New button's menu and create a quick note, which gets filed in the Note section. Using the New tool to create a new note when you're looking at the Contacts screen can get confusing. At first, you may think that the note isn't entered, but it is. Outlook just files it in the Notes module, where it belongs.

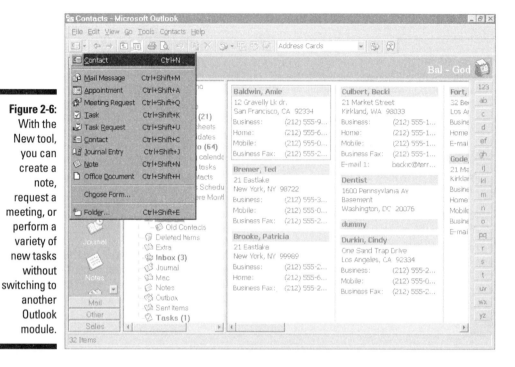

Figure 2-6:
With the
New tool,
you can
create a
note,
request a
meeting, or
perform a
variety of
new tasks
without
switching to
another
Outlook
module.

Turning Parts of the Outlook Screen On and Off

You can work with any part of the Outlook screen in view, or you can turn the screen off. The buttons near the bottom of the View menu allow you to change what you see. Sometimes, for example, you want to look at your Calendar in the largest possible view so you can see a whole month and all its appointments clearly. In that case, you could switch to the Calendar module, and then turn off the Outlook Bar, the Folder List and even possibly the toolbar in order to make lots of room for the Calendar. You also may need to turn on the Folder List when you're moving or copying files, but turn it off when you're scheduling tasks.

For example, to view the Folder List:

✔ Choose View➪Folder List.

✔ Alternatively, if you see a triangle below the title of the Information Viewer, click the title (such as Calendar), and the Folder List appears.

The View menu has icons for both the Outlook Bar and the Folder List; these icons allow you to turn those elements on or off. So if you want to run Outlook with just the Outlook Bar open or just the Folder List, or both, or neither, it's up to you. I think that leaving the Outlook Bar open is the easiest way to go.

Getting Help from the Office Assistant

Even though Outlook is as user-friendly a program as you could hope to find, at times you may want to take advantage of the efficient Windows 95 online help system when you're temporarily stumped (of course, you can turn to this book for help, but sometimes online help is faster).

The Windows Help system was always helpful, but now it's downright sociable. A little animated character pops up in a box and cavorts around when you ask for help; it even does little tricks when you do things like save a file or search for text. Try it!

You can change the type of character you use as your Office Assistant from the Clipit character that Office begins with to the Einstein-like Genius character and my favorite, the Power Pup (see Figure 2-7). All you have to do is right-click the Office Assistant character, choose a new character, and click OK.

Figure 2-7:
The Genius and the Power Pup assistants.

The new Office Assistant character is included because research showed that people treat their computers as though they are other people. No kidding. Most people report more negative things about a computer to a second computer than they will to the computer that they're saying the bad things about; it's like they're trying not to hurt the computer's feelings.

You don't have to worry about hurting the Office Assistant's feelings. Just press the F1 key any time; your Office Assistant pops up and invites you to ask a question (see Figure 2-8). Just type your question in plain English, and the Assistant scratches its head and returns with a list of help topics that are likely to answer your question. If you want to delete a message, for example, just press F1 and type **delete a message**. The list of choices includes everything that has to do with deleting messages.

If you keep the Office Assistant open, some of the questions that you usually answer through dialog boxes are asked by the Assistant (see Figure 2-9). Click the response that you want, just as you would in a regular dialog box.

Figure 2-8:
You can ask
the Office
Assistant a
question in
plain
English.

The Office Assistant will get smarter with time; it's supposed to notice the things you do wrong repeatedly and chime in with suggestions about how to do them better. Microsoft calls this system the Social Interface; some people call it nagging. Remember that the Office Assistant only means to be helpful (just like your mother-in-law).

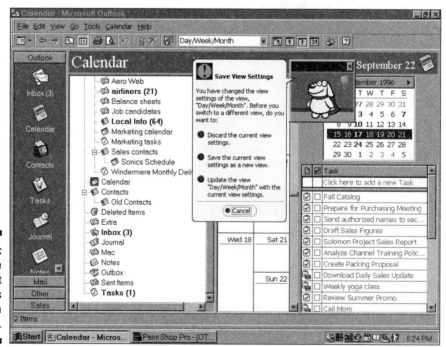

Figure 2-9:
The Office
Assistant
sometimes
acts like a
dialog box.

Chapter 3

No Typing, Please! —
Drag 'til You Drop

• •

In This Chapter

▶ Doing the drag and drop

▶ Creating e-mail messages

▶ Creating Contact records

▶ Creating Journal entries

▶ Drag and drop dead — Deleting

• •

*T*yping — ugh! Who needs it? It's amazing to think that we still use a nine-teenth-century device — the typewriter keyboard — to control our comput-ers on the cusp of the twenty-first century. We appear to be stuck with the QWERTY keyboard for a while longer, but we can give our carpal tunnels a rest now and then by using the mouse, trackball, or glidepoint to drag and drop rather than hunt and peck.

How to Drag

When I say drag, I'm not referring to Monty Python's men in women's clothing. I mean the process of zipping items from one place to another with quick, easy mouse moves rather than slow, laborious menu choices. Throughout the rest of this book I tell you how to do nearly everything in Outlook by the menu method only because it's the clearest way to explain a lot of things in a way that works reliably. But if you want to work quickly in Outlook, drag and drop is the ticket to simple and speedy completion of your tasks.

You have to select an item before you can drag it. That simply means to click the item once.

- *Dragging* means clicking your mouse on something and moving the mouse to another location while holding the mouse button down all the while.
- *Dropping* means letting go of the mouse button.

When you drag an item, you see an icon hanging from the tail of the mouse pointer as you move the mouse across the screen. The icon makes the pointer look like it's carrying baggage, and to some degree that's true; dragging your mouse between Outlook modules "carries" information from one type of item to another.

When you drag and drop items between different Outlook modules, you can keep creating new types of items from the old information, depending on what you drag and where you drop it.

Everything that you can do by using the drag-and-drop method, you can also do through menu choices or keystroke shortcuts, but you lose the advantage of having the information from one item flow into the new item, so you have to retype information. I'm too lazy for that, so I just drag and drop.

Because I'm using this chapter to extol the benefits of drag and drop, I describe every action in terms of a drag-and-drop movement rather than through menu choices or keyboard shortcuts. Throughout the rest of the book, I describe how to do things in terms of menu choices because the menus never change, whereas you can change the names of the icons in the Outlook Bar if you customize them. So when you read other parts of the book, don't think that I'm discouraging you from trying drag and drop; I'm just trying to offer you the clearest explanation I can. (Whew. I'm glad that's off my chest.)

Creating E-Mail Messages

Anything that you drag to the Inbox becomes an outgoing e-mail message. If the thing that you drag to the Inbox contains an e-mail address, such as a contact, Outlook automatically creates the message with that person's e-mail address filled in.

If the item that you drag to the Inbox contains a subject, such as a task, Outlook automatically creates the message with that subject filled in.

From a name in your Address Book

Addressing messages is one of the most useful reasons to use drag and drop in Outlook. E-mail addresses can be cumbersome and difficult to remember, and if your spelling of an e-mail address is off by even one letter, your message won't go through. It's best to just keep the e-mail addresses of the people to whom you sent messages in your Contact list and use those addresses to create new messages.

To create an e-mail message from your Contact list:

1. Click the Contacts icon.

The Contact list appears (see Figure 3-1). You can use any view, but Address Cards view is easiest, because you can click the first letter of the person's name to see that person's card. For more about viewing your Contact list, see Chapter 10.

2. Drag a name from your Contact list to the Inbox icon.

The Message form appears, with the address of the contact filled in.

3. Type a subject for your message.

Keep it simple; a few words will do.

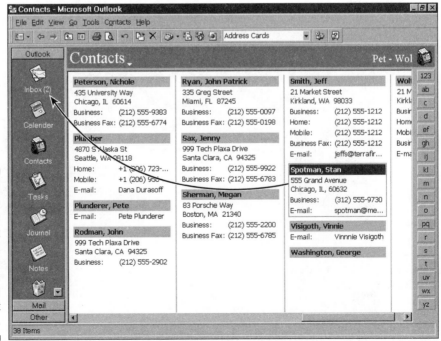

Figure 3-1:
Dragging a contact to your Inbox creates a new e-mail message addressed to that person.

4. Click in the text box and type your message.

You can also format text with bold type, italics, and other effects by click-ing the appropriate buttons on the toolbar.

5. Click Send.

The display returns to the Contact list, and your message is sent.

From an appointment

After you enter the particulars about an appointment, you may want to send that information to someone else, to tell that person what the appointment is about, where it occurs, and when it occurs.

To send an e-mail message with information about an appointment:

1. Click the Calendar icon.

The Calendar appears.

2. Drag the appointment you're interested in from the Calendar to the Inbox icon (see Figure 3-2).

The Message form appears.

Figure 3-2: Dragging an appointment to the Inbox creates a new message.

3. In the To text box, type the name of the person to whom you want to send a copy of the appointment.

Alternatively, you can click the To button and choose the person's name from the Address Book. If you use the Address Book, you have to click To again and then click OK.

4. Click the Send button (or press Alt+S).

Your recipient gets an e-mail message with details about the meeting. You can add additional comments in the text box.

If you plan to invite other people in your organization to a meeting, and you want to check their schedules to plan the meeting, you can also use the Meeting Planner tab of the Appointment form. For this method to work, the people whom you plan to invite to the meeting must be sharing their schedules through Microsoft Exchange Server.

Sending a File by E-Mail

Sometimes, you don't need to type in a message; you just want to send a file by e-mail — that Excel spreadsheet with sales figures, for example, or your new book proposal in Word.

When you send someone a file (or when someone sends you a file), the file travels as a part of the message called an *attachment*. When you attach a file to your e-mail message, the recipient gets a copy of the file, and you still have one, too. The process is like sending a fax, except that no paper is involved, and it's better than a fax because the person who gets the file can make changes in the file.

Dragging a file to the Inbox is a tiny bit more complicated than dragging contacts or appointments because files are located using the My Computer icon, which is in a different section of the Outlook Bar from the Inbox. When you're accustomed to the different groups in the Outlook Bar, it's a breeze to drag and drop files anywhere you want them.

To send a file using e-mail:

1. Click the Other group separator bar in the Outlook Bar.

The My Computer and My Documents folders appear.

2. Click the My Documents icon.

The list of files in the My Documents folder appears.

3. Click the name of the file that you want to send.

The file darkens, indicating that it has been selected (see Figure 3-3).

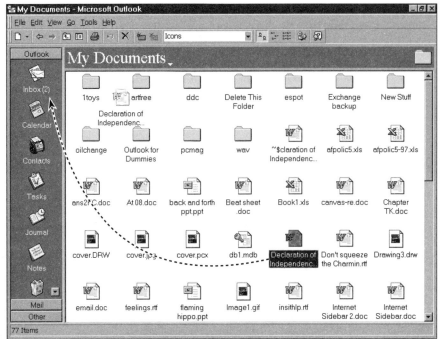

Figure 3-3:
Select the
file that you
want to drag
to the Inbox.

4. Click the Outlook group divider in the Outlook Bar.

The Inbox icon appears, along with all the usual Outlook icons.

5. Drag the file that you selected to the Inbox icon.

The New Message form appears, with an icon in the message space (see Figure 3-4).

6. In the To text box, type the name of the person to whom you want to send a copy of the file.

Alternatively, you can click the To button and choose the person's name from the Address Book. If you use the Address Book, you have to click To again and then click OK.

7. Click the Send button (or press Alt+S).

Your file is on its way.

Isn't that easy? There's actually an even easier way: When you're working on a file in Word, Excel, or PowerPoint, choose Send To➪Mail Recipient, and then perform Steps 6 and 7 of the preceding list.

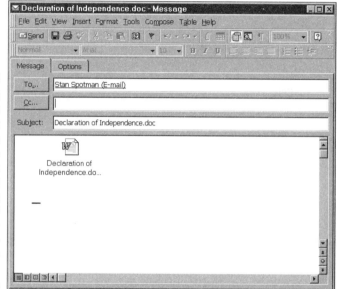

Look out for heavy files!

When it comes to sending e-mail, all files are created equal, but some are much bigger than others. You can e-mail all files, big and small, but the big ones can take a long time to send and receive. If you and the person to whom you're sending a file are on the same network, the size of the file isn't such a big problem. If you're sending the file to someone who gets e-mail from an online service over a regular telephone line, however, it's a good idea to check with that person to see whether he or she is willing to accept a file that could take 10 to 15 minutes, or more, to download. Not all online services let your recipient know the size of the files he or she is getting.

Think about that when you send a file. If the size of the file that you're sending is measured in megabytes, it could take some time for the person to whom you're sending the file to receive it. Some people think that you broke their machines because the file took so long to receive. You can't break someone's machine by sending a file, but there are people to whom you don't want to give that impression. You can use compression programs like PKZIP or WinZip to reduce the size of your files before you send them, but it's still possible to create files that take a long time to send through a phone line even when you compress them.

Creating Contact Records from E-Mail

You can drag an item from any other Outlook module to the Contacts icon, but the only item that makes sense to drag is an e-mail message, so as to create a Contact record that includes the e-mail address. You not only save work by dragging a message to the Contacts icon, but also eliminate the risk of misspelling the e-mail address.

To create a new Contact record:

1. **Click the Inbox icon.**

   A list of your current incoming e-mail messages appears. Select the message for which you want to make a Contact record (see Figure 3-5).

2. **Drag the selected message to the Contacts icon.**

   The New Contact form opens, with the name and e-mail address of the person who sent the message filled in.

3. **If you want to include more information than the e-mail address of the contact, enter that information in the appropriate box on the Contact form.**

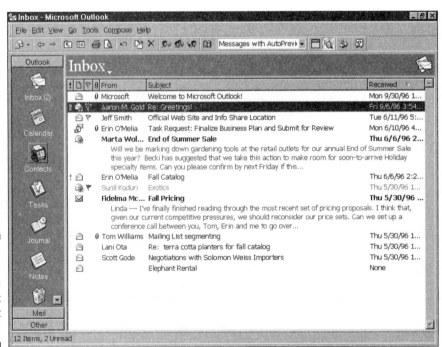

Figure 3-5:
Aaron M.
Gold is
about to get
a Contact
record.

You can change existing information or add information — the company for whom the person works, the postal mail address, other phone numbers, and so on.

If the body of the e-mail message contains information that you want to use as contact information, select that information and drag it to the appropriate box of the New Contact form.

4. **Click the Save and Close button (or press Alt+S).**

   You now have the e-mail address and any other information for the new contact stored for future reference.

Another quick way to capture an e-mail address from an incoming message is to right-click the name of the sender in the From line of the incoming message block. The From line is not a normal text box, so you may not think that right-clicking it would do anything, but it does. A shortcut menu appears. Click Add to Contacts to open the New Contact dialog box. Then follow the last two steps of the preceding list.

Creating a Journal Entry for a Contact

The most useful thing to drag to the Journal icon is a contact listing, which automatically opens a Journal entry in the name of that contact. You can make a note of a phone call or letter you've received from that person, or you can make a note of a conversation you had with that person.

To open a Journal entry:

1. **Click the Contacts icon.**

   The Contact list appears.

2. **Drag a name from your address list to the Journal icon.**

   A Journal Entry form appears, with the contact record that you dragged entered as an attachment.

3. **From the Entry type menu, choose the type of event that you're recording.**

   Phone call is the default choice, because it's most useful (see Figure 3-6). You may also want to use letter, fax, or conversation. The e-mail and other contact information is nice, but most of that information is entered in the Journal automatically, so it's not entirely necessary to make Journal entries for e-mail and other new contact information.

4. **Click Save and Close (or press Alt+S).**

The benefit of creating Journal entries for the phone calls you receive is that you can check your contact entries later and see a record of all the phone calls and other messages you've exchanged.

Figure 3-6:
You can
create a
Journal
from a
Contact
entry to
keep track
of phone
calls or
other types
of
interactions
with people
on your
contact list.

Drag and Drop Dead: Deleting Stuff

If in doubt, throw it out. You know the drill.

Here's how to delete an item using drag and drop.

1. Click the Notes icon in the Outlook Bar.

Your list of notes appears. You can click any icon that has items you want to delete; I'm just using notes as an example.

2. Drag a note to the Deleted Items icon in the Outlook Bar.

Kiss it goodbye — it's gone.

If you change your mind after deleting something, just click the Deleted Items folder; the folder opens and a list of everything that you've deleted is there. It's like being a hit man in the afterlife; you get another chance to see everyone you've disposed of. Except in this case you can bring items back to life; just drag them back to where they came from. Even Don Corleone couldn't do that.

Chapter 4

Files and Folders: A Quick Course in Keeping Things Straight

*F*iles and folders frequently flummox folks who use Windows. Fortunately, Outlook has a good set of tools for managing files and folders, so the issue of file management should be easier to understand if you're using Outlook. But you still need to understand basic file management to take advantage of the improved tools in Outlook.

I'll assume that you're familiar with using files and folders in Windows so that I can focus on showing you the file-management features of Outlook. For an excellent explanation of how to deal with files, see *DOS For Dummies,* Windows 95 Edition, by Dan Gookin, published by IDG Books Worldwide, Inc., which describes the concepts in full detail.

If your experience goes way back to 1993 when people used Windows 3.1 (heaven help 'em!), these critters were called files and directories. When Windows 95 came out, Microsoft started using the word *folders* rather than directories, but folders and directories are exactly the same thing.

Whatever you call them, files and folders still reside on floppy disks, hard drives, and network drives. Floppy disks and hard drives have letter names (A:, B:, C:, and so on), while files and folders are named in plain English.

If your computer is connected to a network, you also have hard drives that belong to the network. These drives are not on your computer; they're somewhere else in the building, but on your computer they show up in Outlook or Windows Explorer as if they were on your own machine. The network makes the hard drives on the network look just like the one inside your machine when you're looking for files, and that's fine. You can treat files on the network just as though they are files on your computer.

Networks also allow you to share files with other people. A network is a little like a library; you can use a file when you need it and then put it back. Later, someone else may come along and use the file; then that person puts the file back so that yet another person can use it. Your network administrator can configure the system to prevent other people from changing your files, or prevent you from changing other people's files.

Managing Your Files

File management is a fancy term for looking at your files and folders and arranging what you have the way you want it. The first step toward managing your files is seeing them.

To see a listing of your files, follow these steps:

1. Choose Go⇨My Computer.

There it is — you see a list of your drives, in all their glory (see Figure 4-1). Why would you want to see a list of your drives? To see a list of your folders, of course.

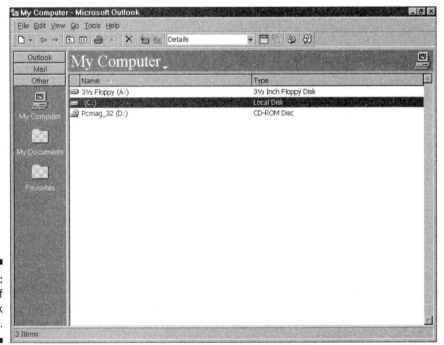

Figure 4-1:
A list of
your disk
drives.

2. Double-click the icon for the C drive.

A list of the folders on your C drive appears. Doesn't that make your day?

3. To view a list of the files in your folders, double-click the icon for the folder whose contents you wish to see (such as the My Documents folder).

You see a listing of all the files in the My Documents folder (see Figure 4-2). If there are subfolders within the My Documents folder, you can see the names of the files in any of those folders by double-clicking on the icon for a folder whose contents you want to see.

I assume that you have a folder called My Documents because Office 97 creates a folder like that during installation. My Documents is the folder where Office 97 programs like to save the documents that you create, unless you tell the programs to save the documents somewhere else. If you don't have a My Documents folder, double-click another folder — whichever folder you want. You get the idea; double-clicking the icon for a folder makes Outlook show you a list of the files in the folder.

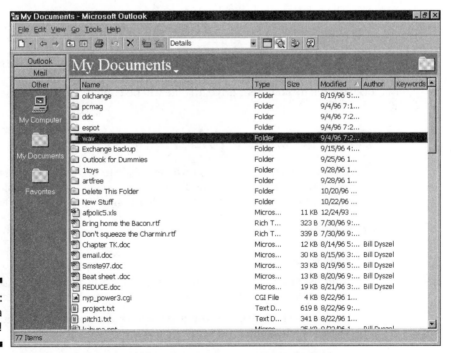

Figure 4-2:
Now that's a
list of files!

Selecting files

After you open a folder to see the list of files in it, you need to select a file or files in order to move, copy, or delete a file or group of files. Here's what you do:

- ✔ To select a single file, click its name.

- ✔ To select several files that are next to one another, click the first one, hold down the Shift key, and click the last one. The first and last file are selected, along with all the files in between.

- ✔ To select several files that are not next to one another, click one and then hold down the Ctrl key while clicking the others.

Moving, copying, and deleting files

To move a file from one folder to another, follow these steps:

1. **Click the file that you want to move.**

   The selected file is highlighted.

2. **Drag the file to the folder where you want to move it.**

If the folder to which you drag the file is on the same drive (such as the C drive) as the folder where the file was originally located, the file will be moved. If you drag the file to a different drive, the file will be copied.

Creating a new folder

There are times when you just need a new place to put things. You may need to create a new folder for a new group of files from a client or to keep the documents concerning a certain project together to make them easier to find.

Here's how you create a new folder:

1. **Choose <u>G</u>o⇨My Computer.**

   Your list of drives appears. You can also click the Other separator bar in the Outlook Bar, and then click the My Computer icon.

2. **Double-click the icon for the drive where you want to create a new folder (such as the C drive).**

   The list of folders on the drive you selected appears.

3. **Choose File⇨New⇨Folder (or press Ctrl+Shft+E).**

   The Create New Folder dialog box appears.

4. **Type the name you want to give to your new folder.**

   The name appears in the dialog box.

5. **Click OK.**

Your new file appears in your list of folders. If you want to create a new folder inside an existing folder, double-click the icon next to the existing folder before choosing File⇨New⇨Folder.

Renaming folders

Marilyn Monroe and John Wayne changed their names from Norma Jean and Marion (guess who was Marion). That just goes to show you that sometimes there's a darn good reason to change a name. You can change the name of any folder to anything you want.

There are some folders that you shouldn't rename, two in particular. Renaming your My Documents folder could make it difficult to find your documents when you're using other Office programs because they normally look in the My Documents folder for the documents they created. You can configure the programs to find the folder by its new name if you rename it, but it's easier to leave it alone. Renaming your Windows directory could cause big problems; your programs may not run and your computer may not start without some serious glaring and grumbling from your computer guru. You're best off to leave those two directories with their original names.

To rename a folder:

1. **Right-click the name of the folder that you want to rename.**

   A menu appears.

2. **Choose Rename.**

   The Rename dialog box appears with the old folder name highlighted.

3. **Type the new name of the folder.**

   The new folder name replaces the old name in the dialog box.

4. **Click OK.**

You can't rename a folder when it's open. If you can see the names of the files in a folder, the folder is open, and you can't rename that folder. You can choose Go⇨Up One Level, select the folder, and try again.

Renaming files

Renaming files is nearly identical to renaming folders, except that folders have no file extensions, which are the three-character suffixes like .DOC or .XLS or .EXE that Windows uses to identify which program should run when you double-click a file to open it. If you try to rename a file that ends in .EXE, Windows warns you that it's a program file and suggests that you think twice before renaming it. As long as you keep the last three letters the same as they started, you should have no problem.

To rename a file:

1. **Right-click the name of the file that you want to rename.**

   A menu appears, with commands including Open, Delete, and Rename.

2. **Choose Rename from the menu.**

   The Rename dialog box appears (see Figure 4-3).

Figure 4-3:
The Rename dialog box lets you change the name of any file.

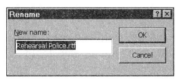

3. **Type the new name of the file.**

   The new folder name replaces the old name in the dialog box.

4. **Click OK.**

When you first open the Rename dialog box, the old name of the file is displayed and is highlighted. As soon as you start typing, the old name disappears; whatever you type as the new name replaces it.

What's in a name: file extensions

Windows 95 normally hides the last three letters of a file's name, known as the file extension. The extension starts with a period and indicates what program created a file. Well, not always; that's the problem. Although the file extension is a leftover from the days of DOS that we'd all rather forget, Windows 95 uses the file extension when it tries to figure out what kind of program created a certain file. That's how Windows 95 knows what program to run when you double-click the name of a file. Windows 95 knows that it should open Word and not Excel when you click a Word file, for example, because Word files have names that end in .DOC. When you rename a file, it's possible to change the file extension, which makes Windows very confused; it may not know what to do with a file that doesn't have exactly

the right extension. The situation is pretty silly. It's as though you picked up a clear Coke bottle with dishwater in it but didn't know that it was dishwater because the label said Coke. You'd know better than to drink it, but Windows 95 wouldn't.

If your machine is showing you the file extensions, be careful not to change the extensions when you're changing file names. You can tell that file names are showing if all the files created by Microsoft Word end in .DOC, for example, and all the Excel files end in .XLS. Changing the extensions of your files can make Windows 95 so confused that it will refuse to view or open certain documents for you if they're not properly named.

Using Views with Files and Folders

There's always been some way to see what files you have and where you have them. The Windows Explorer is the file-management tool that comes with Windows 95. Making sense of your collection of documents gets more complicated after you collect a few hundred files. Sometimes you need to know more than you can get from the simple list of your files that Explorer shows you. Outlook can show you more information about each file, including things like the author, page count, or the time and date that a file was most recently printed.

Outlook allows you to arrange and sort information about your files in many slick ways. I show you the basic, plain-vanilla approaches to viewing your lists of files in this chapter. In Chapter 21, I get into the really cool things that Outlook can do but Windows Explorer can't.

You may not need the fancy stuff, though. The basic file-management tricks in this chapter will take you a long way.

Sorting files in a folder

Every view of your files (except Document Timeline view, which I explain in a minute) is organized in rows and columns. Each row contains the information for one file, and each column contains one type of information about each file listed. You can sort the entire list by the contents of one column with a single mouse click.

To sort files in a folder:

1. **Choose Go⇨My Computer.**

   A list of your drives appears.

2. **Double-click the icon for the C drive.**

   A list of the folders on your C drive appears.

3. **To view a list of the files in your folders, double-click the icon for the folder whose contents you wish to see.**

   You see a listing of all the files in the folder you selected.

4. **Click the name at the top of the column you want to sort by.**

If you have many files, Outlook needs a few seconds to sort them out; it fills the time by showing you a little box containing the letters A, F, and Z. Outlook juggles the letters around and then displays the list of files in the order that you suggested. I usually put my files in name order or date order (by date modified), but you can sort by any column on the screen.

Icons view

The Icons view is a way of displaying your files that consists of no more than filling the screen with icons accompanied by the names of the files they represent. Icons are bigger and friendlier-looking than plain old lists of files, but they don't give you as much information. If you don't want much information, that's good. If you want more information about each file, such as its size and the name of the program that created it, switch to another view, such as Details view.

Here's what you do to see the Icons view:

1. **Choose Go⇨My Computer.**

   Your list of drives appears. If you can see the My Computer icon in the Outlook Bar on the left side of the screen, you can click that instead.

2. **Double-click the name of one of your drives, such as the C drive.**

   Your list of folders appears.

3. **Double-click the name of a folder, such as My Documents.**

   A list of the files in the folder appears.

4. **Choose View⟹Current View⟹Icons.**

   A list of icons appears (see Figure 4-4). The word *Icons* appears in the Current View menu in the toolbar. Just to the right of the Current View menu is a set of three buttons, each of which bears a small diagram of a group of icons. Clicking any of the three buttons changes the type of Icon view that you see: large icons, small icons, or a list of icons. You can change among these views at will.

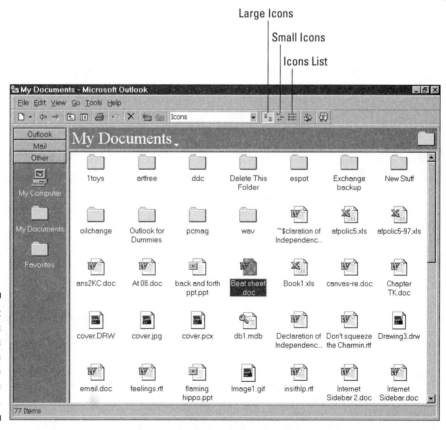

Figure 4-4: The Icons view is less informative but easier to read than other views.

Details view

Details view is a plain old list of file names, sizes, dates, and so on — in other words, it gives you all the, uh, details. Lists in Details view look just like the lists that Windows Explorer gives you, but the Outlook version can do much more (see Chapter 5 for more about views).

To see your files in Details view:

1. **Choose Go➪My Computer.**

   Your list of drives appears. If you can see the My Computer icon in the Outlook Bar on the left side of the screen, you can click that instead.

2. **Double-click the name of one of your drives, such as the C drive.**

   Your list of folders appears.

3. **Double-click the name of a folder, such as My Documents.**

   A list of the files in that folder appears.

4. **Choose View➪Current View➪Details.**

Details view is the view that I choose to use most of the time, because it shows me all the files in the folder I've chosen and gives me the most information at a glance.

By Author view

Guess how By Author view groups your files? If it's good enough for the library to organize by author, it's good enough for me.

To see your files in the By Author view:

1. **Choose Go➪My Computer.**

   Your list of drives appears. If you can see the My Computer icon in the Outlook Bar on the left side of the screen, you can click that instead.

2. **Double-click the name of one of your drives, such as the C drive.**

   Your list of folders appears.

3. **Double-click the name of a folder, such as My Documents.**

   A list of the files in the folder appears.

4. **Choose View➪Current View➪By Author.**

   A list of your files appears, grouped by author (see Figure 4-5).

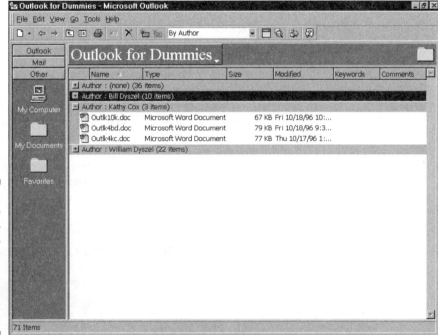

Figure 4-5:
The By Author view groups your files by the name of the person who created them.

If you're the only person who uses your computer, you really don't want to use the By Author view. You're the only author, so you'd see all the files in whatever order they happen to be in. Viewing By Author is more useful when you share files on a network with many other people. Then questions of authorship are important. You'll also find viewing files By Author to be handy if you consolidate the work of several people; this way, you know at a glance which file came from whom.

By File Type view

By File Type view groups your files according to what kind of program created the file. Files created by Microsoft Word are one type; files created by Excel are another file type. Some file types can be created by more than one program, but Windows always associates files of a certain type with only one program.

To use the By File Type view:

1. Choose Go⇨My Computer.

Your list of drives appears. If you can see the My Computer icon in the Outlook Bar on the left side of the screen, you can click that instead.

2. Double-click the name of one of your drives, such as the C drive.

Your list of folders appears.

3. Double-click the name of a folder, such as My Documents.

A list of the files in the folder appears.

4. Choose View⇨Current View⇨By File Type.

A list of your files appears grouped according to the program that created them (see Figure 4-6).

You want to use By File Type view to give yourself a shorter list to look at when you're trying to find a file in a folder. If you're looking for an Excel file in a folder that has 2 Excel files and 98 Word files, it's easier to find 1 of 2 files in the Excel group than 1 of 100 in the entire folder, right?

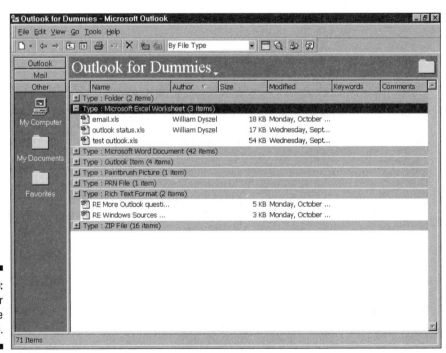

Figure 4-6:
See your
files By File
Type.

Document Timeline view

The Document Timeline view is an interesting new way to view your files according to the last date on which they were modified. Because you can click the heading of the Date Modified column to sort your files by date, you actually don't need Document Timeline view, but the Document Timeline is much cooler to look at than a simple list of file names. That's good enough for me.

To use the cool Document Timeline view:

1. **Choose Go⇨My Computer.**

   Your list of drives appears. If you can see the My Computer icon in the Outlook Bar on the left side of the screen, you can click that instead.

2. **Double-click the name of one of your drives, such as the C drive.**

   Your list of folders appears.

3. **Double-click the name of a folder, such as My Documents.**

   A list of the files in the folder appears.

4. **Choose View⇨Current View⇨Document Timeline.**

The Document Timeline appears with icons representing each of your files organized by the date when they were last modified (see Figure 4-7).

Four buttons appear just to the right of the Current View menu in the toolbar when you use Document Timeline view. The leftmost button centers the timeline on today's date. You can also scroll left and right to see files modified on earlier and later dates. The next button shows you just one day; clicking a date in the top line of the timeline takes you to that date. The next button shows you seven days' worth of documents; the button after that shows a month's worth of documents.

The Document Timeline is helpful when you can't remember what you called a file but you know when you used it last. You can just look at the date you remember using the file in the timeline and you'll find your document.

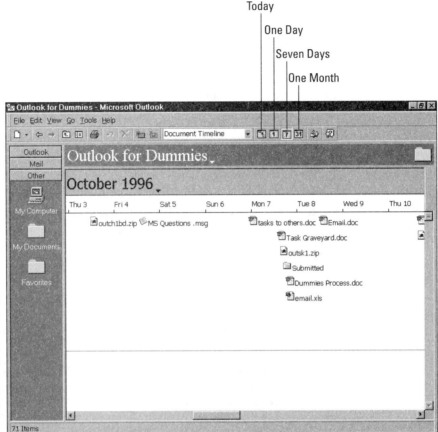

Figure 4-7:
The
Document
Timeline
shows you
your files in
chronological
order.

Programs view

Way back at the beginning of this chapter, I talk about the fact that some files
are programs; they make the computer do actual work. Sometimes, the programs are useful (games and cool screen savers); other times, they just create
boring stuff like letters and spreadsheets. Either way, be careful when you
delete or rename program files; you might lose a program you need. Windows
warns you when you're deleting a program file, so you'll know to be careful.

To see your files in Programs view:

1. **Choose Go⇨My Computer.**

   Your list of drives appears. If you can see the My Computer icon in the Outlook Bar on the left side of the screen, you can click that instead.

2. **Double-click the name of one of your drives, such as the C drive.**

   Your list of folders appears.

3. **Double-click the name of a folder, such as My Documents.**

   A list of the files in the folder appears.

4. **Choose View⇨Current View⇨Programs.**

A list of the program files in the directory you're viewing appears (see Figure 4-8).

Many folders don't have any programs in them, so don't be surprised if you get a blank screen when you try Programs view. If you don't see any files that end in the letters .EXE, you don't have any Program files.

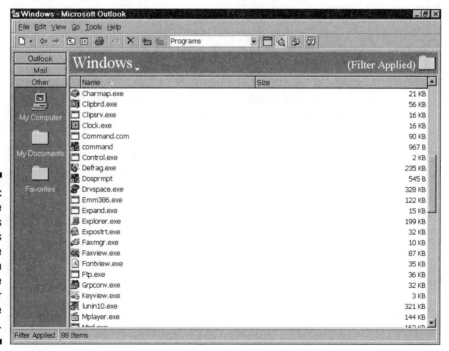

Figure 4-8: The Programs view shows you the program files in the folder you've chosen.

Why bother?

You can also use Windows Explorer in Windows 95 to deal with files and folders, but I believe that Outlook does the job much more sensibly. You also have options for arranging your view of your files and folders in Outlook that simply don't exist in Windows Explorer.

Windows 95 has started hiding the inner workings of the computer just to make you more comfortable, but you can peek behind the scenes if you really want to see how things happen. Windows 95 also allows you to give your files sensible names that have more than eight characters, which you could not do with older versions of Windows. Sensible file names make recordkeeping easier for people, but many

people still find the concepts of drives and folders to be nonsensical.

People work on computers every single day and many still don't understand the machines too well, but they get along fine anyway, so don't worry. On the other hand, if you understand how your drives and folders are organized, the knowledge can help in a pinch. The system of files and folders is simple once you think about it a bit. It's like a road map that seems complicated at first, but once you've learned to use a map you can get where you're going faster. Because Outlook presents your system of files and folders more understandably, the whole issue of keeping track of your files seems much simpler.

Final Facts on Filing

If you like to get down to the nitty-gritty in dealing with files and folders, you'll like using Outlook because its file-management tools are so powerful, including the capability to add fields and save custom views. For a taste of the really cool file-management tricks that you can do with Outlook, see Chapter 19.

If you move or copy files only on pain of death or when bribed with chocolate, you'll like using Outlook because you can create a few simple views (or have someone else create and save some simple views for you) and not be bothered with all the ugly details of files, folders, and whatnot. You can have it both ways, but only in Outlook; the other Office 97 programs can't do the tricks that Outlook can!

Chapter 5

How You See It: Views and New Views

*W*hen you boil it down, the two biggest things that you do in Outlook are entering information and viewing it. This chapter is about viewing information any way you want to look at it, which makes the information easier for you to use and understand.

Any body of information can have a variety of looks. Each look is referred to as a *view* in Outlook parlance. You don't have to think much about views if you'd rather not, because when you buy Outlook, dozens of views are included. Simply choose the one you want. I describe the main views in this chapter.

Types of Views

Choosing a view is like renting a car. You can choose a model with the features that you want, whether the car is a convertible, a minivan, or a luxury sedan. All cars are equipped with different things — radios, air conditioning, power cup holders, and so on — that you can use or not use, as you please. Some offer unlimited free mileage. Outlook views are much more economical, though; in fact, they're free.

Every module in Outlook has its own selection of views. The Calendar has (among others) a view that looks calendarlike. The Contacts module includes a view that looks like an address card. The Journal and the Tasks modules include a Timeline view. All modules allow you to use at least one type of Table view, which organizes your data in the old-fashioned row-and-column arrangement.

Each type of view is organized to make something about your collection of information obvious at first glance. You can change the way that you view a view by sorting, filtering, or grouping.

You don't have to do anything to see a view; Outlook is *always* displaying some kind of view. The view is the thing that takes up most of the screen most of the time. The view (or the Information Viewer, in official Microsoftese) is one of only two parts of Outlook that you can't turn off. (You also can't turn off the menu bar.)

Each view has a name, which is displayed at the top of the screen in the Current View box in the toolbar. Click the Current View box, and a menu drops down, listing other views that are available to you in the module that you're using.

Table view

All modules contain some version of the Table view. A Table view is square — all rows and columns. If you create a new item by adding a new task to your Tasks list, for example, a new row turns up in the Table view. There's one row for each task in Table view (see Figure 5-1).

The names of Table views often contain the word *list,* as in Simple List, Phone List, or just List. That word means that they're a plain-vanilla table of items, just like a grocery list. Other Table view names start with the word *By,* which means that items in the view are grouped by a certain type of information, such as by entry type or by name of contact. I discuss grouped views later in the chapter and show you how to group items your own way.

Icons view

Icons view is the simplest view — just a bunch of icons with names thrown on the screen (see Figure 5-2).

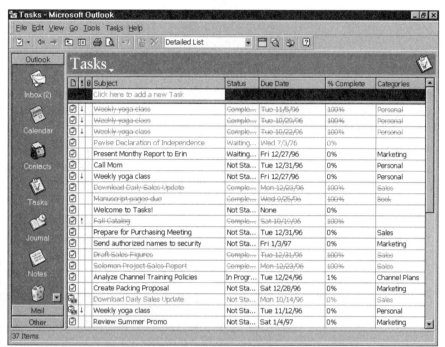

Figure 5-1:
The Tasks
module in a
Table view.

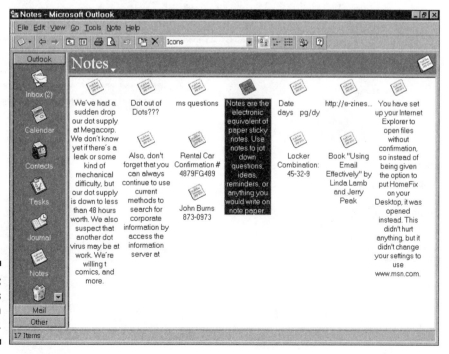

Figure 5-2:
The Notes
module in
Icons view.

The only Icons views that come with Outlook are used for viewing notes and file folders. Icons view doesn't show a great deal of information, and some people like it that way. I like to see more detailed information, so I stay with Table views. There's nothing wrong with using Icons view most of the time; you can easily switch to another view if you need to see more.

Timeline view

Timeline views show you a set of small icons arranged across the screen. Icons that are higher on the screen represent items that were created or tasks that were begun earlier in the day. Icons that are farther to the left were created on an earlier date (see Figure 5-3).

The Task Timeline in the Tasks module also draws a line that represents the length of time that it takes to perform an item if the start and end times of a task have been specified previously.

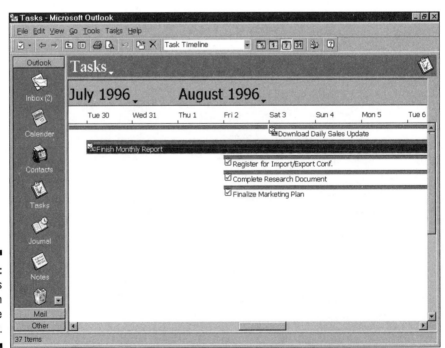

Figure 5-3:
Tasks
arranged in
the Timeline
view.

A Timeline view includes four toolbar buttons that allow you to change the length of time you want to view. Your choices are Today, 1-day (not necessarily today), 7-day, and 31-day (or one month). As you can do in all other view settings, you can click to move between 1-day and 7-day views and back, like changing television channels.

Card view

Card views are designed for the Contacts module. Each Contact item gets its own little block of information (see Figure 5-4). Each little block displays a little or a lot of information about the item, depending on what kind of card it is. (See Chapter 10 for more about the different views in the Contacts module).

The Address Cards view shows you only a few items at a time, because the cards are so big. To make it easier to find a name in your Contact list that's not displayed on the screen, you can type the first letter of the name that your contact is filed under to see that person's address card.

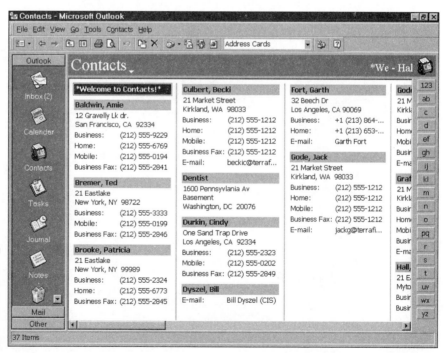

Figure 5-4:
See your
Contacts in
Address
Cards view.

Day/Week/Month view

Day/Week/Month view is another specialized view, designed particularly for the Calendar.

Like a Timeline view, Day/Week/Month view adds 1-day, 7-day, and 31-day (month) buttons to the toolbar to allow you to switch between views easily. The 1- and 7-day views also display a 3-month calendar. You can click any date in the monthly calendar to switch your view to that date (see Figure 5-5).

Playing with Columns in Table View

Table views show you the most detailed information about the items that you've created; they also allow you to organize the information in the greatest number of ways with the least effort. Okay, Table views look a little dull, but they get you where you need to go.

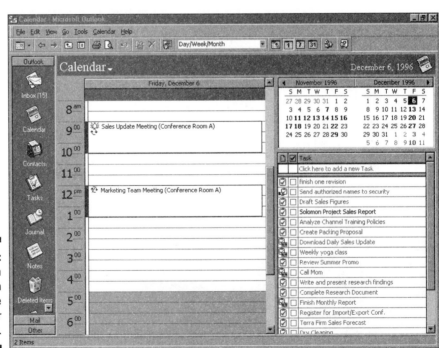

Figure 5-5:
Starting a
day in
the life
of your
calendar.

Table views are organized in columns and rows. Each row displays information for one item: one appointment in your Calendar, one task in your Tasks list, or one person in your Contact list. Adding a row is easy. Just add an item, press Ctrl+N, and then fill in the information you want for that item. Getting rid of a row is easy, too. Just delete the item. Click your mouse to select the item and then press the Delete key.

The columns in a Table view show you pieces of information about each item. Most Outlook modules can store far more pieces of information about an item than you can display on screen in row-and-column format. The Contact list, for example, holds more than 90 pieces of information about every person in your list. If each person is represented by one row, you would have to have more than 90 columns to display everything.

Adding a column

Outlook starts you out with 11 columns in the Phone List view of your Contact list. (Remember that the names of Table views usually have "list" in them somewhere.) If you want more columns, you can easily add some. You can display as many columns as you want in Outlook, but you may have to scroll across the screen to see the information that you want to see.

To add a column in any Table view:

1. **Choose View➪Field Chooser.**

   You can also right-click the heading of any column and choose Field Chooser from the shortcut menu. The Field Chooser dialog box appears.

2. **Choose the type of field that you want to add.**

   The words `Frequently-Used Fields` appear in the text box at the top of the Field Chooser. Those words mean that the types of fields most people like to add are already listed. If the name of the field that you want to add isn't listed in one of the gray boxes at the bottom of the Field Chooser dialog box, pull down the menu that `Frequently-Used Fields` is part of and see what's available.

3. **Drag the field into the table.**

You have to drag the new item to the top row of the table, where the heading names are (see Figure 5-6). Notice that the names in the Field Chooser are in the same kind of gray box as the headers of each column of your table. (If they look alike, they must belong together, like Michael Jackson and Lisa Marie. Right? . . . maybe that's not the best example.)

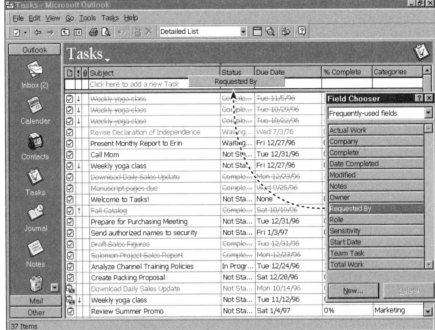

Figure 5-6:
The
Requested
By field is
dragged to
the top row
of the table.

Moving a column

Moving columns is even easier than adding columns. Just drag the heading of the column to where you want it (see Figure 5-7).

Columns = fields

I promised to tell you how to add a column, and now I'm telling you about fields. What gives? Well, columns are fields, see? No? Well, think of it this way.

In your checkbook, your check record has a *column* of the names of the people to whom you wrote checks and another *column* that contains the amounts of those checks. When you actually write a check, you write the name of the payee in a certain *field* in the check; the amount goes in a

different *field*. So you enter tidbits of information as *fields* in the check, but you show them as *columns* in the check record. That's exactly how it works in Outlook. You enter somebody's name, address, and phone number in *fields* when you create a new item, but the Table view shows the same information to you in *columns*. When you're adding a column, you're adding a field. Same thing.

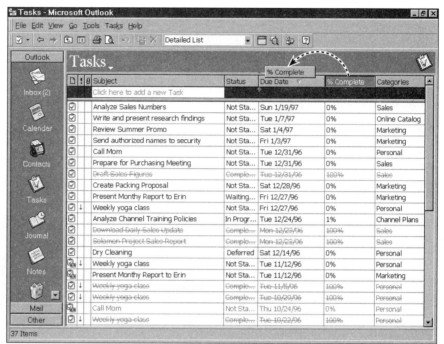

Figure 5-7:
Moving the
% Complete
column.

Two little red arrows appear as you're dragging the heading to show you where the column will end up when you release the mouse button.

Formatting a column

Some fields contain too much information to fit in their columns. Dates are prime offenders. Outlook normally displays dates in this format: Fri 7/4/97 4:14 PM. I normally don't care what day of the week a date falls on, so I reformat the column to 7/4/97 4:14 PM and save the other space for something that I really want to know.

To change the formatting of a column:

1. Right-click the heading of a column.

A menu appears.

2. Choose Format Columns.

The Format Columns dialog box appears (see Figure 5-8).

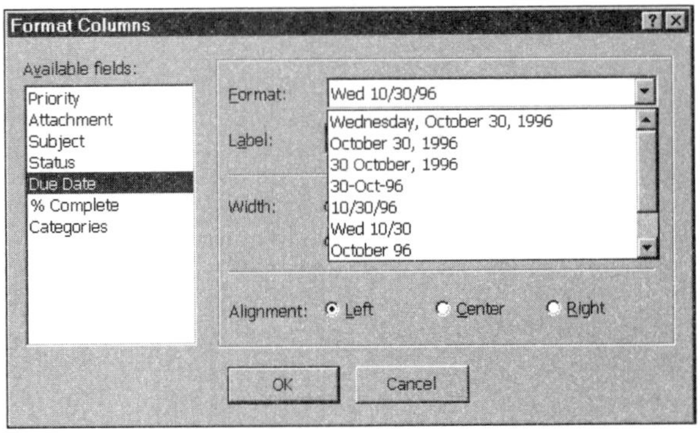

Figure 5-8:
The Format
Columns
dialog box.

3. **Choose a format type from the Format menu.**

Pick whatever suits your fancy. Some columns contain information that can be formatted only one way, such as names and categories. Information in number columns (especially dates) can be formatted in a variety of ways.

4. **Click OK.**

Your column is reformatted.

Changing a column format affects only that column in that view of that module. If you want to change the formats of other views and modules, you have to change them one at a time.

Widening (or shrinking) a column

Widening (or shrinking) a column is even easier than moving a column. Here's how:

1. **Move the mouse pointer to the right edge of the column that you want to widen (or shrink) until the pointer becomes a two-headed arrow.**

Making that mouse pointer turn into a two-headed arrow takes a bit of dexterity. If you find the procedure to be difficult, you can use the Format Column procedure described in the preceding section. Type a number in the Width box — bigger numbers for wider boxes and smaller numbers for narrower boxes.

2. **Drag the edge of the column until the column is the width that you desire.**

The two-headed arrow creates a thin line that you can drag to resize the column (see Figure 5-9).

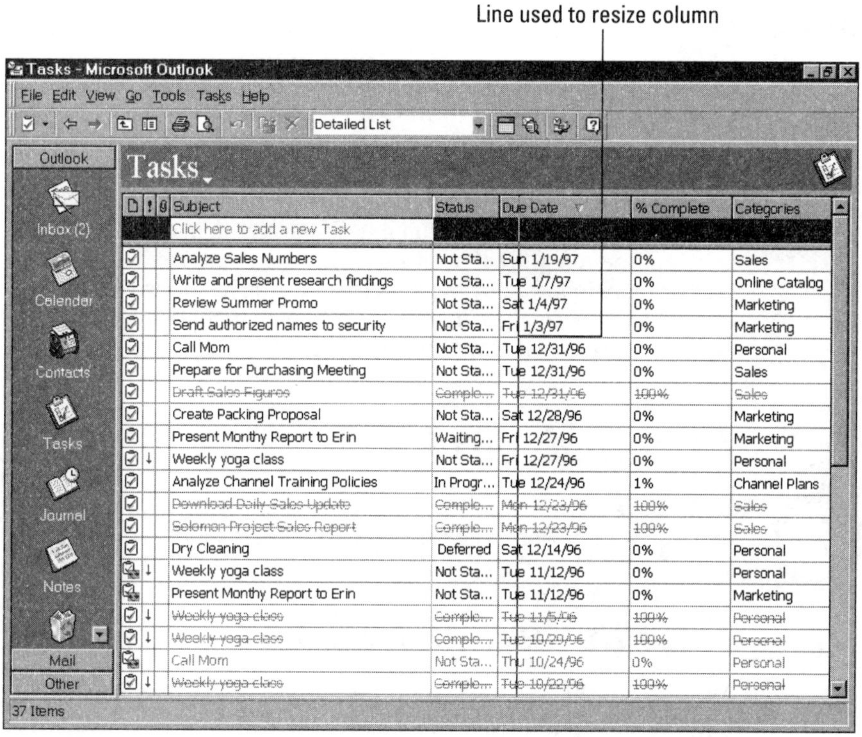

Line used to resize column

Figure 5-9:
Widening
the Status
column.

What you see is what you get.

Removing a column

You can remove columns that you don't want to look at.

To remove a column:

1. **Right-click the heading of the column that you want to remove.**

   A menu appears.

2. **Choose Remove This Column.**

   Zap! It's gone!

Don't worry too much about deleting columns. Remember what I said in the
"Columns = fields" sidebar? When you zap a column, the field remains in the
item. You can use the column-adding procedure (described earlier in this
chapter) to put it back.

Sorting

Sorting just means putting your list in order. In fact, a list is always in some kind of order. Sorting changes the order.

You can tell what order your list is sorted in by looking for triangles in headings. A heading with a triangle in it means that the entire list is sorted by the information in that column. If the column has numbers in it, and if the triangle's large side is at the top, the list begins with the item that has the largest number in that column, followed by the item that has the next-largest number, and so on, ending with the smallest number. Columns that contain text get sorted in alphabetical order. *A* is the smallest letter, and *Z* is the largest.

From Table view

By far the easiest way to sort a table is to simply click the heading of a column that you want to sort. The entire table is sorted on the column that you clicked.

From the Sort dialog box

Although clicking on a column is the easiest way to sort, it allows you to sort on only one column. You may want to sort on two or more columns.

To sort on two or more columns:

1. **Choose <u>V</u>iew⇨<u>So</u>rt.**

   The Sort dialog box appears.

2. **From the Sort Items By menu, choose the first field that you want to sort by.**

   Choose carefully; a much larger list of fields is in the list than is usually in the view. It's confusing.

3. **Choose Ascending or Descending sort order.**

   That means to choose whether to sort from smallest to largest or largest to smallest.

4. **Repeat Steps 2 and 3 for each additional field that you want to sort.**

   As the dialog box implies, the first thing that you select is the most important. The entire table is sorted according to that field and then by the fields that you pick later, in the order in which you select them. If you sort your phone list by company first and then by name, for example, your list will begin with the names of the people who work for a certain company, displayed alphabetically, followed by the names of the people who work for another company, and so on.

5. Click OK.

Your list is sorted.

Grouping

Sorting and grouping are similar. Both procedures organize items in your table according to the information in one of the columns. Grouping is different from sorting, however, in that it creates bunches of similar items that you can open or close. You can look at only the bunches that interest you and ignore all the other bunches.

For example, when you balance your checkbook, you probably *sort* your checks by check number. At tax time, you *group* your checks; you make a pile of the checks for medical expenses, another pile of checks for charitable deductions, and another pile of checks for the tax-deductible money that you spend on *...For Dummies* books. Then you can add up the amounts that you spent in each category and enter those figures in your tax return.

Grouping views with drag and drop

The simple way to group items is to open the Group By box and drag a column heading into it (see Figure 5-10).

1. Click the Group By Box button in the toolbar.

The table drops down slightly and a box appears above the table saying, `Drag a column header here to group by that column`.

2. Drag to the Group By box the header of the column that contains the data you want to group by.

You can drag several fields up to the Group By box to create groups based on more than one column (see Figure 5-11).

Group By box   Group By Box button

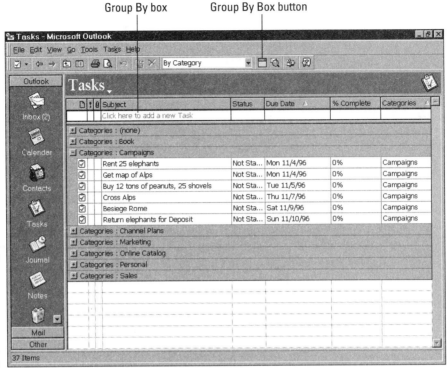

Figure 5-10:
A grouped
view based
on one
column
heading.

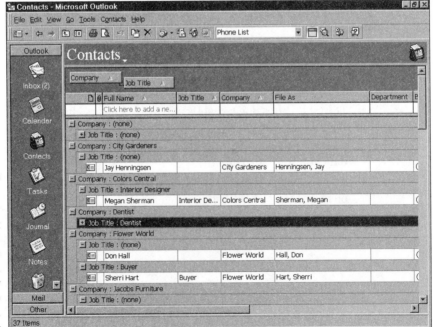

Figure 5-11:
Your
Contact list
grouped
by two
headings,
Company
and Job
Title.

Using the Group By dialog box

Just as you have a second way to sort your listing, you have a second way to group your listing. Just use the Group By dialog box.

To group your list:

1. **Choose View➪Group By.**

   The Group By dialog box appears.

2. **Choose the first field that you want to group the view by.**

   The list has more fields than are showing in the table. If you choose to group by a field that's not showing in your table, you can check the Show Field in View check box (see Figure 5-12).

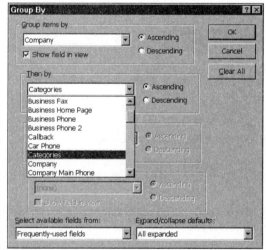

Figure 5-12: The Group By dialog box with the Show Field in View box checked.

3. **Choose any other fields that you want to group the view by.**

   If you group by too many columns, your list will be harder to use, rather than easier.

4. **Click OK.**

Your list is grouped by as many fields as you want.

Viewing grouped items

A grouped view shows you the names of the columns that you used to create the group view. If you click the Contacts icon and choose By Company view (which is a grouped view), you see gray bars with an icon at the right. The word Company is next to it because that's the column that the view is grouped on, and then the name of each company in the list.

The icon at the left end of the gray bar contains either a plus sign or a minus sign. A plus sign means that there's more to be seen. Click the plus sign, and the group opens, revealing the other items that belong to the group. A minus sign means that there's no more to see; what you see is what you get in that group.

If you click the gray bar itself but not the icon, you select the entire group. You can delete the group if you select the gray bar and press the Delete key. When a group bar is selected, it's dark gray rather than light gray, like all the others.

Viewing headings only

You can click the plus and minus signs one at a time to open and close individual groups, or you can open or close all the groups at the same time.

To open or close groups:

1. **Simply choose View➪Expand/Collapse Groups.**

   I think Expanding and Collapsing are dramatic words for what we're doing with these groups. It's not like Scarlett O'Hara getting the vapors; it's just hiding or revealing the contents of a group or all the groups.

2. **To open a single group that you have selected, choose Collapse This Group or Expand This Group.**

3. **To expand or collapse all the groups, choose Expand All Groups or Collapse All Groups.**

What could be easier?

Creating Custom Table Views

If you're used to saving documents in your word processor, then you're familiar with the idea of saving views. When you make any of the changes to a view that I describe earlier in this chapter and then change to another view, Outlook asks whether you want to discard the changes to the view, save the changes as a new view, or make the changes the new way to see the current view. If you plan to use a certain view over and over, it's worth saving.

Here's a simple example of how to save changes to a view. You can do it in any view that's based on a table.

From an existing view

To save changes to a Table view:

1. **Choose any Table view.**

2. **Make changes in the view.**

   Dragging a column to a new position is one change you can make.

3. **Switch to any other view.**

   The Save View Settings dialog box appears, asking whether you want to discard, save, or update the current view (see Figure 5-13).

Figure 5-13:
Care to save
a view?

4. **Choose Save the Current View Settings As a New View.**

   The Copy View dialog box appears.

5. **Type the name that you want to use for the new view.**

   The name that you choose will appear in the toolbar and the View menu.

6. **Click OK.**

I think that changing a view and saving the changes is the easiest way to create new views, because you can see the results before you decide to save the view. If you create a view that you don't like, choose Discard the Current View Settings when the dialog box appears and create a new view.

Using the Define Views dialog box

You can create a new view from scratch by using the Define Views dialog box. Choose View➪Define Views and follow the prompts. This procedure is a little more complicated than simply changing and saving views, but you have more detailed control of the results. When you're comfortable with Outlook, you may want to give the Define Views method a try, but I think that you can to do most of what you need to do just by changing and saving views.

A Bridge from the Views

You can create an endless number of ways to organize and view the information that you save in Outlook. How you decide to view information depends on what kind of information you have and how you plan to use what you have. You can't go too wrong with views, because you can easily create new views if the old ones get messed up. So feel free to experiment.

Chapter 6

Creating Your Own Forms

● ●

● ●

Christmas cookies come in all kinds of shapes — stars, reindeer, Christmas trees, and so on. The cookies get their shapes from a cookie cutter; if you ever make cookies for the holidays, you know how it works. Even though the cookies are different shapes and colors, they're still made of the same ingredients, and they all have a similar taste.

The data that you put in an Outlook item is shaped by a form, which does the same job on data that a cookie cutter does on cookie dough: shapes it and gives it a certain appearance — a standardized format of lines and boxes and text blocks, and such.

Every time you choose File⇨New in Outlook, or double-click an item to open it, a form pops up. Forms allow you to create a new item or edit information in an old item. Forms can be customized to suit your needs (or at least your taste). The forms that come with Outlook are shaped and designed to handle the information that most people use most of the time, but you can create your own forms that allow you to deal with the data you want in the shape in which you want it.

You can't create forms from scratch in Outlook (you need a database program like Microsoft Access for that), just as most people can't create their own cookie cutters. But you can bend a cookie cutter that you already have into a shape you want, and you can adjust one of the existing Outlook forms to meet your needs. Actually, you'll get much better results from customizing Outlook forms than you would by bending your cookie cutters out of shape.

After you customize a form, you can give it a different name from the old form so that you'll have two forms: the original Outlook form and the one that you customized. You can make the forms look entirely different when you use them, even though they're based on the same form.

The best reason to customize a form is to add fields that aren't available in the original form. Fields are categories of information that you need to use, such as phone numbers, names, and addresses. In this section, I show you an example of a form customized to suit a car salesperson. The customized form uses all the information from the original Outlook form and adds a few fields that are specific to the needs of someone who is selling cars.

Adding a Standard Field to a Form

When you first install Outlook, hundreds of standard fields are already set up for you to use. Standard fields are made to store the kind of information that people often need to use like names, addresses, dates, and so on. You can choose to add any of them to your forms, or you can create custom fields. I discuss how to create custom fields later in this chapter.

To add a standard field to an Outlook form:

1. Choose View⇨Folder List.

The Folder List appears (see Figure 6-1), giving you a more detailed view of your Outlook folders. You use the Folder List to create a new folder. I suggest that you create a new folder for this example.

Figure 6-1:
The Folder List, with the Contacts folder highlighted.

2. Right-click the Contacts folder.

A shortcut menu appears. The commands in the menu allow you to create a subfolder, as well as to move, copy, rename, or delete an existing folder.

3. Choose Create Subfolder.

The Create New Folder dialog box appears (see Figure 6-2).

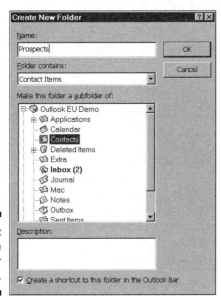

Figure 6-2:
The Create
New Folder
dialog box.

4. Type a name for the folder.

I use **Prospects** for this example.

5. Click OK.

The new folder that you created appears in the Folder List.

6. Click the new folder.

If the Contacts folder has a plus sign next to it, click the plus sign. Subfolders of the Contacts folder appear.

7. Choose File⇨New⇨Contact.

The Contact form appears.

8. Choose Tools⇨Design Outlook Form.

The form switches into Forms Designer mode (see Figure 6-3). The form looks similar to what it looked like before choosing Tools⇨Design Outlook Form, but five new pages — called P.2 through P.6 — appear. These pages are blank pages that you can customize with new fields, new colors, and so on.

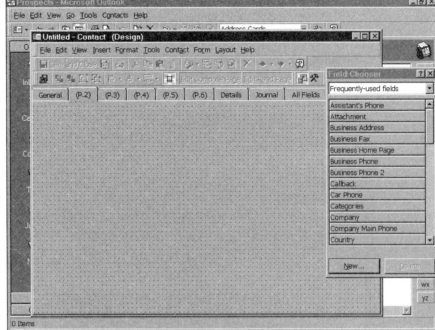

9. **Click (P.2) or any other blank page.**

It's your choice; you can add fields to any of the new pages.

10. **(Optional) To make this page invisible, choose Form⇨Display This Page.**

The parentheses disappear from around P.2. The new pages that appear when you click Design Outlook Form are in parentheses, whereas the ones that appeared originally aren't. That's how you can tell which pages will be visible when you finish customizing the form.

If you want, you can leave all pages visible; but one reason to create a custom form is to reduce the number of steps required to view, enter, or edit the information on the form. You also may be creating this form for other people to use, so you want to keep your form clear and simple. One-page forms are clearer and simpler than multipage forms.

You can click any page and make the page invisible to the user. You can't edit the first page, but you can make it invisible and add the same fields to a different page that you design. You can have a page with just name, address, and home phone, and then make the first page invisible to the user by clicking the General tab, and then choosing Form⇨Display This Page. (The command toggles the page on and off.)

11. **Choose Form⇨Rename Page.**

The Rename Page dialog box appears (see Figure 6-4).

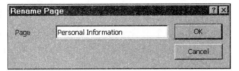

Figure 6-4:
The Rename
Page dialog
box.

12. **Type a new name for the page.**

    I use **Personal Information** as a good name for this page, but any name
    you choose will work.

13. **Click OK.**

    The page tab now has the name that you entered in the Rename Page
    dialog box.

14. **Choose Form⇨Field Chooser.**

    The Field Chooser appears. It's time to add some fields to the new page;
    that's what customizing a form is all about.

    I think that the Field Chooser is confusing. You never see all the fields that
    are available; you see only a certain subset. The words below `Field
    Chooser` tell you which subset you're seeing. In this case, I use the Per-
    sonal fields subset (see Figure 6-5).

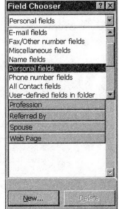

Figure 6-5:
The Field
Chooser
contains
more fields
than you
can see.

You can choose Frequently-Used fields to limit what Outlook shows you to
a small range of fields, or All Contact fields to choose from every kind of
field that Outlook allows in this type of form.

15. Choose Personal Fields and select Referred By.

The fields that Outlook classifies as Personal fields appear in the Field Chooser. Many fields are available, but the one I want for this example happens to be in the Personal fields category. The Referred By field stores the name of the person who referred the customer.

16. Drag the Referred By field onto the page.

When you drag a field onto the page in Forms Designer mode, it automatically aligns properly on the page. To add more fields to your form, keep dragging them in from the Field Chooser (see Figure 6-6).

17. Choose File⇨Publish Form As.

The Publish Form As dialog box appears. *Publishing* is the Outlook term for making a form available in a certain folder or group of folders. Outlook will publish your new form to whatever folder you clicked before beginning to design your form unless you click the Publish In button and choose a different folder.

18. Type a name for your new form.

The name **New Prospect** is a good one for this form. The form name will appear in the menus when you create a new item for this folder.

Publish button

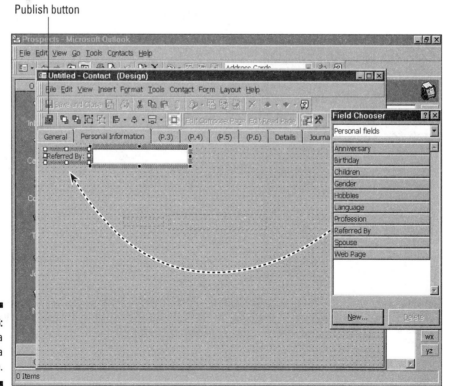

Figure 6-6:
Dragging a
field into a
form.

Editing as design

The term *Outlook Forms Designer* turns up in Outlook often enough to make you think there's a separate program lurking about, ready to help you design forms. Outlook doesn't really let you design forms from scratch; it lets you modify existing forms. When you invoke the Outlook Forms Designer by choosing Tools⇨Design Outlook Form, you're really editing the form in a special way that allows you to create a form that looks and acts differently than the form you began with.

19. Click Publish In.

Nothing visible happens, but your form is published to the folder that you designated: in this case, the Prospects folder.

20. Choose File⇨Close.

A dialog box appears, asking Do you want to save changes?

21. Click Yes to save changes.

A dialog box appears, asking Do you want to save this contact with an empty file as field?

22. Click Yes.

The Forms Designer closes.

The form now contains your additional standard field.

Adding a User-Defined Field to a Form

You can choose from hundreds of standard fields when you first use Outlook, but that's just the beginning. User-defined fields let you add types of information to your forms that weren't included with Outlook.

Here's how to create a user-defined field and add it to a form:

1. Choose File⇨New⇨Contact.

The Contact form appears.

2. Choose Tools⇨Design Outlook Form.

The form switches into Forms Designer mode. The form looks similar to what it looked like before choosing Tools⇨Design Outlook Form, but five new pages — called P.2 through P.6 — appear. These pages are blank pages that you can customize with new fields, new colors, and so on.

3. **Click the tab of an unused page.**

   You can add fields to any of the new pages.

4. **Choose Form⇨Display This Page.**

   The parentheses disappear from the name of the page in the tab, showing you that this page will be visible when you finish customizing the form.

5. **Choose Form⇨Field Chooser.**

   The Field Chooser appears.

6. **Click New in the Field Chooser dialog box.**

   The New Field dialog box appears (see Figure 6-7).

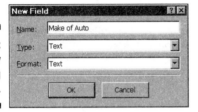

Figure 6-7:
The New
Field dialog
box.

Now to create a User-Defined field: A *User-Defined field* is a field that you dream up to put in your form because you need to add a type of data for which Outlook doesn't have a standard field.

7. **Type a name for a new field.**

   Outlook doesn't include a field called Make of Auto, so type **Make of Auto**. You can use any name up to 32 characters.

8. **Click OK.**

   Your new field appears in the Field Chooser, and the words User-Defined Fields appear at the top of the Field Chooser as the field type.

9. **Drag the new field onto the form page.**

   The new field aligns itself automatically.

10. **Click the Publish button at the far left of the Design Form toolbar.**

    You can also choose File⇨Publish Form As. The Publish\Form As dialog box appears, with the current name of the form already filled in.

11. **Click Publish.**

Changes that you made to your form are now stored and will appear the next time you use the form.

Using the Form You've Designed

It's easy to use a form you've designed in any folder to which you published the form. Whatever name you gave to the form will turn up on the Outlook main menu whenever you choose the Outlook folder that you published the form to.

Here's how you use a custom form:

1. **Choose the menu immediately to the left of Help in the menu bar.**

   In the Calendar, Contacts, Tasks, and Journal modules, that menu is called Calendar, Contacts, Tasks, and Journal, respectively. In the Inbox module, the menu is called Compose. (This arrangement sounds as though it doesn't make sense, and it doesn't. All the custom forms turn up in the second-to-last menu, but the menu doesn't always have the same name.)

2. **Choose the custom form name that appears at the bottom of the menu.**

   If you created the form called New Prospect earlier in this chapter, when you choose the Contacts menu, the name New Prospect appears at the bottom of the menu (see Figure 6-8); choose it.

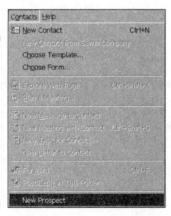

Figure 6-8:
When you publish a custom form, the name of your form appears at the bottom of the menu.

3. **Fill out the form.**

4. **Click Save and Close (or press Alt+S).**

You can have more than one custom form assigned to a folder. You can create a Vacation Request folder, for example, and store Vacation Request, Vacation Approved, and Vacation Denied forms in the same folder.

Making a Custom Form a Folder's Default Form

Every time you choose a folder in Outlook and choose File⇨New a form pops up to invite you to enter the kind of data that is used in that folder. You can also pick another form to use by choosing the form by name from the menus. If you want your custom form to be the one that Outlook offers when you choose File⇨New, you need to designate the form to be the default form for that folder.

Here's how you designate a form to be the default form for a folder:

1. **Choose View⇨Folder List.**

   The Folder List appears.

2. **Click the folder for which you want to change the default form.**

   For this example, that folder is the Prospects folder.

3. **Choose File⇨Folder⇨Properties for *Name of folder*.**

   The folder's Properties dialog box appears (see Figure 6-9).

4. **Click the When Posting to This Folder drop-down list.**

   Select the name of your custom form.

5. **Click OK.**

Now every time you choose File⇨New in that folder, your customized form appears.

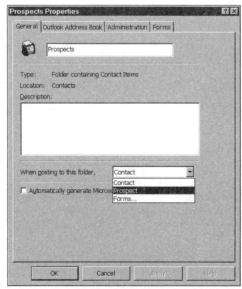

Figure 6-9:
Use the folder's Properties dialog box to set the folder's default form.

Part II
E-Mail and Contacts: Not Just Playing Post Office

The 5th Wave   By Rich Tennant

Dear Margaret,
What I have to say to you is very personal...

In this part . . .

Office boundaries can extend worldwide anymore, and keeping in touch with co-workers at home and away can be difficult without an integrated message-sending and contact-tracking system like Outlook. This part shows you many ways to dress up your e-mail, maintain contact with your contacts, and span the globe through the Internet without leaving your desktop.

Chapter 7

E-Mail: Basic Delivery

*I*f you're as lazy as I am, electronic mail — e-mail — is a dream. I love getting mail — fan mail, junk mail, official mail, anything but bills. But regular paper mail stacks up in ugly piles, and I always lose the important stuff. E-mail is quick to read, easy to find, and simple to answer. Outlook makes e-mail even easier to read, create, and answer. You don't even have to organize your e-mail in Outlook; it organizes itself!

Front Ends and Back Ends

You need two things to send and receive e-mail:

✔ A program that helps you create, save, and manage your messages

✔ A program that actually transports the messages to or from the other people you exchange messages with

Some technical people call these two parts the front end and back end, respectively. Outlook is a front end for e-mail; it helps you create, format, store, and manage your messages, but it has very little to do with actually getting your messages to your destination. That work is done by a back-end service like Microsoft Exchange Server, cc: Mail, or Lotus Notes in your office, or by an online service like CompuServe or The Microsoft Network.

Outlook can serve as the front-end for many, but not all, mail services. In the near future you'll be able to use Outlook to manage the mail you send and receive on America Online. The exact details of how you do this aren't clear just yet; America Online is still working out the fine points. Check with AOL to see when support for Outlook will be available.

If you feel that you're the last person on earth without Internet e-mail capability, you've got that capability now with Outlook. To run Outlook, you must have Windows 95. There's an icon on the Windows 95 Desktop for The Microsoft Network. If you don't have an Internet e-mail service, it's easy to get one; just click The Microsoft Network icon. The friendly Microsoft prompts then welcome and guide you through the process of collecting your credit card number and, of course, collecting your money. A few keystrokes, and voilà — you have e-mail service faster than you can say "billionaire Bill Gates."

Don't get me wrong; I don't want to give too much hype to MSN. If there were an easier way to get online access I'd recommend it, but Microsoft has made it fiendishly simple to sign up for MSN and the price is competitive with all the other services. You can use CompuServe or AT&T WorldNet for Internet access and e-mail, or any of a thousand other services, but MSN is the easiest to join. I tell you more about online services in Chapter 12.

You may already be set up on an office e-mail system, such as Microsoft Mail or cc:Mail. If so, I assume that you have a computer guru around to set you up on those systems, because that stuff can get kind of messy. You can definitely use CompuServe but setting up Outlook to send and receive e-mail from CompuServe can be a little tricky. You can also switch to a mail service other than the ones I've mentioned, if that suits your fancy, but making other systems work with Outlook isn't always simple, and I prefer to do things the easy way.

In many ways, electronic mail is better than regular paper mail (a.k.a. snail mail). E-mail is delivered much faster than paper mail — almost instantaneously. I find that speedy delivery is really handy for last-minute birthday greetings. E-mail is also incredibly cheap; in fact, it's free much of the time.

What's my e-mail address?

When you have an e-mail account, you want to tell other people your e-mail address so that they can send stuff to you. E-mail addresses are a little like long-distance telephone numbers. If you live in Chicago, and you're calling someone in New York, you tell that person that your number is (312) 555-9780; if the other person lives in Chicago, you leave off the (312) and just tell him or her to call you at 555-9780. If you work in the same office, you say that you're at extension 9780; the other person knows the rest.

Likewise, your e-mail address comes in short, medium, and long versions for different people, depending on how much of the address they share with you. If you use The Microsoft Network and your account name is Jane_Doe,

your e-mail address to the world at large is Jane_Doe@msn.com. (Don't_forget_that_ punctuation; computers still aren't smart enough to know that Jane_Doe with the underscore and Jane Doe with no underscore are the same person.) Other members of The Microsoft Network address mail to you as Jane_Doe. (The underscore isn't required; I'm just using it as an example of things that stop a computer cold but that you and I wouldn't notice.)

The same goes if you're on an office e-mail system. If you work for International Widgets Corporation, you may be Jdoe@widgets.com. (Check with your company's computer guru about your corporate e-mail address.) Your co-workers can send you messages at Jdoe.

Creating Messages

If you can type a name, you can send an e-mail message. If you type just the name, your recipient gets an e-mail message containing nothing but a name, so you really need to type a name and a message.

To create a new e-mail message, follow these steps:

1. **Choose <u>Go</u>⇨Outbo<u>x</u> (or press Ctrl+Shift+O).**

   The e-mail Outbox appears. You can also go to the Inbox (Ctrl+Shift+I).

2. **Choose <u>File</u>⇨<u>New</u>⇨<u>M</u>ail Message (or press Ctrl+N).**

   The New Message form appears (see Figure 7-1).

3. **Click the To text box and type the e-mail address of the person to whom you're sending your message.**

   You can also click the To button itself, find the name of the person to whom you're sending the message in the Address Book, and then click OK. Or you can use the AutoName feature described in the "What's in a name? AutoName!" sidebar later in this chapter.

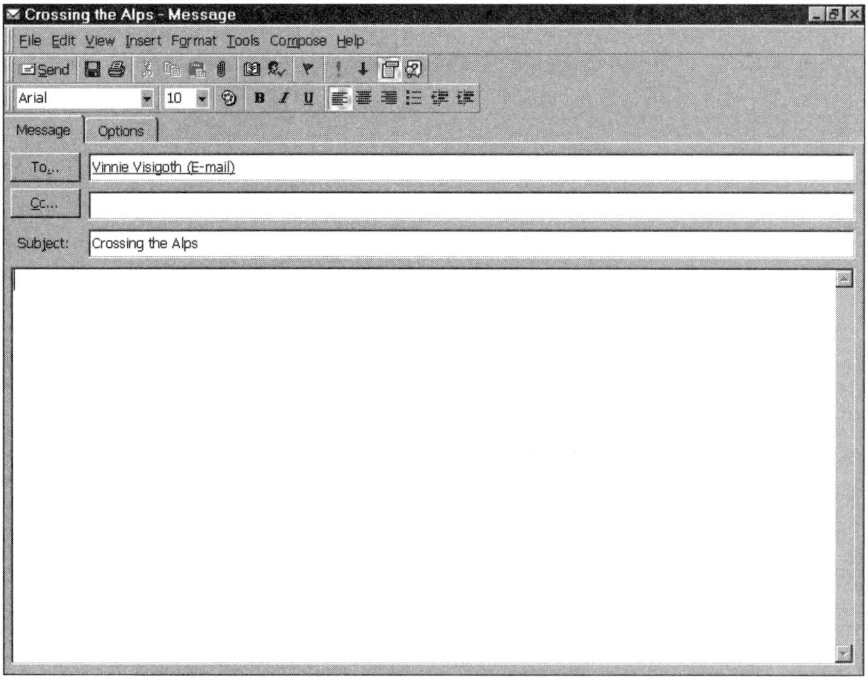

Figure 7-1:
The New
Message
form.

4. Click the Cc... text box and type the e-mail address of the people to whom you want to send a copy of your message.

If you're sending messages to multiple people, separate their addresses with either a comma or a semicolon.

5. Type the subject of the message in the Subject box.

Your subject can be up to 256 characters long, but keep it shorter. A snappy, relevant subject line makes someone want to read your message; a long or weird subject line doesn't. (Well, you never know with a weird subject line — but don't send weird e-mail at the office, unless everybody does.)

6. Type the text of your message in the text box.

If you use Microsoft Word 97 as your word processor, you can also set up Outlook to use Word 97 as your e-mail editor. You can include formatting, graphics, tables, and all the tricks available in Word to make your e-mail more attractive. When you use Word as an e-mail editor, you don't do anything different — you just see the Word toolbars in the Outlook e-mail form when you're creating e-mail. You can use all the tools you see to add formatting to your e-mail. I've listed a few formatting tricks you can use in Chapter 9. You can also read *Word 97 For Windows For Dummies* (from IDG Books Worldwide, Inc.) for more complete information about using Word 97.

What's in a name? AutoName!

One neat feature of Outlook is that you can avoid memorizing long, confusing e-mail addresses of people to whom you send mail frequently. If the person to whom you're sending a message is entered in your Contact list (see Chapter 10 for more information about contacts), and you've included an e-mail address in the Contact record, all you have to type in the To box of your e-mail form is the person's name, or even just a part of the person's name. Outlook helps you fill in the rest of the person's name and figures out the e-mail address. You know that you got it right when Outlook underlines the name with a solid black line after you press the Tab key or click outside the To box. If Outlook underlines the name with a red wavy line, Outlook thinks that it knows the name you're entering, but the name isn't spelled quite right, so you need to correct the spelling. If Outlook doesn't put any underline below the name, it's telling you that it has no idea to whom you're sending the message but that it will use the name that you typed as the literal e-mail address, so you have to be doubly sure that the name is correct.

Be careful how you format e-mail to send to people on the Internet. Not all mail systems can handle graphics or formatted text like boldface or italics, so the masterpiece of correspondence art that you send to your client on the Internet may arrive as gibberish. If you don't know what the other person has on his or her computer, go light on the graphics. When you're sending e-mail to your colleagues in the same office, or if you're sure that the person you're sending to also has Outlook, the formatting and graphics should look fine.

7. **Click the Send button (or press Alt+S).**

   Your mail is sent to the Outbox. If you're on an office network, your mail will go to from your Outbox to the Inbox of the person you're sending to automatically. If you're using an online service like MSN or CompuServe, you need to press F5 to send it along.

Setting the priority of a message

Some messages are more important than others. The momentous report that you're sending to your boss demands a different level of attention than the wisecrack that you're sending to your friend in the sales department. Setting the importance level to High tells the person getting the message that your message requires attention.

Here's how you set the priority of a message:

1. **Choose Go⇨Outbox (or press Ctrl+Shift+O).**

   The Outbox screen opens, showing your outgoing mail (see Figure 7-2).

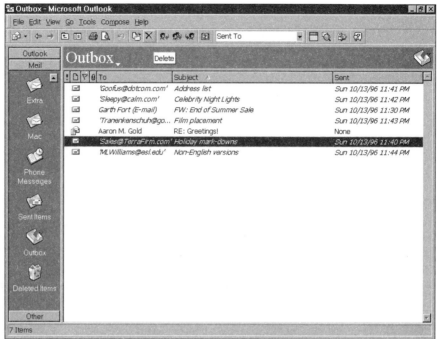

Figure 7-2:
The Outbox
with
messages.

2. Double-click the title of the message for which you want to set the importance level.

The Message form opens, looking just like it did when you created the message. You can also set the importance level while you're writing the message. You can use either of two buttons in the Message form toolbar to designate the importance of the message as High or Low. Just click one of the importance buttons and then choose File➪Close (or press Alt+F4) to close. If the toolbar is turned off or missing, follow the rest of the steps.

3. Click the Options tab just below the toolbar.

The Options tab (see Figure 7-3) allows you to define qualities about your message that are optional (clever name, eh?).

4. Click the triangle at the right end of the Importance box.

A menu appears.

5. Choose High, Normal, or Low.

Normally, Importance is set to Normal, so you don't have to do anything. Putting a Low importance on your own messages seems to be silly, but you can also assign importance to messages that you receive in your Inbox, to tell yourself which messages can be dealt with later, if at all.

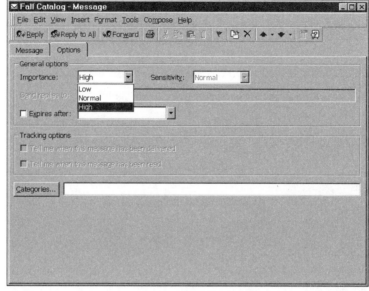

Figure 7-3:
Use the
Options tab
to set the
priority of
your
message.

6. **To close the message screen, choose File⇨Close (or press Alt+F4).**

7. **If the Office Assistant asks** Do you want to save changes?, **click Yes.**

I've told you how to change the priority of a message by opening it from the Outbox, so Outlook sees what you've done as a change to the message and asks permission to save the changes. You can also set the priority of your message as you create it by clicking the Options tab and choosing the priority before clicking Send.

Setting the sensitivity of a message

You may want your message to be seen by only one person, or you may want to prevent your message from being changed by anyone after you send it. Sensitivity settings allow you to restrict what someone else can do to your message after you send it and who that someone else can be.

1. **Choose Go⇨Outbox (or press Ctrl+Shift+O).**

The Outbox screen opens, showing your outgoing mail.

2. **Double-click the title of the message for which you want to set the sensitivity level.**

The Message form dialog box opens. You can set the sensitivity while you write the message or change the sensitivity after you write the message but before you send it.

3. **Click the Options tab just below the toolbar.**

The Options page appears (see Figure 7-4).

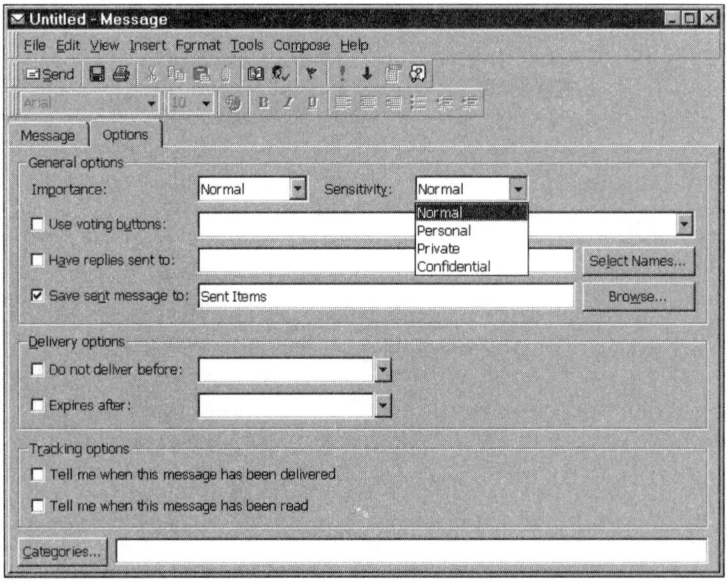

Figure 7-4:
Click the
Options tab
to set the
sensitivity of
your
message.

4. **Click the scroll-down button, which is the triangle at the right end of the Sensitivity box.**

A menu scrolls down with the words Normal, Personal, Private, and Confidential. Most messages you send will have Normal sensitivity, so that's what Outlook uses if you don't say otherwise. The Personal and Confidential settings only notify the people getting the message that they may want to handle the message differently than a Normal message. Some organizations even have special rules for dealing with Confidential messages. Marking a message Private means that no one can modify your message when they forward it or reply to it.

5. **Choose Normal, Personal, Private, or Confidential.**

6. **To close the message screen, choose File➪Close (or press Alt+F4).**

7. **If the Office Assistant asks** Do you want to save changes?, **click Yes.**

Outlook sees what you've done as a change to the message and asks permission to save the changes.

You can also set the sensitivity of your message as you create it by clicking the Options tab and choosing the sensitivity before clicking Send.

Adding an Internet link to an e-mail message

All Office 97 programs automatically recognize the addresses of items on the Internet. If you type the name of a Web page, such as http://www.pcstudio.com, Outlook changes the text color to blue and underlines the address, making it look just like the hypertext you click on to jump between different pages on the World Wide Web. That makes it easy to send someone information about an exciting Web site; just type or copy the address into your message. If the recipient is also an Outlook user, he or she can just click the text to make the Web browser pop up and open the page you told them about.

Reading and Replying to E-Mail Messages

Outlook has a couple of ways to tell you when you receive an e-mail message. In the Outlook Bar, a number in parentheses next to the Inbox icon tells you how many unread e-mail messages you have (see Figure 7-5). The word Inbox in the Folder List changes to boldface type when you have unread e-mail, and if you look in the Inbox, the titles of unread messages are in bold as well.

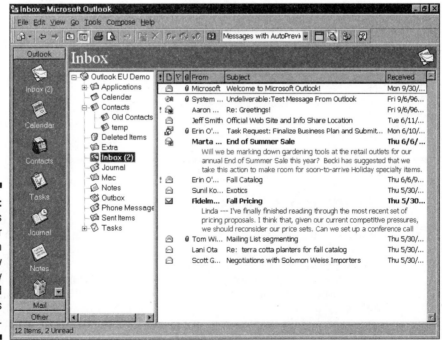

Figure 7-5:
Numbers next to your Inbox icon tell you how many unread messages are there.

To open and read an e-mail message, follow these steps:

1. **Choose Go⇨Inbox (or press Ctrl+Shift+I).**

   The Inbox screen opens, showing your incoming mail.

2. **Double-click the title of the message that you want to read.**

   The message opens, and you can see the text of the message (see Figure 7-6). If the message is really long, press the down-arrow key or the PgDn key to scroll through the text.

3. **To close the Message screen, choose File⇨Close (or press Alt+F4).**

The Message screen closes and you see the list of messages in your Inbox.

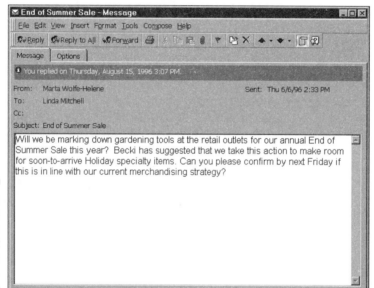

Figure 7-6:
Double-click a message to open it and read the contents.

Previewing message text

When you start getting lots of e-mail, some of it will be important, but some of it will be relatively unimportant, if not downright useless. When you first see the mail in your Inbox, it's nice to know which messages are important and which are not, so that you can focus on the important stuff. You can't count on the people who send e-mail to you to say, "Don't read this; it's unimportant" (although a Low priority rating is a good clue). Outlook tries to help by allowing you to peek at the first few lines of a message, so that you'll know right off the bat whether it's worth reading.

To see previews of your unread messages:

1. **Choose Go▷Inbox (or press Ctrl+Shift+I).**

   The Inbox screen opens, showing your incoming mail (see Figure 7-7).

2. **Choose View▷Current View▷Messages with AutoPreview.**

   The list of messages in your Inbox appears with the first few lines of each unread message displayed in blue.

Every module in Outlook has a collection of views that you can use to make your information easier to use. The view called Messages with AutoPreview is the best way to look at your incoming e-mail. In Chapter 8, I show you some of the other views that can make your collection of e-mail messages more useful.

Sending a reply

The thing I love about e-mail is that it's so easy to send a reply. You don't even need to know the person's address when you're sending a reply; just click the Reply button, and Outlook takes care of it for you.

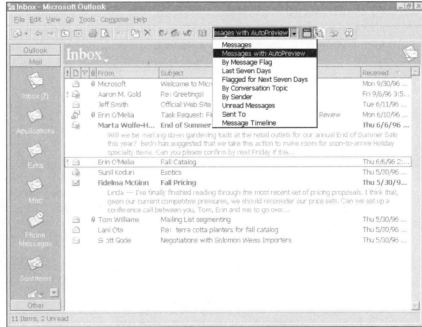

Figure 7-7:
You can see a preview of your messages with AutoPreview.

I'm seeing a preview of Internet gobbledygook

If you receive a great deal of e-mail from the Internet, the first few lines of your messages may be nothing but computerese. That's because Internet e-mail bounces between computers all over the country — and sometimes all over the world — before it gets to you. The lines of gibberish at the beginning of your Internet e-mail messages are directions used by the computers that the messages bounced among so that the message ends up bouncing to you successfully. Because the opening lines are computerese, Outlook's AutoPreview is less helpful with Internet e-mail; instead, use it for messages on your corporate network.

Here's how you reply to a message:

1. **Choose Go⇨Inbox (or press Ctrl+Shift+I).**

   The Inbox screen opens, showing your incoming mail.

2. **Double-click the title of the message to which you want to reply.**

   The message you double-clicked opens and you can see the contents of the message.

   If the message is already open, you can skip the first two steps and go directly to Step 3 (just click Reply).

3. **To reply to the people who are named in the From line, click the Reply button (or press Alt+R).**

4. **To reply to the people who are named in the Cc line as well as the From line, click the Reply to All button (or press Alt+L).**

   The Reply screen appears (see Figure 7-8).

   You may get (or send) e-mail that's addressed to a whole bunch of people all at once. At least one person must be named in the To line; more than one person can be in the Cc line, which is for people to whom you're sending only a copy. Very little difference exists between what happens to mail that's going to people in the To line and mail that's going to the people in the Cc line — all of them can reply to, forward, or ignore the message. You don't always need to reply to the people on the Cc line, or you may want to reply to only some of them. If you do that, you must click the Reply button (not Reply to All) and add them again to the Cc line.

5. **Type your reply in the Message box.**

   Don't be alarmed that there's already text in the text box — that's the text of the message to which you're replying. Your blinking cursor is at the top of the screen, so anything that you type precedes the other person's

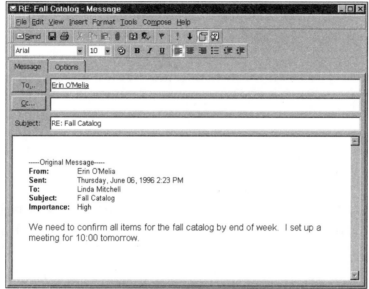

Figure 7-8:
The Reply
screen.

message. (This arrangement means that the person who gets your message can review the original message, which helps them remember exactly what they said when they get your reply.)

6. Click the Send button (or press Alt+S).

On your office network, clicking Send speeds the message to its intended recipient.

If you're a stand-alone user who's sending mail on an online service like The Microsoft Network or CompuServe, you must also press F5 to send your message.

7. Choose File⇨Close (or press Esc) to close the Message screen.

The Message form disappears and your Inbox reappears.

Using a link to the Web from your e-mail

When you open a message, sometimes you see blue underlined text with the name of a Web page or other Internet resource, such as www.pcstudio.com. If you want to look at that page, all you have to do is double-click on the text and, if everything is installed correctly, your Web browser will pop up and open the Web page whose name you've clicked on.

After you open the page, you can save the page to your Favorites folder to allow you to find it again easily.

That's Not My Department: Forwarding Mail

You may not always have the answer to every e-mail message that you get. You may need to pass a message along to somebody else to have it acted upon, so pass it on.

To forward a message:

1. **Choose Go⇨Inbox (or press Ctrl+Shift+I).**

   The Inbox screen opens, showing your incoming mail.

2. **Double-click the title of the message to which you want to reply.**

   The Message screen opens (see Figure 7-9). You can forward the message as soon as you read it. If you've already opened the message, you can skip the first two steps.

3. **Click the Forward button (or press Alt+W).**

   The Forward screen appears (see Figure 7-10). The subject of the original message is now the subject of the new message, except that the letters *FW* (for Forward) are inserted at the beginning.

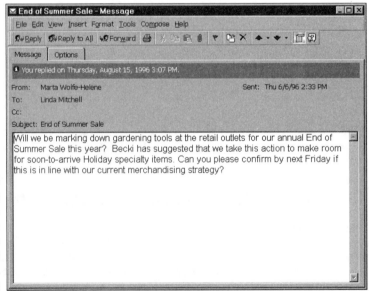

Figure 7-9:
The
message
you wish to
reply to is
opened.

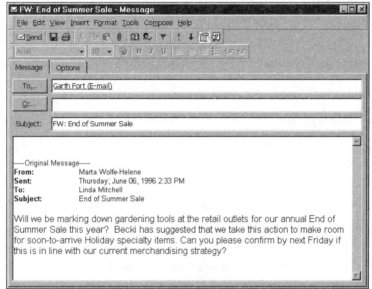

Figure 7-10:
The Forward
screen.

4. **Click the To text box and type the e-mail address of the person to whom you're forwarding the message.**

   If the person to whom you're forwarding is entered in your Contact list, just type the person's name; Outlook figures out the e-mail address for you.

5. **Click the Cc text box and type the e-mail addresses of the people to whom you want to forward a copy of your message.**

   Many people forward trivia, such as jokes of the day, to scads and scads of their friends by e-mail. Most recipients are included as Cc addresses.

   Remember, business e-mail etiquette is very different than home e-mail etiquette. Many employers have strict policies about appropriate use of their corporate e-mail systems. If you work for such a company, be aware of your company's policies.

   If you want to pester your friends by sending silly trivia from your home computer to their home computer (like I do), that's your own business.

6. **In the text box, type any comments that you want to add to the message.**

   The text of the original message appears in the text box, preceded by the words Original Message and a couple of blank lines. You can preface the message that you're forwarding if you want to give that person a bit of explanation — for example, **This is the 99th message I've had from this person.**

7. **Click the Send button (or press Alt+S).**

Your message is on its way.

Deleting Messages

You can zap an e-mail message without a second thought; you don't even have to read the thing. As soon as you see the Inbox list, you know who's sending the message and what it's about, so you don't have to waste time reading Burt's Bad Joke of the day. Just zap it.

If you accidentally delete a message you didn't want to lose, click the Deleted Items icon; you'll find all the messages you've deleted in the last few months. To recover a deleted message, just drag it from the Deleted Items list to either the Inbox icon or the Outbox icon.

Here's how you delete a message:

1. **Choose Go⇨Inbox (or press Ctrl+Shift+I).**

   The Inbox screen opens, showing your incoming mail.

2. **Click the title of the message that you want to delete.**

   You don't have to read the message, you can just delete it from the list.

3. **Choose Edit⇨Delete (or press Delete).**

When you delete messages, Outlook doesn't actually eliminate deleted items; it moves them to the Deleted Items folder. If you have unread items in your Deleted Items folder, Outlook annotates the Deleted Items icon with the number of unread items, the same way that it annotates the Inbox with the number of unread items. You can get rid of the annotation by choosing Tools⇨Empty "Deleted Items" Folder. Or you can just ignore the annotation.

Saving Interrupted Messages

If you get interrupted while writing an e-mail message, all is not lost. You can just save the work that you've done and return to it later. Just choose File⇨Save (or press Ctrl+S), and your message is saved to the Inbox (unless you had reopened the message from the Outbox, as shown in Figure 7-11, then it saves the unfinished message to the Outbox).

When a message is ready to be sent, its name appears in the Outbox in italics. If you've saved it to work on later, its name appears in normal text, not italics. If you're not finished with the message and plan to return to it later, save it (press Ctrl+S). If the message is ready for prime time, send it (press Alt+S).

Figure 7-11:
You can
save
incomplete
messages
and return
to complete
them later.

Saving a Message as a File

You may create or receive an e-mail message that's so wonderful (or terrible)
that you just have to save it. You may need to print out the message and show
it to someone else, save it to a floppy disk, or export it to a desktop-publishing
program.

To save a message as a file, follow these steps:

1. **Choose File⇨Save As (or press F12).**

   The Save As dialog box appears.

2. **Click the triangle at the end of the Save In box (called the scroll-down
   button) to choose the drive to which you want to save your file.**

   If you do all your work on drive C, Outlook chooses drive C first, so you
   don't have to do anything. To save to a floppy disk, choose the A drive.

3. **Click the name of the folder in which you want to save the file.**

   A list appears of all files in the folder that you select.

4. **Click the File Name text box and type the name that you want to give the file.**

   Type any name you want, up to 256 characters.

5. **If you want to change the type of the file, click the triangle at the end of the Save as Type box and choose a file type.**

   If you're using Word as your e-mail editor, you'll see the entire range of file types that you can create in Word. If not, the list offers text, RTF (that stands for Rich Text Format, which is text with formatting), MSG (the Outlook message format), and Outlook Template (see Figure 7-12). Use *.RTF or *.MSG. The Outlook Template format is for a message you want to use over and over again in Outlook.

6. **Click Save (or press Enter).**

   The message is saved to the file and folder you clicked in Steps 2 and 3.

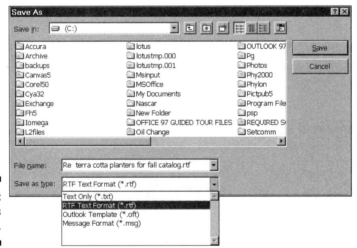

Figure 7-12:
The Save As
dialog box.

Postscript

Sending e-mail is simple. Keeping track of all the tens of millions of people to whom you want to send e-mail to is a bigger task. Fortunately, Outlook does both things, so you can go to one program to get the names of the people you know, to find the things that you know about them, and to send them e-mail asking them to tell you more.

Chapter 8
E-Mail: Special Delivery

*O*utlook can do all sorts of tricks with the mail you send out, as well as with the messages you receive. You can flag messages with a reminder, delay your messages for later delivery, or set your messages to expire if they're not acted upon by a certain time.

As the automobile ads say, "Your mileage may vary." Outlook is just the pretty face on an elaborate arrangement of other items that make e-mail work. Outlook is like the dashboard of your car; you can use the dashboard to make the car do what you want it to do, but the things that your car can do depend more on what's under the hood than what's on the dashboard. In the same way, some features of Outlook work only if the system that's backing it up supports those features, too. Some features work only if the person to whom you're mailing uses a system that supports advanced features as well.

Microsoft Exchange Server is the name of a program that must be running on the network you're logged onto in order to take full advantage of many features of Outlook, such as delaying delivery of messages or diverting messages to someone else. In this book, I won't go into great depth about features you may not have. I show you the possibilities; then you can give some of the slicker features a try. If the features work, you'll know that everything's lined up right and you have the necessary bells and whistles. If the features don't work, no loss — you'll have to wait until everybody's as well-equipped as you are (or until you get better equipped yourself).

Nagging by Flagging

Some people like to use their list of e-mail messages as a to-do list. You can flag messages to remind yourself about things that you have to do. You can also plant a flag in a message you send to someone else to remind them of a task that they have to do.

Adding a flag to an e-mail message

E-mail messages are the only items that you can flag. You can add reminders to tasks and appointments to achieve the same effect. Reminders can be set for a specific time of day, while flags are set by day, but not time of day.

To attach a flag to your e-mail messages (ones you send and ones that you're sent):

1. **Choose** <u>G</u>o↔<u>I</u>nbox (**or press Ctrl+Shift+I**).

   The Inbox screen opens, showing your incoming mail (see Figure 8-1).

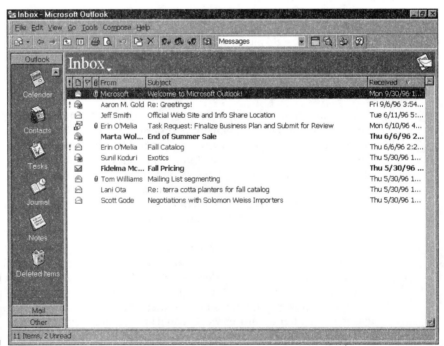

Figure 8-1:
The Inbox
screen.

2. Double-click the message that you want to flag.

The Message dialog box appears.

3. Choose Edit⇨Message Flag (or press Ctrl+Shift+G).

The Flag Message dialog box appears (see Figure 8-2).

Figure 8-2:
Need to add
a flag?

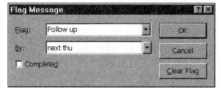

4. Click the triangle at the right end of the Flag text box and choose one of the menu items or type your own choice.

A handy flag is "Follow Up," to remind you to confirm an appointment or other arrangement.

5. Click the By box and type the date on which you want the reminder flag to appear.

You can type the date **5/5/97**; Outlook understands. You can type **first monday of may**; Outlook understands. You can type **a week from Monday**; Outlook understands that to mean "seven days after the Monday that comes after today." You don't even have to worry about capitalization. Don't type **I hate mondays**, though; Outlook doesn't understand that. (I do.)

6. Click OK.

When the date you entered in the Flag Message dialog box arrives, a reminder dialog box pops up to help jog your memory.

Changing the date on a flag

Procrastination used to be an art; Outlook makes it a science. When someone nags you with flags, you can still put it off. Yes, dear, you *can* do it later.

To change the date on a flag:

1. Choose Go⇨Inbox (or press Ctrl+Shift+I).

The Inbox screen opens, showing your incoming mail (see Figure 8-3).

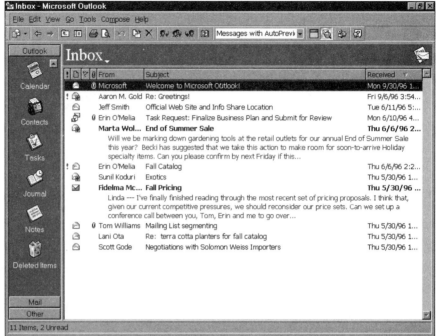

Figure 8-3:
A mass of
messages,
ready for
flags.

2. **Double-click the message that you want to flag.**

   The Message dialog box appears.

3. **Choose Edit⇨Message Flag (or press Ctrl+Shift+G).**

   The Flag Message dialog box appears (see Figure 8-4).

 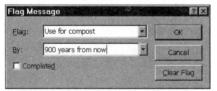

Figure 8-4:
The Flag
Message
dialog box.

4. **Click the By box and type the new date when you want the reminder
   flag to appear.**

   Type the date when you'll feel ready to be flagged again. **900 years from
   now** will work — really!

5. **Click OK.**

Of course, there's a catch. You can always change the date on the flags that you've set, but if someone sends you a message, flags it, and marks it "Private," you can't change the contents of the flag. Rats!

Making a Sent Message Unavailable after a Specified Date

Some messages don't make sense to the reader if they're read too late. A message saying `If you get back from your trip before Monday, we're having an important meeting on Monday at 2:00 p.m.` can be marked to disappear on Monday if the person to whom it's addressed hasn't read it.

Expiring messages are one of those advanced features that work only when the networks that both the sender and the receiver are using are equipped for it.

To set the timing on a message:

1. Choose Go➪Outbox (or press Ctrl+Shift+O).

The Outbox screen opens, showing your outgoing mail (see Figure 8-5).

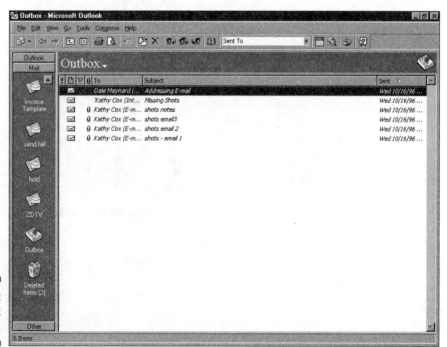

Figure 8-5:
The Outbox
screen.

2. **Double-click the title of the message for which you want to set the expiration date.**

   The Message form opens.

3. **Choose the Options tab just below the toolbar.**

   The Options page appears (see Figure 8-6).

4. **Click the Expires After check box in the Delivery Options section and enter the expiration date in the Expires After text box.**

   You can type the date, such as **July 4, 1997**, the **first Friday of July**, or **Next Friday**. You can also click the triangle at the right end of the Expires After box and choose the date from the pull-down calendar.

5. **To close the Message screen, choose File⇨Close (or press Alt+F4).**

6. **A dialog box appears, asking** Do you want to save changes? **Click Yes.**

Expiration can also be set when you're creating the message. Just follow Steps 3 through 5 while creating the message.

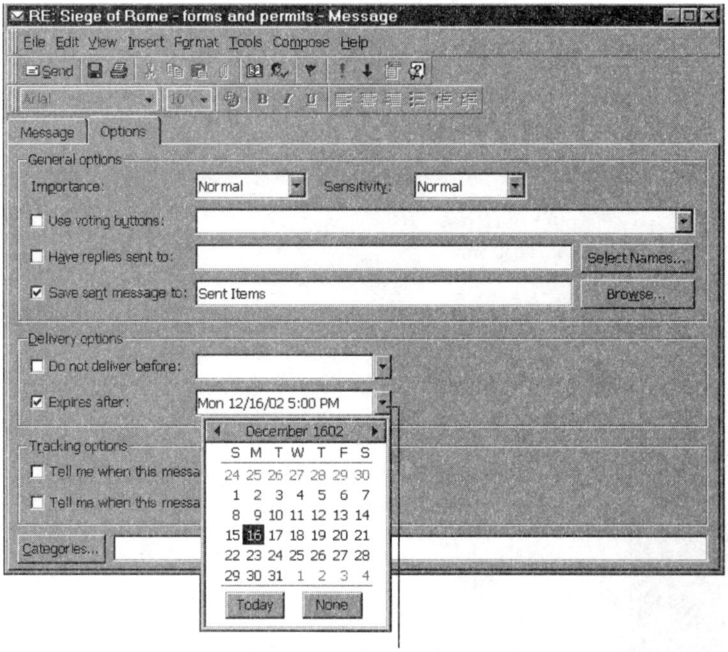

Figure 8-6:
The Options
page.

Click the scroll down bar (triangle) to see the pull-down calendar

Saving Delivery for a Later Date

Maybe you want your message to arrive later, closer to the time when it matters. Maybe you want the message to land in the boss's Inbox just after you leave on vacation.

Oops! Better make sure that your network is equipped for this feature before you try anything sly. If your network is running Microsoft Exchange Server you can use the Delayed Delivery feature. Check with your local network guru to see if you can delay delivery of messages.

To set your message for a later delivery date:

1. **Choose Go⇨Outbox (or press Ctrl+Shift+O).**

   The Outbox screen opens, showing your outgoing mail.

2. **Double-click the title of the message for which you want to set the expiration date.**

   The Message form opens.

3. **Choose the Options tab just below the toolbar.**

   The Options page appears.

4. **Click the Do Not Deliver Before check box in the Delivery Options section of the page.**

   A check mark appears in the Do Not Deliver Before check box.

5. **Enter the expiration date in the Do Not Deliver Before text box.**

   Type the date or click the scroll-down button (triangle) at the right end of the Do Not Deliver Before text box and choose the date from the drop-down calendar (see Figure 8-7).

6. **To close the message screen, choose File⇨Close (or press Alt+F4).**

7. **A dialog box appears asking if you want to save changes. Click Yes.**

Your message will be delivered at the time you request.

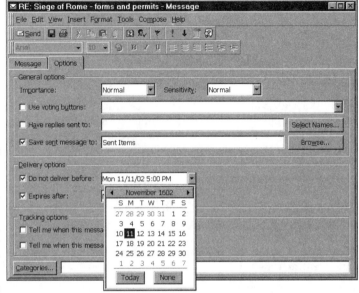

Figure 8-7:
Use the Do
Not Deliver
Before
check box
to set your
delivery
options.

Diverting Message Replies to Another User

When you send a message to a large group of people and ask for replies, you may not want to deal with all the replies. You can set up the message so that replies go to someone else. This way, your recipients can click Reply instead of having to look up the person to whom they're supposed to send the reply.

This feature requires that you, the people you're sending the message to, and the person who's getting the replies be on a network that uses Microsoft Exchange Server. Check with your system administrator to see whether you're equipped for this feature.

To divert your messages to another user:

1. **Choose Go⊏>Outbox (or press Ctrl+Shift+O).**

   The Outbox screen opens, showing your outgoing mail.

2. **Double-click on the title of the message for which you want to divert message replies.**

   The message you double-clicked opens.

3. **Choose the Options tab just below the toolbar.**

   The Options dialog box appears.

4. **Click the Have Replies Sent To check box.**

   A check mark appears in the Have Replies Sent To check box (see Figure 8-8).

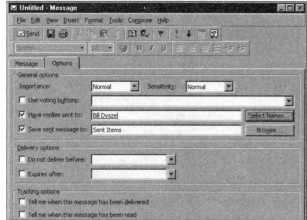

Figure 8-8:
Enter the
name of the
person to
whom you
wish to
divert
replies on
the Options
tab.

5. **Click the Select Names button.**

   The Address Book dialog box appears.

6. **From your address list, choose the name of the person to whom you're diverting replies.**

   This person must be in your Address Book. If not, he or she may not be set up to get diverted messages from you.

7. **Click OK.**

   All replies will be diverted to the person you selected.

Saving Copies of Your Messages

There's nothing handier than knowing what you've sent and when you sent it. You can save all your outgoing mail in Outlook so that you can go back and look up the messages you've sent. Outlook starts out saving sent items when you first install the program, but you can turn this feature on and off, so before you go changing your options, look in your Sent Messages folder to see whether it contains messages.

To save copies of your messages:

1. **Choose Go⇨Outbox (or press Ctrl+Shift+O).**

   The Outbox screen opens, showing your outgoing mail.

2. **Choose Tools⇨Options.**

   The Options dialog box appears, displaying two rows of tabs.

3. Click the Sending tab.

The Sending page appears (see Figure 8-9).

Figure 8-9:
You can
decide
whether or
not to save
copies of
the
messages
you send to
the Sent
Messages
folder by
using the
Options
dialog box.

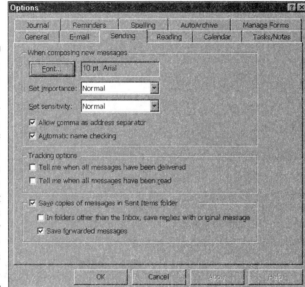

4. Click the Save Copies of Messages in Sent Items Folder check box.

If the box already contains a check mark, leave it alone. If you click the box when it's already checked, you turn off your "vote" for saving messages. Don't worry if you make a mistake; you can always change it back. Just make sure there's a check in the box if you want to save messages.

5. Click OK.

Outlook saves two months' worth of saved messages and sends older messages to an archive file to save memory in your computer.

Automatically Adding Your Name to the Original Message when Replying

When you reply to a message, it helps to include parts of the original message that you're replying to, so that the person reading your message knows exactly what you're responding to. The trick is: How will the reader know which comments are his or hers and which are yours?

Outlook allows you to preface your comments with your name or any text that you choose. If you want to be understood, it's best to use your name. If you want to confuse the issue, use a phrase like "Simon says."

To tag your replies with your name:

1. Choose Go⇨Outbox (or press Ctrl+Shift+O).

The Outbox screen opens, showing your outgoing mail.

2. Choose Tools⇨Options.

The Options dialog box appears.

3. Click the Reading tab.

The Reading page appears (see Figure 8-10).

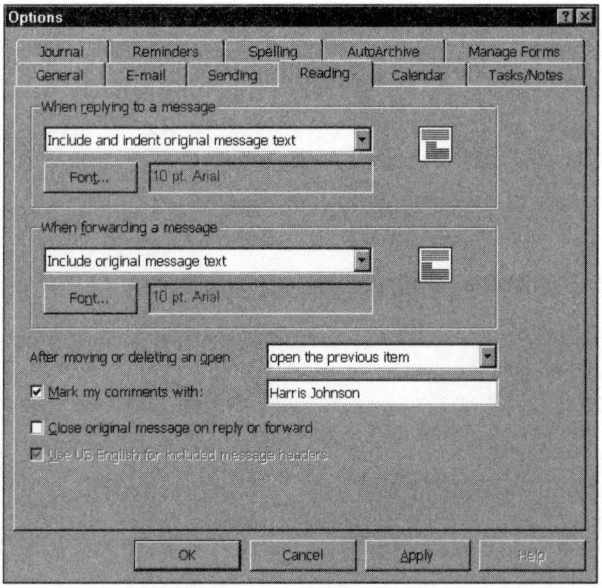

Figure 8-10:
To use your
name as a
prefix to all
text you
type in your
message
replies,
check the
Mark My
Comments
With box
and enter
your name
in the text
box to the
right.

4. Click the Mark My Comments With check box.

Be sure that the check box isn't already checked or you will remove the check.

5. In the Mark My Comments With text box, enter the text that you want to accompany your annotations.

Your best bet is to enter your name here. Whatever you enter will be used as the prefix to all text you type when replying to messages.

6. Click OK.

You can select and delete the text of the original message when you create a reply, but including at least a part of the message you're replying to makes your response easier to understand. You also have the option of selecting and deleting the parts of the original text that aren't relevant to your reply.

Setting Your Options

You can control the appearance of the messages that you forward, as well as your replies. If all your e-mail stays in your office among other Office 97 users, you can make your text look pretty incredible in messages you send to one another by adding graphics or wild-looking fonts or special effects like blinking text. If you're sending mail to poor ol' Internet users or to people on an online service such as CompuServe (see Chapter 12 for more about e-mail to online services and the Internet), you need to pay attention to how messages look to those people. To set your options:

1. **Choose Go➪Outbox (or press Ctrl+Shift+O).**

   The Outbox screen opens, showing your outgoing mail.

2. **Choose Tools➪Options.**

   The Options dialog box appears (see Figure 8-11).

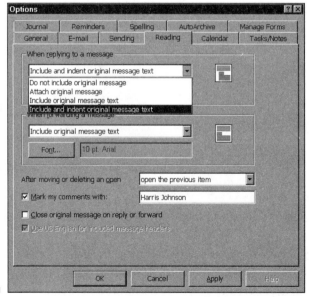

Figure 8-11: Change the appearance of your outgoing messages by selecting what you need in the Options dialog box.

3. **Click the scroll down bar (triangle) at the right end of the When Replying to a Message box.**

   A menu of options drops down. When Outlook is first installed, Include and Indent Original Message Text is the default option. The diagram to the right of the scroll-down menu illustrates how the message will be laid out when you choose each option.

4. **Choose the style that you prefer to use for replies.**

   The little diagram to the right of the menu changes when you make a choice to show you what your choice will look like. If you don't like the choice that you've made, try another and see how it looks in the diagram.

5. **Click the triangle at the right end of the When Forwarding a Message box.**

   The When Forwarding a Message box has one choice fewer than the When Replying to a Message box does, but the two menus work the same way, and they both have that little diagram of the page layout off to the right.

6. **Choose the style that you prefer to use for forwarding messages.**

   Just pick one; you can always change it.

7. **Click OK.**

You can do all sorts of fancy, exciting, and even useful tricks with e-mail by taking advantage of Outlook's options. If the advanced options seem confusing, you can easily ignore them. Just click Reply and type your answer.

Sending Attachments

If you've already created a document that you want to send to somebody, you don't have to type the document all over again in a message; just send the document as an attachment to an e-mail message. You can attach any kind of file — word-processing documents, spreadsheet files, presentations from programs such as PowerPoint. Any kind of file can be sent as an attachment.

To send an attachment:

1. **Choose Go⇨Inbox (or press Ctrl+Shift+I).**

   The Inbox screen opens, showing your incoming mail.

2. **Choose File⇨New⇨Mail Message (or press Ctrl+N).**

   The New Message form appears.

3. Choose Insert➪File or click the paper-clip button in the Message form toolbar.

The Insert File dialog box appears (see Figure 8-12). It looks just like the dialog box that you use for opening files in most Windows 95 programs, and it works like opening a file, too. Just click the name of the file you want to send and press Enter.

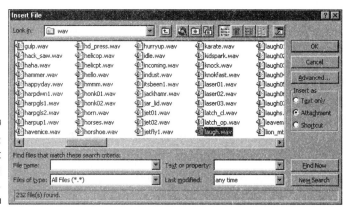

Figure 8-12:
The Insert
File dialog
box.

4. In the list of files, click the name of the file that you want to send.

An icon appears in your text representing the file you've attached to your message.

5. Click OK.

Your Message form now contains an icon. The name of the icon is the same name as the file that you selected, which means that the file is attached. When you send this e-mail message, a copy of the file that you selected will go to your recipient.

6. Type your message (if you have a message to send).

You may not have a message; perhaps you only want to send the attachment. If what you want to say is in the attachment, that's fine, but remember that the contents of an attachment don't show up on the recipient's screen until he or she double-clicks to open the attachment.

7. Click the To button.

The Select Names dialog box appears.

8. Select a name from your mailing list.

If the name of the person to whom you want to send your message isn't in the list, you can click the Cancel button and return to the Message form. Then just type the e-mail address in the To text box.

9. **Click the To button.**

   The name of the selected person appears in the To box of the Select Names dialog box.

10. **Click OK.**

    The name of the selected person is now in the To box of the message.

11. **Click the Subject text box and type a subject for your message.**

    Subjects are optional, but if you want somebody to read what you sent, including a subject helps.

12. **Click the Send button.**

    Your message and its attachment are sent.

Those are just a few of the tricks that you can do with the mail you send. You can also do tricks with the mail you get; I cover those tricks in Chapter 9.

"THAT'S RIGHT, MS. BINGAMAN, HE'S COLLECTING A ROYALTY FROM EVERYONE ON EARTH, AND THERE'S NOTHING WE CAN DO ABOUT IT."

Chapter 9
Sorting Your Mail

*T*here's good news and bad news about e-mail. The good news is that e-mail is free; you can send as much as you want for virtually no cost. The bad news is that e-mail is free; anybody can easily send you more e-mail than you can possibly read. Before long, you need help sorting it all out so you can deal with messages that need immediate action.

Outlook has some handy tools for coping with the flood of electronic flotsam and jetsam that finds its way into your Inbox. You can create separate folders for filing your mail, and you can use Outlook's view feature to help you slice and dice your incoming messages into manageable groups.

If you leaped to adopt Outlook as soon as it was released in late 1996 (it was a leap year, after all), you'll find that one great message-management feature that had been advertised wasn't included: the Rules Wizard. The Rules Wizard allows you to give Outlook instructions about how to treat all your incoming messages; Outlook can take care of your messages before you see them. For example, you can have messages from your clients sent to a different folder than messages from your colleagues. You can have mail that comes from people you don't know routed differently than mail from people you do know, in order to minimize distractions from junk mail. You have to visit the Microsoft Web site by choosing Help⇨Microsoft on the Web. You can then download the Rules Wizard to take advantage of it.

Creating a New Mail Folder

The simplest way to manage incoming mail is to just file it. Before you file a message, though, you need to create at least one folder in which to file your messages. You have to create a folder only once; it's there for good after you create it. You can create as many folders as you want; you may have dozens or just one or two.

I have folders for filing mail from specific clients, for example. All the e-mail I've received in connection to this book is in a folder called Outlook for Dummies (clever title, eh?). Another folder called Personal contains messages that aren't business related.

To create a folder for new mail:

1. **Click the Inbox icon.**

   The list of messages in your Inbox appears.

2. **Choose File⇨New⇨Folder (or press Ctrl+Shft+E).**

   The Create New Folder dialog box appears.

3. **Click the word Inbox in the list of folders at the bottom of the Create New Folder dialog box.**

   The word Inbox is highlighted (see Figure 9-1).

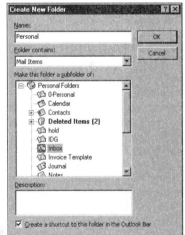

Figure 9-1:
The Create
New Folder
dialog box
with the
word Inbox
highlighted.

4. In the Name text box, type a name for your new folder, such as Personal.

You can name the subfolder anything you like. You can also create many folders for saving and sorting your incoming e-mail. Leaving all your mail in your Inbox gets confusing. On the other hand, if you create too many folders, you may be just as confused as if you had only one.

5. Click the checkbox that says Create a Shortcut to this Folder in the Outlook Bar.

A checkmark appears.

6. Click OK.

You now have a new folder named Personal (or whatever name you entered) for filing messages you want to save for future reference. I like to use three or four mail folders for different types of mail to make it easier to find what I'm looking for.

Moving messages to another folder

Filing your messages is as easy as dragging them from the folder they're in to the folder where you want them. Just click the Inbox to look at your messages when they arrive, and then drag each message to the folder where you want your messages to stay.

To move messages to another folder:

1. Choose Go⇨Inbox (or press Ctrl+Shift+I).

Your list of incoming mail messages appears.

2. Click the title of the message that you want to move.

The message is highlighted.

3. Drag the message to the icon on the Outlook Bar for the folder in which you wish to store it.

Your message is moved to the folder to which you dragged it. If you created a folder named Personal (or anything else) in the step above, you can drag the message there.

Creating extra folders is only·one method of organizing your incoming messages. You can also create views of each folder that display your messages in useful ways. You can group messages by the name of the person who sent it by choosing View⇨Current View⇨By Sender, for example, which makes it unnecessary to create a folder for each person who sends you mail. For a variety of ways to view your messages, see the end of this chapter.

Creating and using a template

Templates are prepared forms designed to save you time by automatically inserting the kind of information you use over and over and allowing you to fill in the information that changes. (Of course, templates aren't just for e-mail; you can use a template in any Outlook folder.) A good analogy is the paper message form that you use for taking telephone messages. Outlook allows you to do the same thing and send the message to the person who's supposed to get it. If you take messages for your boss, you can use the While You Were Out template to take down the message information and forward it to her by e-mail. That way, you both have a record of what calls came in and which ones you sent along. If you're used to using templates in Microsoft Word, it's the same idea.

Templates are still a little strange in Outlook. Technically, templates can be saved in any Outlook module — E-mail, Contacts, Tasks, Journal, or any other. But most of the templates that Microsoft includes with Outlook have a To box and work like an e-mail message. So E-mail is the natural place for messages based on Outlook templates.

To use a template:

1. Choose File➪New➪Choose Template.

A box appears, containing an icon for each template (see Figure 9-2). You can recognize template files by the .OFT extension.

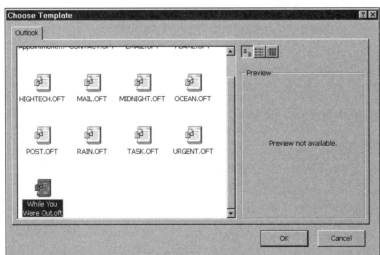

Figure 9-2:
The Choose
Template
dialog box.

2. Double-click the template that you want.

The template you choose appears. For this example, I chose the While You Were Out template (see Figure 9-3).

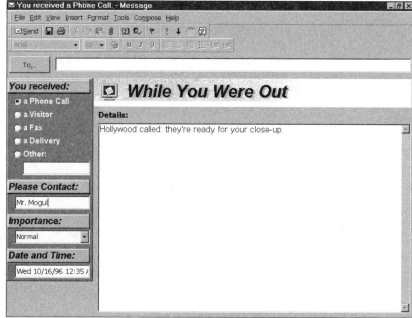

Figure 9-3:
The While
You Were
Out
template.

3. Fill in the information in the form.

Templates can be customized to fit any need. Just click any box where you could put information and enter your desired text.

4. Click the To button.

The Select Names dialog box appears (see Figure 9-4).

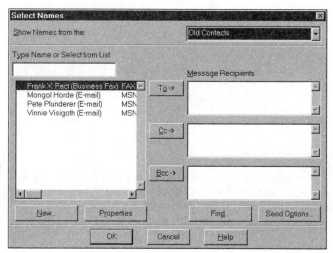

Figure 9-4:
The Select
Names
dialog box.

5. **Choose the name of the person to whom you want to send the message.**

   If the name of the person to whom you want to send your message isn't in the list, click the triangle at the right end of the <u>S</u>how Names From the text box and choose Contacts or Personal Address Book to see whether the name you want is there.

6. **Click the T<u>o</u> button.**

   Yes, I know, you clicked the To button before. This one enters the person's name in your e-mail message.

7. **Click OK.**

   The Select Names dialog box disappears, and the template reappears.

8. **Click Send.**

   If your computer is on a network at your office, your message is on its way. If you're using Outlook at home, you'll have to send your message by choosing <u>T</u>ools⇨<u>C</u>heck for New Mail. (I know "Check for New Mail" doesn't sound like what you'd do to send mail, but that's the name for the command.) You can also press F5.

Viewing Your Messages

You can use at least ten views of your messages, beginning with the set that comes with Outlook. You can modify each view by sorting on any column of information in any view by clicking the title of that column. You can also create a grouped view by using the Group By button. Also, you can save any view that you've dreamed up by saving and naming the view when Outlook prompts you each time you change views. Any of these views works in any mail folder, and the mechanics of using views of your mail are the same as the mechanics of using views in other Outlook modules. For an overview of views in Outlook, see Chapter 5.

The easiest way to change views is to click the triangle next to the name of the view in the toolbar and select another view from the drop-down menu. I'm describing the menu method of changing views here simply for reliability. The toolbar can be turned off, but the menus will always be there.

Messages view

Messages view is the no-frills picture of your Inbox — From, To, Subject, just the basics. Messages that you haven't read yet are listed in boldface type; the others are listed in plain type.

To see your Inbox in Messages view:

1. **From the Inbox, Choose View⇨Current View.**

   The list of views available in the current module appears. You need to be in the Inbox to view your incoming messages.

2. **Choose Messages.**

   The Messages view of your Inbox appears, listing your messages by author, subject, and date (see Figure 9-5). You can view any of them by double-clicking the title, or you can get a short preview by switching to AutoPreview.

I like to leave my Inbox in the Messages view or the AutoPreview view. Because I've set up folders for sorting other personal mail, I normally move incoming messages to other folders where I manage them by applying different views.

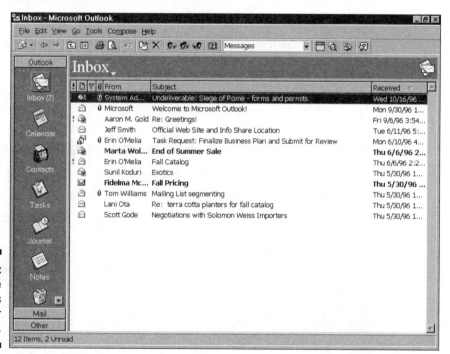

Figure 9-5:
The
Messages
view of your
Inbox.

AutoPreview view

When you don't have time to read all the messages you get, a preview is helpful. The first few lines can give you a hint as to which messages you want to read. AutoPreview shows you these first few lines. To use AutoPreview:

1. **Choose <u>V</u>iew⇨Current <u>V</u>iew.**

   The list of available views appears.

2. **Choose Messages with AutoPreview.**

Your messages appear with AutoPreview (see Figure 9-6).

Normally, you see previews only of messages that you haven't read yet. You see only the titles of messages that you have read. Actually, Outlook assumes that you've read any message you've opened. You can also mark a message read or unread by right-clicking it and choosing Mark as Read or Mark as Unread. I sometimes mark messages as Read, and then delete them when I've judged from their preview or return address that I'm not interested in reading them. Sometimes I'll mark a message Unread after I have read it if it's a long message that I'd like to devote more time to later. Marking a message unread makes the blue AutoPreview text appear, which helps jog my memory.

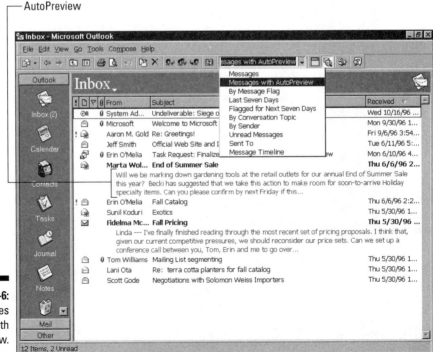

Figure 9-6: Messages with AutoPreview.

Flagged view

You can flag incoming messages to help you keep track of what you have to do in response to each message. Flagged view groups your messages according to whether flags are set on the messages, and lists what kinds of flags are set and when they're due. For more about flagging, refer to Chapter 8.

To use the Flagged view (also called the By Message Flag view):

1. Choose View⇨Current View.

The list of current views appears.

2. Choose By Message Flag.

Your messages appear organized in two groups, Flagged and normal (see Figure 9-7). Normal in this case means it's not flagged.

Some experts say that the most efficient way to deal with all your incoming messages is to file them according to what you need to do with them and then act upon them according to each message's priority and timing. Message flags are one handy way of getting a handle on what you have to do with the messages that you get. By Message Flag view automatically organizes your messages according to the action that they demand, making you instantly efficient, right?

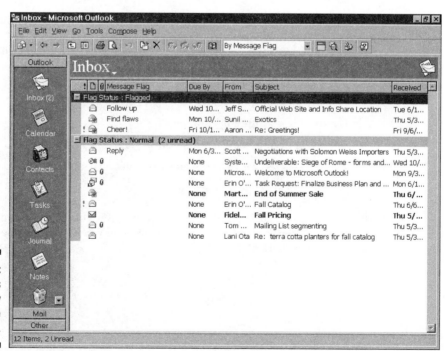

Figure 9-7:
Messages
in By
Message
Flag view.

Last Seven Days view

When you're asked to take immediate action on a message you received a few days ago, it's not always easy to find the message that told you what to do, especially if you get lots of e-mail. Last Seven Days view shows you only the messages that you got within the past week. It's easier to find an item in a short list than in a long one.

To use the Last Seven Days view:

1. **Choose View⇨Current View.**

   The list of current views appears.

2. **Choose Last Seven Days.**

   You see the messages you received over the last seven days.

The Last Seven Days list limits your view to messages that arrive in a seven-day time period; it does not sort according to what's in them or who sent them. You can sort your messages according to the name of the sender or the subject of the message by clicking the titles at the top of the columns in the view.

Flagged for Next Seven Days view

If you're flagging messages that are really important, the messages that you've flagged to get your attention in the next few days are likely to require your attention first. For a quick look at the hottest of the hot items, use Flagged for Next Seven Days view.

To see the Flagged for Next Seven Days view:

1. **Choose View⇨Current View.**

   The list of current views drops down.

2. **Choose Flagged for Next Seven Days view.**

   Your messages appear in Flagged for Next Seven Days view (see Figure 9-8).

Like Flagged view, Flagged for Next Seven Days view cuts to the essentials: who sent the message, the subject of the message, and when action is due on the message that is marked.

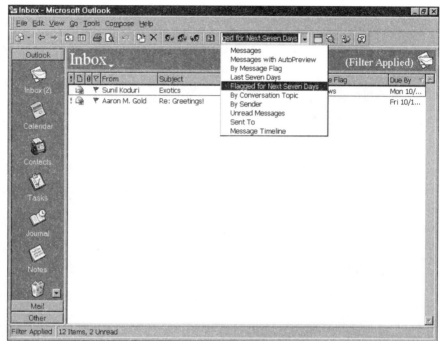

By Conversation Topic view

You should always include a subject line that's easy to understand, so that the person who gets your message will know at first glance the topic of your message and what to do about it. With any luck, other people will do the same thing for you. Then you can really get some mileage from your messages by sorting them in By Conversation Topic view.

To sort messages By Conversation Topic:

1. Choose View⇨Current View.

The list of current views appears.

2. Choose By Conversation Topic view.

Your messages appear in By Conversation Topic view (see Figure 9-9).

When you select By Conversation Topic view, Outlook groups your messages according to their subject lines and puts a plus or minus sign next to their titles. Plus signs tell you that more messages will appear under that title if you click on the plus. A minus sign next to a title means that there are no more messages to be seen under that title.

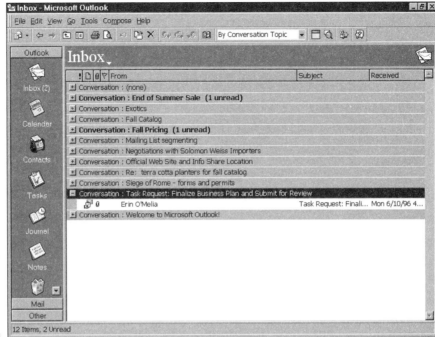

Figure 9-9:
The By
Conversation
Topic view.

When groups of people carry on discussions by e-mail, they normally just click the Reply button and type their two cents' worth, so all the messages have the same subject line. After a while, the messages resemble a conversation, with each message responding to the contents of one or more of the earlier messages. These e-mail conversations are often called *threads*.

When you participate in an e-mail conversation, it's best if you don't edit the subject line unless you plan to change the subject. That way, everybody else in the conversation knows that you're participating in the same conversation.

By Sender view

When the boss calls and asks, "Did you get the e-mail message about bonuses that I sent you three weeks ago?" you probably don't want to spend a great deal of time sorting through everybody else's messages from the past three weeks. The quickest way to answer the boss's question promptly is to switch to By Sender view.

To use the By Sender view:

1. **Choose <u>V</u>iew⇨Current <u>V</u>iew.**

   The list of current views appears.

2. **Choose By Sender view.**

   Your messages appear in the By Sender view (see Figure 9-10).

You can instantly find the boss's name in By Sender view. Double-click the message titled `Bonuses`. Then you can tell the boss, "I certainly did; it's right here in front of me." You'll be able to reply so quickly that the boss will be glad to give you that bonus.

Unread Messages view

You don't have to read every message that comes across your screen, but Murphy's Law says that the most important information will be in a message that you haven't read yet. The Unread Messages view gives you a quick peek at the things that you haven't taken a quick peek at yet.

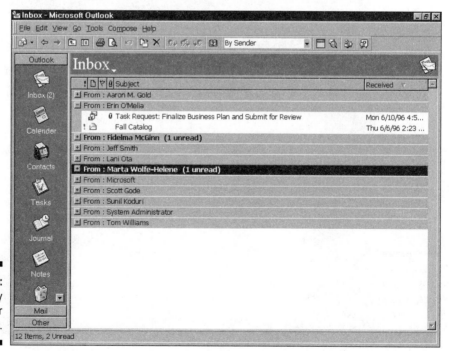

Figure 9-10: The By Sender view.

To see the Unread Messages view:

1. **Choose View➪Current View.**

   The Current View menu appears.

2. **Choose Unread Messages view.**

   Your unread messages appear (see Figure 9-11).

Don't leave your Inbox in the Unread Messages view all the time because messages will seem to vanish when you finish reading them. It's easier to use Messages view most of the time and switch to Unread Messages view now and then as a strategy for finding things.

Sent To view

It may seem silly to have a view of your Inbox sorted according to the name of the person each message is sent to. After all, it's your Inbox; everything should be sent to you, or it wouldn't be here, right?

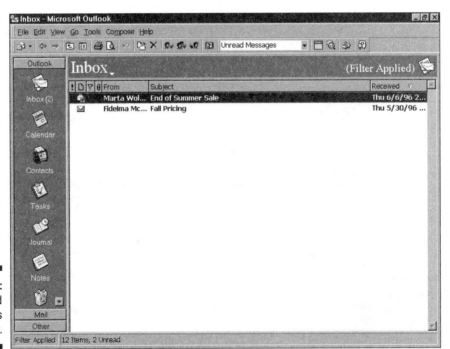

Figure 9-11:
The Unread
Messages
view.

You have two reasons for using Sent To view. Some messages that come to you are addressed to everybody at your company, for example, so it's good to know that certain messages shouldn't be taken personally. The second reason is that the same set of views is available in the Inbox and the Sent Items folder. The Sent Items folder is where Outlook keeps copies of messages that you've sent to other people. Knowing what you sent to whom can come in very handy.

To use the Sent To view:

1. **Choose <u>V</u>iew⇨Current <u>V</u>iew.**

   The list of current views appears.

2. **Choose Sent To view.**

   Your list is rearranged according to whom the message was sent (see Figure 9-12).

Sent To view is only sorted, not grouped, which means that the messages appear in order of the names of the people who sent them. A grouped view would display the name of each person who has sent you mail as the heading of a group. If you click the Subject column, you'll lose the benefit of having the list sorted by sender. If your Sent To list appears to be sorted incorrectly, just click the word To at the top of the To column.

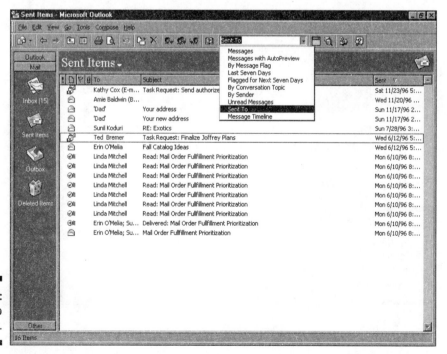

Figure 9-12:
The Sent To
view.

Message Timeline view

Message Timeline view is one of the most interesting views in Outlook; it draws you a graph of all your messages according to when they arrived. Message Timeline view is designed to help you find messages when you can remember when they arrived but not why they arrived or who sent them.

To use Message Timeline view:

1. **Choose View⇨Current View.**

   The list of current views appears.

2. **Choose Message Timeline view.**

   The Message Timeline view appears (see Figure 9-13).

The little icons that represent the messages are actually shortcuts to the messages that they represent. You can open a message by double-clicking the icon for that message. You can also right-click the message icon to reply to, delete, or move a message to another folder.

Figure 9-13:
The
Message
Timeline
view.

Chapter 10

Your Little Black Book: Creating Contact Lists

· ·

In This Chapter

▶ Storing names and addresses

▶ Viewing contacts

▶ Sorting a view

▶ Rearranging views

▶ Using grouped views

▶ Creating your own groups

▶ Saving a view

▶ Deleting a saved view

▶ Finding contacts

· ·

*H*ardly anybody works alone. Even if you work at home, you always have people you need to keep track of: people you sell things to, buy things from, have lunch with, or any of dozens of things you need to do with other people. All that personal information can be hard to store in a way you can find and use again quickly when you need it. And the things you need to know about people in different parts of your life are different. So you need a tool that's flexible enough to let you organize names, addresses, and all that other information in ways that make sense in different contexts.

For example, I work as a computer consultant and write for computer magazines. The information I need to keep about consulting clients (systems, software, hours, locations, and networks) is different than information I need for dealing with people in the book-publishing business (editors, deadlines, topics, and so on). I'm also still active as a professional singer and actor, so my contacts in those businesses are two entirely different kettles of fish. But when someone calls on the phone, or when I want to do a mailing to a group from one world or another, I need to be able to look the person up right away, regardless of category.

Outlook is flexible enough to let me keep all my name and address information in a single place but sort, view, find, and print it differently, depending on what kind of work I'm doing. You can also keep lists of family and friends stored in Outlook right alongside your business contacts and still distinguish them from one another quickly when the need arises.

Storing Names, Numbers, and Other Stuff

Storing lots of names, addresses, and phone numbers is no big trick, but finding them again can take magic unless you have a tool like Outlook. You may have used other programs for storing names and related numbers, but Outlook ties the name and number information together more tightly with the work you do that uses names, addresses, and phone numbers, such as scheduling and task management.

If you've ever used a little pocket address book, you pretty much know how to use the contacts feature of Outlook. Simply enter the name, address, phone number, a few juicy tidbits, and there you are!

To store a name in the Outlook Contacts module, follow these steps:

1. **Choose Go⟿Contacts.**

   The Contact list appears (see Figure 10-1).

2. **Choose File⟿New⟿Contact.**

   The New Contact form appears.

   To be really quick about it, click File⟿New⟿Contact or press Ctrl+Shift+C instead to see the form shown in Figure 10-2.

3. **Click the Full Name button.**

   The Check Full Name dialog box appears (see Figure 10-3):

   - Click the triangle (called the scroll down button) on the right edge of the Title button and choose a title from the list that drops down, such as Mr., Ms., or Dr., or type one in, such as **Rev., Ayatollah,** or whatever.

   - Click in the First text box and enter the contact's first name.

   - Click in the Middle text box and enter the contact's middle initial (if any). If there's no middle initial, you can leave it blank.

   - Click in the Last text box and enter the contact's last name.

   - Click in the Suffix drop-down list and choose a suffix, such as Jr., III, or type one in the box, such as **Ph.D., D.D.S.,** or **B.P.O.E.**

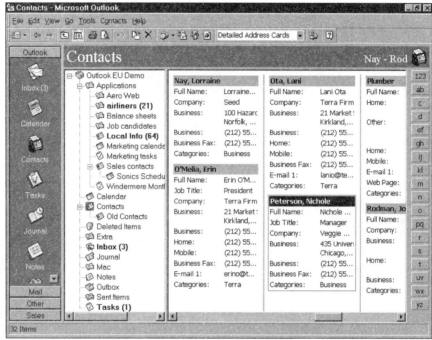

Figure 10-1:
The Contact
list in the
Contacts
module.

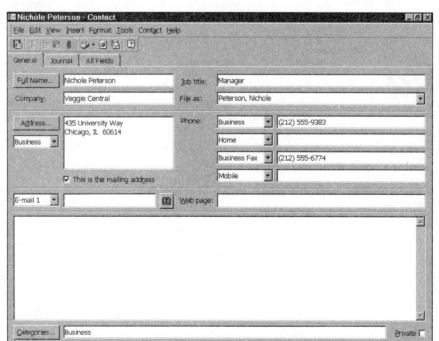

Figure 10-2:
The New
Contact
form.

• Click OK. The Check Full Name dialog box closes and you are back in the New Contact form, where the name you entered is now shown in both the F<u>u</u>ll Name and Fi<u>l</u>e As text boxes.

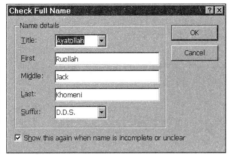

Figure 10-3:
The Check
Full Name
dialog box.

4. **Click in the appropriate box and type in the information requested on the New Contact form.**

   If the information is not available, for example, if the contact has no job title, leave the box blank. A triangle after the box indicates a drop-down list with choices you can select from. If your choice is not listed, enter your choice into the box.

   • If you've entered a name in the F<u>u</u>ll Name box, the Fi<u>l</u>e As box will already contain that name.

   • If you want this person filed under something other than his or her name, click in the Fi<u>l</u>e As box and type in your preferred designation. For example, you may want to file your dentist's name under the term "Dentist" rather than by name. If you put Dentist in the Fi<u>l</u>e As box, the name turns up under Dentist in the alphabetical listing rather than under the name itself. Both the F<u>u</u>ll Name and the Fi<u>l</u>e As designation exist in your Contact list. That way, for example, you can search for your dentist either by name or the word "Dentist."

5. **Click the A<u>d</u>dress button to open the Check Address dialog box.**

   • Click the <u>S</u>treet text box and type in the contact's street address.

   • Click the <u>C</u>ity text box and type in the contact's city.

   • Click the St<u>a</u>te/Province text box and type in the contact's state.

   • Click the <u>Z</u>IP/Postal Code box and type in the contact's postal code.

   • Click the triangle at the right end of the C<u>o</u>untry box and choose the contact's country if Outlook has not already chosen the correct one.

   See Figure 10-4 for a look at a completed Check Address dialog box.

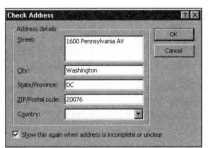

Figure 10-4:
The Check
Address
dialog box.

6. **Click the check box on the New Contact form next to** This Is the Mailing Address **if the address you've just entered is the address you plan to use to send mail to the contact.**

7. **Click in the text box to the right of the Business phone box and type in the contact's business phone number.**

8. **Click in the text box to the right of the Home phone box and type in the contact's home phone number.**

   For numbers other than Business and Home phones, click on the triangle to the right of the phone number type block and choose the kind of number you're entering. Then enter the number.

   Four phone number blocks are on the New Contact form. Any of them can be used for any of the 20 phone number types that are available in the drop-down list. You can also add custom fields so that you can include more than four phone numbers for a single contact. For the person who has everything, you can create custom fields for their Ski Phone, Submarine Phone, Gym Phone — as many as you want. For more about Custom Fields, see Chapter 24.

   You can choose any of 20 dozen phone number types to enter, depending on what types of phone numbers your contacts have (see Figure 10-5).

9. **Click in the text box to the right of the e-mail address list box and enter your contact's e-mail address.**

   If your contact has more than one e-mail address, click the triangle at the right edge of the E-mail-1 box (see Figure 10-6) and change it to E-mail-2, and then click in the text box and type in the address.

10. **Click in the _W_eb Page text box if the contact has a Web page and enter the URL address for that page if you want to be able to link to that page directly from the Address Card.**

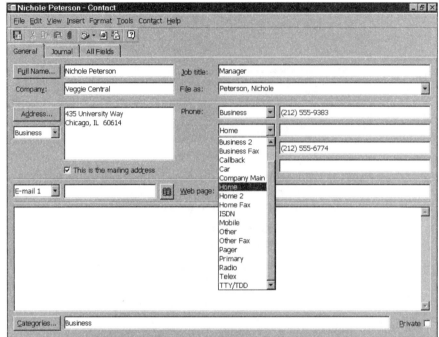

Figure 10-5:
You can always get your contact at one of these types of phone numbers.

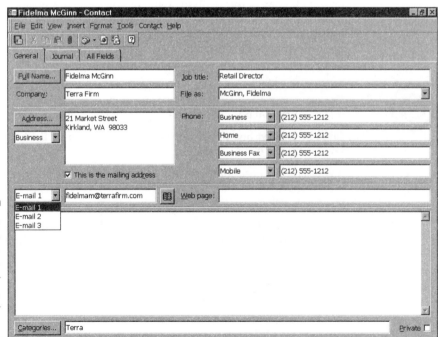

Figure 10-6:
You can enter more than one message for each person in your Contact list.

URL is a fancy name for the address of a page on the World Wide Web. When you see ads on TV that refer to www.discovery.com or www.dummies.com, what you're seeing is a *Uniform Resource Locator* or URL. You can view a Web page by entering the URL for the page in the Address box of your Web browser. If a person or company in your Outlook Contact list has a Web page, you can enter the URL for that page in the Web Page box. To view the Web page for a contact, select the contact and choose Contact➪Explore Web Page (or press Ctrl+Shft+X); your Web browser opens and loads the contact's Web page.

11. Click in the large text box at the bottom of the form and type in anything you want.

You can enter directions, details about meetings, the Declaration of Independence, anything you want (preferably, something that can help you in your dealings with the contact).

Format the text in the big text box (see Figure 10-7) by using the formatting buttons on the toolbar, if you want. The formatting tools on the toolbar are just like the ones all the other word-processing programs use: font, point size, bold, italic, justification, and color. Select the text you want to format and change formatting. You can change the formatting of a single letter or the whole text box. You can't format the text in the smaller data text boxes in the other parts of the Contact form, only in the big text box at the bottom of the form. If your formatting toolbar isn't showing, choose View➪Toolbars➪Formatting from the Contact form menu.

Big Text Box

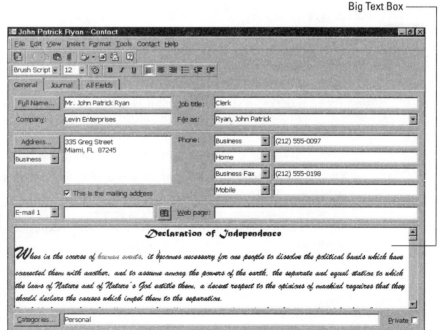

Figure 10-7:
Have fun
with
formatting in
the Contact
text box.

12. **Click the Categories button at the bottom left of the screen to assign a category to the contact, if you like.**

    Assigning categories is another trick to help you find things easily. See the section in Chapter 14, "Assigning a Category to Your Notes" as an example of how to use categories with any Outlook item. Once you've assigned categories to Outlook items, you can easily sort or group the items according to the category you've assigned.

    Choose one of the existing categories if one suits you, and then click OK (see Figure 10-8).

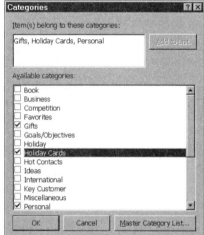

Figure 10-8:
Put your contact in a category for easy reference.

13. **If none of the existing categories suits you, click Master Category List in the lower-right corner to see the Master Category list box.**

    Type a category of your choice in the New box (see Figure 10-9). Be sure not to add too many new categories as that could make it hard to find things.

14. **Click Add and then click OK to return to the Categories list.**

    Choose the new category from the list if you want. You can choose more than one category at a time.

15. **Click the Private box in the lower right corner of the New Contact form if you're on a network and you don't want others to know about your contacts.**

Figure 10-9:
Enter your
own
category in
the Master
Category
List.

16. **Click the Journal tab at the top left of the form to open the Journal page and set your Journaling Preferences.**

    Journaling is a handy feature that lets you keep track of all your activities with any person, place, or thing you deal with on your computer. You may as well turn Journaling on in case you want to use it later.

    • To activate your journal, click in the check box that says Automatically Record Journal Entries for this Contact.

    • When you're first entering a contact, it's best to leave the Show Journal Entries choice as All (see Figure 10-10). If you don't want to show all Journal entries related to the contact, click the triangle (scroll button) at the right of the Show Journal Entries menu and choose an entry you'd like to display.

17. **When you're done, click Save and Close (Alt+S).**

After you enter anything you want or need (or may need) to know about people you deal with at work, you're ready to start dealing.

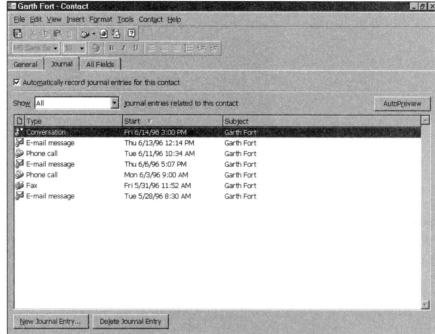

Figure 10-10:
With the Journal on, you have a complete record of all your activities with this contact.

Viewing Contacts

Once you have entered your contact information, Outlook lets you see the information arranged in many different and useful ways, called *views*. Viewing your contact information and sorting the views are quick ways to get the big picture of the data you've entered (see Chapter 5 for more information on views). Outlook comes with anywhere from 5 to 12 predefined views in each module. You can easily alter any predefined view; then you can name and save your altered view and use it just like the predefined views that come with Outlook.

To change the view of your Contact list:

1. **Choose Go⇨Contacts.**

   The Contact list box appears.

2. **Choose View⇨Current View and pick the view you want.**

   You can shift between views like you can switch television stations, so don't worry about changing views and changing back. Another way to change the view is to click the triangle at the right of the Current View window and click the name of the view from the menu. Figure 10-11 shows the Current View window and its list of views for Contacts. The Detailed Address Cards view is listed.

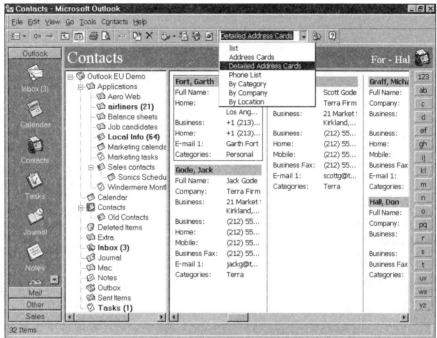

Figure 10-11:
The Detailed
Address
Cards view.

3. **Click Address Cards from the drop-down menu (or whatever other view you want).**

   You can also choose Detailed Address Cards, Phone List, By Category, By Company, By Location, or whatever other views are listed.

4. **Choose Discard the Current View Settings from the dialog box that appears (see Figure 10-12).**

Figure 10-12:
Decide what
to do with
your View
Settings.

   Whenever you make changes to an Outlook view and then change views, Outlook asks if you want to save changes to the view.

5. **You see the Address Cards view as shown in Figure 10-13 (or whatever other predefined view you select).**

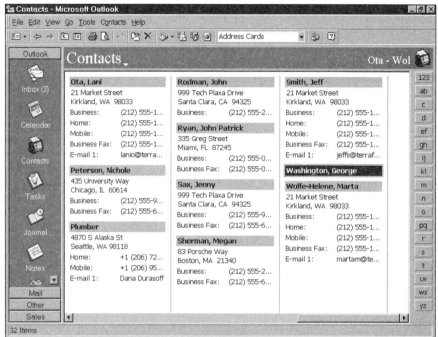

Figure 10-13:
Your
contacts in
Address
Cards view.

To use one of the other views, repeat the steps above and choose the view you want.

Sorting a view

Some views are organized as simple lists, such as the Phone List view of the Contacts module. Figure 10-14 shows the Phone List: a column of names on the left, followed by a column of Job Titles, Company Names, and so on.

If you're missing one view that is arranged in columns, all you have to do to sort on that column is to click once on the title of the column. For example, suppose you want to see the names of the people who work for IBM who are entered in your Contact list. One easy way to see all their names at once is to sort on the Company column:

1. Click the triangle at the right of the Current View menu.

The list of views appears.

Figure 10-14:
The Phone
List view.

2. Choose the Phone List view.

Your list of contacts appears in the Phone List view.

3. Click the head of the Company column.

You see a little icon with the letters AFZ and an arrow. That tells you that Outlook is sorting the column in alphabetical order. If you only have a few items to sort, the icon may flash by so quickly you don't notice it. When you have a really long list to sort, the icon may stay there for several seconds as Outlook sorts your list.

After you've sorted your list, it's easier to find the name of somebody by scrolling down to that part of the alphabet. If you sort the company, all the contacts line up in order of company name, so you can scroll down to the section of your list where all the people from a certain company are listed.

Rearranging views

You can rearrange views simply by dragging the column title and dropping the title where you want it. For example, to move the Job Title column in the Phone List view:

1. **Click the Contacts icon in the Outlook Bar.**

   Your list of contacts appears.

2. **Click on the Job Title heading and drag it on top of the column to its right.**

   You see a pair of red arrows pointing to the border between the two columns to the right of the Job Title column. The red arrows tell you where Outlook will drop the column when you release the mouse button. (See Figure 10-15.)

3. **Release the mouse button.**

   The Job Title column is now to the right of the Company column rather than the left. If it makes more sense to you to have Company to the left of Job Title, you can set up your view in Outlook to do just that.

You can use the same process to move any column in any Outlook view. Because the screen is not as wide as the list, you may need to move columns around at times to see what you really want to see. For example, the Phone List in Figure 10-14 shows 8 columns, but the list in that view really has 11 columns. You must use the scroll bar at the bottom of the list to scroll to the right to see the last column, Categories. If you want to see the Categories column at the same time as the Name column, you have to move the Categories column to the left.

Figure 10-15:
You can rearrange columns in any Outlook view by dragging the column heading to the location you desire.

When you make changes to a view and then switch to a different view, a dialog box appears asking you to Discard, Save, or Update the Current View (refer to Figure 10-12). For example, if you move the Job Title column to the right of the Company column, as I do in Figure 10-15, then choose View⇨Current View⇨ Address Cards to switch to the Address Cards view, the Save View Settings dialog box of Figure 10-12 appears.

- ✔ If you choose Discard, your new arrangement of columns disappears; the next time you use that view, the columns return to where they were before you moved them.

- ✔ If you choose Save the view, Outlook asks you to assign it a new name. You then have one more named view to choose from on your Current View menu — the view you saved.

- ✔ If you choose Update the view, when you next use the view, the view contains your changes but has the same name you started with.

If this is all too confusing, don't worry; you never have to change views if you don't want to. If you always answer "Discard" to the question about saving views, you'll be safe. If you're more adventurous and like to mess around with your views, that's fine; you can always change them back.

Using grouped views

Sometimes sorting just isn't enough. Contact lists can get pretty long after awhile; you can easily collect a few thousand contacts in a few years. Sorting a list that long means that, if you're looking for stuff starting with the letter *M,* the item you want to find will be about three feet below the bottom of your monitor screen, no matter what you do.

Groups are the answer, and I don't mean Outlook Anonymous. Outlook already offers you several predefined lists that use grouping.

You can view several types of lists in Outlook: A sorted list is like a deck of playing cards laid out in numerical order, starting with the deuces, then the threes, then the fours, and so on up through the picture cards. A grouped view is like seeing the cards arranged with all the hearts in one row, then all the spades, then the diamonds, then the clubs. There are also several other view types that don't apply to contacts, like Timeline and Address Cards.

Gathering items of similar types into groups is handy for tasks like finding all the people on your list who work for a certain company when you want to send congratulations on a new piece of business. Because grouping by company is so frequently useful, the By Company view (see Figure 10-16) is set up as a pre-defined view in Outlook.

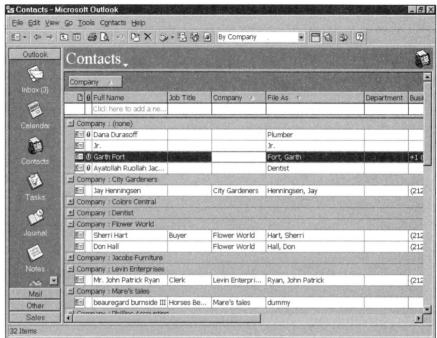

Figure 10-16:
The By
Company
view.

To use the By Company view:

1. **Choose Go⇨Contacts.**

   The Contacts module opens with its current view displayed.

2. **Choose View⇨Current View⇨By Company.**

   If you've made any changes in the view you were just using, a dialog box appears, asking you Discard, Save, or Update the Current View. Choose Discard.

   Each gray bar labeled Company: (name of company) has a little box at the left with a plus or minus sign on it. Click on a plus sign to see additional names in that category; a minus sign indicates that no more entries are available.

3. **Click on the plus icon to see entries for the company listed on the gray bar.**

This grouping thing gets really handy if you've been assigning categories to your contacts as you've created items. If you're clever about how you use and add categories that fit the work you do, grouping by category can be a huge time-saver.

If the predefined group views don't meet your needs, you can group items according to just about anything you want, assuming that you've entered the data.

To see the By Category view:

1. **Choose Go⬏Contacts.**

   The Contacts view appears.

2. **Choose View⬏Current View⬏By Category.**

   If you've made changes to the current Contacts view, a dialog box will appear asking you Discard, Save, or Update the Current View. Choose Discard.

   Each gray bar has an icon on the left side with a plus or a minus, followed by Category: *name of Category.* A minus means that there are no entries hidden under that company's heading; a plus means that more entries are available (see Figure 10-17).

3. **Click on a plus icon to see more entries for the Category listed on the gray bar.**

Grouping is a good way to manage all Outlook items, especially contacts. Once you get a handle on using groups you'll save a lot of time when you're trying to find things.

Figure 10-17:
By Category view; if you have a plus sign to the left, you need to click it to see more entries.

Creating your own groups

The group thing doesn't end with predefined groups. You can easily decide to group Contact views according to your own whims. Just push a button, drag and drop, and you have a group of your very own.

The key to making your own groups is the *Group By* Box. Just open the Group By Box and drag a column head into the box the same way you do to rearrange the columns. Voilà! A whole new way to group things!

To use the Group By Box:

1. Choose View⇨Group By Box (see Figure 10-18).

The Group By Box appears. Be sure that the Group By Box isn't open already; you know if it's open because the little icon next to Group By Box on the View menu is lighter in color if the box is already open; the icon darkens if the box is closed. Just click the icon a couple of times to see if it's light or dark.

Figure 10-18:
The Group
By Box icon
is lighter if
the box is
already
open.

A Group By icon is also located just right of the Current View menu; it does exactly the same thing when you click it.

If no grouping is set, a light gray box appears below the word Contacts in the Information Viewer. The box reads `Drag a column header here to group by that column`. I couldn't have put it better myself.

2. Drag a column header to the gray box to group by that column (duh! Aren't you glad you have me to tell you this stuff!).

For example, drag the Job Title column header to the Group By Box. Your contacts are grouped by Job Title (see Figure 10-19).

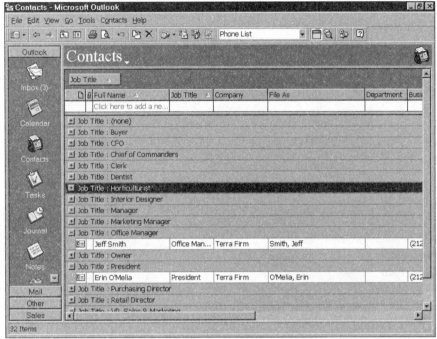

Figure 10-19:
Your
contacts
arranged by
Job Title.

You don't like the way you've grouped your contacts? So! Group them another way — any way you like. Just repeat the preceding steps, dragging your preferred header to the Group By Box.

Saving a view

You can change views more often than you change underwear, but now and then you may create a view that you want to stay with for awhile so Outlook lets you name and save your views. (You can keep changing the underwear, though.)

To save a view:

1. **Create a custom view by dragging any column head to a new location or to the Group By Box.**

   The view appears with the change you made.

2. **Click on the Current View menu and choose an existing view, such as the Phone List view (see Figure 10-20).**

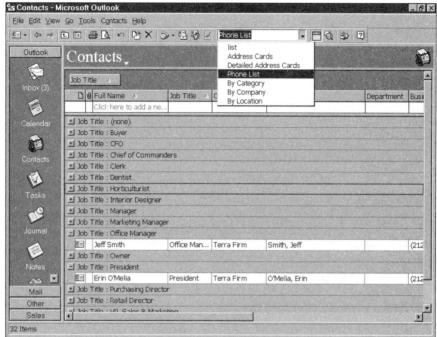

Figure 10-20:
Choosing
the Phone
List view.

A dialog box appears, asking if you want to Discard, Save, or Update the current view.

3. Choose Save the Current View Settings as a New View from the dialog box that appears and click OK (see Figure 10-21).

Figure 10-21:
Saving your
view.

The Copy View dialog box appears.

4. Click in the text box under Name of New View and enter the name you wish to call the view (see Figure 10-22).

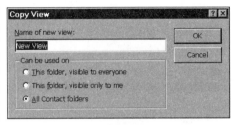

Figure 10-22:
Name your
new view in
the Copy
View dialog
box.

You're better off giving your saved views names that describe the view. You can name them anything you want, but if you name your views after the Seven Dwarfs, for example, you may get very confused.

(In case you misplaced your documentation, they're Sleepy, Dopey, Sneezy, Grumpy, Happy, Bashful, and Doc — not exactly names that you use at work every day, except maybe for Grumpy. Okay, you may be sleepy, dopey, sneezy, happy, and bashful, too, Doc, but that doesn't mean you should name your views that way.)

5. Click OK (leave the rest of the settings alone for the moment).

Your new view has been saved and is ready for action.

Deleting a saved view

Now, I don't want to say "I told you so." But there's a good chance that somewhere along the line you named a view something you couldn't figure out later (in one of your sleepy times, I bet). Or maybe you just saved and named a view you simply don't want anymore. Life is like that; easy come, easy go.

Fortunately, getting rid of an unwanted view in Outlook is much simpler than disposing of most household pests and a lot easier than getting gum off your shoe.

To delete a saved view:

1. Choose View⇨Define Views.

The Define Views dialog box appears (see Figure 10-23).

2. Click on the name of the view you wish to delete and then click the Delete button.

The Are You Sure dialog box appears (see Figure 10-24).

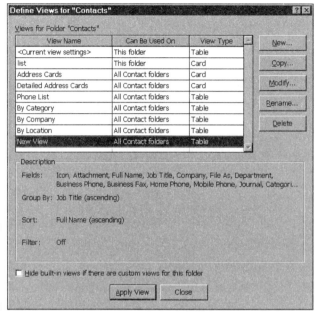

Figure 10-23:
The Define
Views dialog
box.

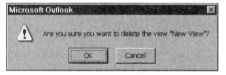

Figure 10-24:
Are you
sure?

When Outlook asks "Are you sure," that means take a breath and think about it. After you wipe out a view, you may find it difficult to go back and reconstruct it. Be careful not to zap views that you may need later.

3. If you're sure, click OK.

4. Click Close.

Because it's so easy to add and delete named views, you can feel free to create all the custom views you want.

Finding Contacts

The whole reason for entering names and such in a Contact list is so that you can find them again. Otherwise, what's the point of all this rigmarole?

Finding names in the Outlook Contacts module is child's play. The easiest way is to look in the Address Cards view under the last name.

To find a contact by last name:

1. **Choose Go⬄Contacts.**

   Your list of contacts appears.

2. **Choose View⬄Current View⬄Address Cards.**

   The Address Cards view appears (see Figure 10-25).

The Address Cards view has a set of lettered tabs along the right edge. You can click on a tab to go to that lettered section, but there's an easier way: Simply type the first letter of the name you're looking for. For example, if you're looking for Pat Kirtland (and you've let Outlook make his File As name Kirtland, Pat), type the letter **K**. You'll see the names that start with K.

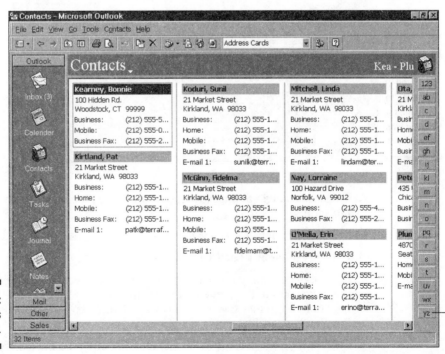

Figure 10-25:
The Address
Cards view.

Lettered tabs

Of course, you may need to search for a contact name based on something like the company the contact works for. Or you may want to find all the people on your list who live in a certain state. Or people who put you in a certain state of mind (if you've included that in their Contact record). To do this, you use the Find Items tool.

To search for a contact using the Find Items tool:

1. **Click Tools⇨Find Item on the menu bar (or press Ctrl+Shift+F).**

   The Find Dialog box appears.

2. **Click the scroll down button (triangle) at the right end of the Look For text box.**

   A menu drops down from the Look for text box (see Figure 10-26).

3. **Choose Contacts from the menu.**

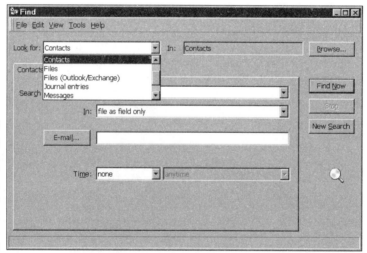

Figure 10-26: Choose what kind of item you're looking for with the Find Items tool.

4. **Click the triangle at the right end of the In text box under the Contacts tab setting.**

   You see a list of fields (see Figure 10-27).

5. **Choose Frequently-Used Text Fields.**

   Other choices limit your search to a single field. If you're really sure that the thing you want is in one of those fields, go ahead and choose that field, but your search may come up empty-handed. When in doubt, choosing Frequently-Used Text Fields is a safe bet.

6. **Click in the Search for the Word(s) text box and type the text you want to find.**

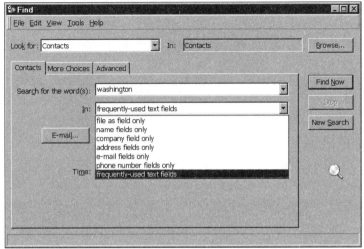

Figure 10-27:
The Find
dialog box.

If you're looking for your friend George Washington's phone number, type
Washington.

7. **Click the Find Now button.**

Outlook starts out by saying There are no items to show in this
view, but give it a second; some searches take a little time. (How long does
it take you to find the remote control for your VCR?)

If the mouse pointer has turned into an hourglass, Outlook is still out
looking. If the hourglass goes away and nothing's turned up, that's it.

If your search is successful, a list of contacts that match the text you
entered appears at the bottom of the dialog box.

8. **Double-click on the name of the contact in the list at the bottom of the
dialog box to see the Contact record.**

If you get nothing, check to see if you picked the right section or if the
thing you're searching for is spelled exactly right.

Remember, it's hard to be as stupid as computers; close doesn't count with
them. If you saw Grge Wshngtn you'd know to look for George Washington. Not
a computer; George would have to have his vowels removed before a computer
would see those two words the same way.

On the other hand, if you only have a scrap of the name you're looking for,
Outlook can find that scrap wherever it is. A search for "Geo" would turn up
George Washington as well as any other Georges in your Contact list, including
Phyllis George and George of the Jungle (if they're all such close, personal
friends of yours that they're in your Contact list).

Chapter 11

Personal Distribution Lists and Address Books

● ●

In This Chapter

▶ Creating a Personal Distribution List

▶ Adding names to your Personal Address Book

▶ Editing a Personal Distribution List

▶ Why all these Address Books?

▶ Importing a Schedule+ Address Book

● ●

*I*f you send regular messages to the same groups of people, Personal Distribution Lists save time. Whether you regularly harangue all the members of Congress or all the members of your company softball team, you can create a list of names and e-mail addresses and then address those people as a unit — that's what a Personal Distribution List is.

Creating a Personal Distribution List

You can create Personal Distribution Lists only in the Personal Address Book (see Chapter 10 for more about Address Books). You can't clump people up in the Contacts module and address them as one person. You can send a single e-mail message to a group of people by adding all their names in the To box of a message, but only the Personal Address Book can store a Personal Distribution List. This arrangement is left over from Exchange Inbox — the Microsoft program that came before Outlook. The Personal Address Book isn't as pretty as the Outlook Contact list, but it gets the job done.

To create a Personal Distribution List:

1. Choose Tools⇨Address Book.

The Address Book dialog box appears. You can also bring up the Address Book by clicking the Address Book button in the toolbar, just to the left of the Current View list (when you're using the Inbox module).

2. Choose File⇨New Entry.

The New Entry dialog box appears.

3. Choose Personal Distribution List from the Select the Entry Type box.

4. Click OK.

The New Personal Distribution List Properties dialog box appears (see Figure 11-1).

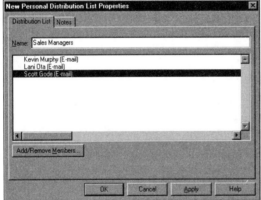

Figure 11-1:
The New Personal Distribution List Properties dialog box.

5. Type a name for your new distribution list.

Pick a memorable name that describes what's in the group. Try Sales Managers, Art Directors, or Serfs — whatever describes the members of the group.

6. Click Add/Remove Members.

The Edit Members Of dialog box appears (see Figure 11-2). The Edit Members Of dialog box is really a different version of the Address Book, including the names of all the people listed in a certain Address Book; the name of the Address Book that they're listed in appears in the top-right corner of the dialog box.

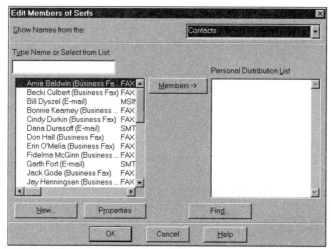

Figure 11-2:
Editing your
distribution
list.

7. **Click the name of a person you want to add to your personal address list.**

   You can select multiple names by holding down the Ctrl key while clicking each name. You can select a row of consecutive names by clicking the first name that you want to select and then holding down the Shift key while clicking the last name.

8. **Click the Members button.**

   The name or group of names that you selected appears in the Personal Distribution List box on the right side of the dialog box.

9. **Click OK.**

   Your Personal Distribution List is available for your use.

You can also add one Personal Distribution List to another. You can have groups called Hourly Employees and Salaried Employees, for example, and add them both to a group called All Employees. Then you can send only one message to reach all members of both groups. You only have to edit the smaller group when a new employee is hired or some other change is made; the larger group such as the All Employees group automatically includes whatever changes you've made in any smaller groups that belong to it.

Using a Personal Distribution List

Suppose that you want to send a message to the members of the All Employees group. If you've created a Personal Distribution List, you can send a single message and reach everybody.

To send a message to your Personal Distribution List:

1. **Choose File⇨New⇨Mail Message.**

   The Untitled Message form appears.

2. **Click the To button.**

   The Select Names dialog box appears (see Figure 11-3), showing the list of names from your Contacts module.

A Personal Distribution List

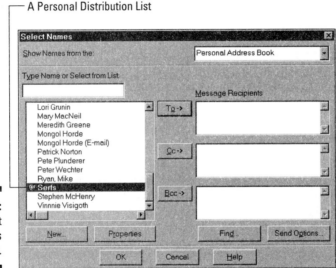

Figure 11-3:
The Select
Names
dialog box.

3. **Choose Personal Address Book from the Show Names From The drop-down list.**

   The names in your Personal Address Book appear in the left window of the Select Names dialog box, as do the names in any Personal Distribution Lists that you've created. You can store a Personal Distribution List only in the Personal Address Book, not the Contact list. If you think that's nonsensical, you're right; I do, too.

   Your Personal Distribution Lists appear in the list in boldface, with a little two-faces icon.

4. **Click the name of the Personal Distribution List that you want to use.**

   You can choose more than one list at a time or include several lists by holding down the Ctrl key while clicking.

5. Click the To button.

If you want to send a copy of the message to members of a list, click the Cc or Bcc button (Bcc stands for blind copies — copies sent to folks that you don't want to appear on the open copy list).

6. Click OK.

The New Message form appears, with the list you selected displayed in the To box. Now you can type your subject and message and then send your e-mail.

Editing a Personal Distribution List

People come and people go in Personal Distribution Lists, just like everywhere else. It's a good thing that you can edit the lists.

To edit your Personal Distribution List:

1. Choose Tools⇨Address Book.

The Address Book dialog box appears. You can also bring up the Address Book by clicking the Address Book button in the toolbar, just to the left of the Current View menu (when you're using the Inbox module).

2. Choose Personal Address Book from the Show Names From The drop-down list.

The names of the people and Personal Distribution Lists that you've entered appear in the Names column of the dialog box (see Figure 11-4).

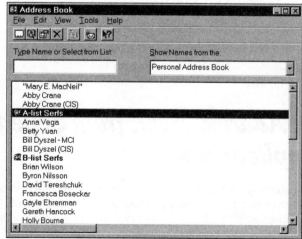

Figure 11-4:
Your
Personal
Distribution
Lists show
up in the
Address
Book
dialog box.

3. **Double-click the name of the Personal Distribution List that you want to edit.**

   The Properties dialog box appears, displaying the names of the people in the distribution list.

4. **Click Add/Remove <u>M</u>embers.**

   The Edit Members Of dialog box appears. The current names of members are listed on the right side of the dialog box; people in your Address Book who are not members of the list are on the left.

5. **Click the name of a person you want to add to the Personal Distribution List.**

   You can choose more than one person by holding down the Ctrl key while clicking each name.

6. **Click the <u>M</u>embers button.**

   The names of the people you selected now appear in the Personal Distribution List column.

7. **In the Personal Distribution List column, click the name of anyone you want to remove from the list.**

8. **Press the Delete key.**

   The name that you selected is deleted.

9. **Click OK.**

   The Edit Members Of dialog box disappears.

10. **Click OK.**

    The Properties dialog box disappears.

11. **Choose <u>F</u>ile⇨Close (or press Alt+F4).**

    The Address Book closes.

Your Address Book is now updated and corrected for the next time you need to send a message.

Importing an Address Book from Schedule+ and Other Applications

If you've been using another personal information manager, such as Schedule +, you can import your files from the old program and use the contacts that you already have. Importing is much easier than typing hundreds of contacts again.

Some of the programs that you can import files from include

- ✔ Act!
- ✔ Ecco
- ✔ Lotus Organizer
- ✔ Schedule +
- ✔ SideKick

You can also import files from any of a number of other programs that can export standard text files.

To import a file:

1. Choose File⇨Import and Export.

The Import and Export Wizard appears. A *Wizard* is a series of dialog boxes with instructions to guide you through a sequence of choices to help you complete a process that requires several parts. The process of importing files and having Outlook convert them into a Contact list varies depending on what kind of file you're importing, how the information in the file is arranged, and how you want Outlook to treat it.

2. Follow the directions that the wizard gives you for the program you're importing from.

You may need to install some special tools from the Office 97 CD-ROM to import your file. Follow the prompts of the Import and Export Wizard.

Why All These Address Books?

I like many things about Outlook, but not the collection of Address Books. The Address Books are a crazy-quilt arrangement of several separate, independent lists of names and e-mail addresses. It's nuts. I hope Microsoft will simplify the issue of dealing with Address Books in some future version, but in the mean-time, I'll try to help you make sense of it all.

The Outlook Contact list contains all kinds of personal information, whereas an Address Book focuses on e-mail addresses. An Address Book can also deal with the nitty-gritty details of actually sending your message to an e-mail service with the right routing information. In most cases, Outlook figures out the routing information, but there are cases in which you have to define the routing for a certain address, especially if you're using CompuServe as your e-mail delivery service.

Here's the lowdown on your plethora of Address Books:

- ✔ **The Personal Address Book:** The Personal Address Book is your very own list of e-mail addresses of the people to whom you send mail. It is not the same as the Outlook Contact list; individual names can be included in either, neither, or both the Personal Address Book and the Contact list.

- ✔ **The Contacts Address Book:** The Contacts Address Book is really the list of e-mail addresses from the Contact list. Outlook automatically creates the Contacts Address Book to allow you to add the names of people in your Contact list to a Personal Distribution List.

- ✔ **The Global Address Book:** If you're using Outlook on a corporate network, The Global Address Book, which is maintained by your system administrator, normally contains the names and e-mail addresses of all the people in your company. The Global Address Book makes it possible to address an e-mail message to anybody in your company without having to look up the e-mail address.

- ✔ **Additional address books:** If you create additional folders for Outlook contacts, those folders also become separate Address Books. Your system administrator can also create additional Address Books.

If you're lucky, you'll never see the Address Book; all the addresses of all the people you ever send e-mail to are listed in the Global Address Book that somebody else maintains, such as on a corporate network. Under those circumstances, Outlook is a dream. You don't need to know what an Address Book is most of the time; you just type the name of the person you're mailing to in the To box of a message. Outlook checks the name for spelling and takes care of sending your message. You'd swear that there's a psychic midget inside your computer who knows what you need.

Under less-than-ideal conditions, when you try to send a message, Outlook either complains that it doesn't know how to send the message or can't figure out whom you're talking about. Then you have to mess with the address. That situation happens only when the address isn't listed in one of the Address Books or isn't in a form that Outlook understands.

The other situation in which you need to deal with Address Books is when you want to create a Personal Distribution List, as you do in this chapter, to save yourself the trouble of adding addresses to a message one by one.

Chapter 12

Online and Internet Service Providers

1 f you want to use Outlook to send and receive e-mail, you'll need an outside service unless your computer is attached to a corporate network with an Outlook-compatible e-mail system. You can use online services, such as The Microsoft Network or CompuServe, or an Internet service provider (ISP) such as AT&T WorldNet Service or Netcom.

If you are using Outlook on a computer that is attached to an office network, you'll probably get e-mail and Internet capability through your network, so you can skip this chapter. Check with your network administrator to see what features are available to you.

Everything about the Internet and online services changes quickly. When it comes to the best way to get and use an online service, what's true as I'm writing this chapter may no longer be true when you read it. I'll tell you how it is as of very early 1997.

When it comes to supporting Outlook, America Online was a bit late to the party, but AOL users can expect to use Outlook for exchanging AOL e-mail very soon. AOL is working on a program for retrieving and reading mail through Outlook that should be available by the time you read this. I think AOL is the most fun online service as well as the biggest by a long shot, having about 10 million members, but I've never been fond of how little you can do with AOL e-mail messages once they arrive. Adding Outlook to the picture will be a big help. Check with AOL to see if you can get their program to make Outlook compatible with AOL.

The Microsoft Network (MSN): Built-in Compatibility

So we come to the No. 3 online service: The Microsoft Network (not a Microsoft network but *The* Microsoft Network, or MSN).

If you don't have an online service or an Internet service provider, and you're using Outlook, MSN is by far the easiest online service *and* e-mail provider *and* Internet service provider to join and use. It's like falling off a log. I'm not sure that I like how easy it is, but hey, what do I know? Maybe if I had a few billion dollars to gain in the deal like Microsoft, I'd think differently.

In its first year as an online service, MSN was pretty weak and Microsoft knew it. The company completely relaunched the service, so now we'll see. MSN doesn't offer as many fun things to do as AOL does or as useful a collection of information as CompuServe does. But the service is there, and it's The Microsoft Network, so it automatically becomes No. 3. Because MSN and Outlook are both Microsoft products, it's no surprise that they work well together.

MSN is an absolute no-brainer to join and use. You may not even be aware that you're using it until the bill comes. (The old Microsoft Network forgot to bill people for a long time; that was nice while it lasted.) But at $19.95 a month for unlimited service, you can hardly go wrong. Lots of other Internet service providers also offer service for that price, but they don't include the files and conferences and other benefits of an online service like MSN.

Signing up

There's already an MSN icon on your desktop when you first install Windows 95. All you have to do to sign up with MSN is click the icon and follow the instructions. The new version of MSN that Microsoft launched in late 1996 requires you to insert a CD-ROM to set it up. If you follow the instructions you see after you click the MSN icon, Microsoft will send you everything for starting your account and getting a password for MSN.

Setting up Outlook

After you've signed up for The Microsoft Network or any other service provider, you have to make the provider you chose work with Outlook. I show you how to set up Outlook with The Microsoft Network, because it's the easiest service to use with Outlook. Setting up another service for your e-mail follows a similar process, but you need to check with your e-mail and Internet service provider for specific details.

To set up Outlook to get mail from The Microsoft Network:

1. **Choose Tools⇨Services.**

   The Services dialog box appears. If the dialog box already displays The Microsoft Network Online Service, click Cancel. You're done.

2. **If MSN is not displayed, click Add.**

   The Add Service to Profile dialog box appears (see Figure 12-1).

Figure 12-1:
The Add
Service to
Profile
dialog box.

3. **Double-click The Microsoft Network Online Service.**

   The Services dialog box reappears, now displaying The Microsoft Network Online Service.

4. **Click OK.**

   The dialog box disappears and you see the Outlook Main Screen again.

5. **Choose File⇨Exit and Log Off.**

   You have to restart Outlook when you add a new service such as MSN.

6. **Double-click the Outlook icon to restart Outlook.**

   You can now use Outlook to send and receive mail on The Microsoft Network as well as on the Internet.

You can have more than one online service set up to send and receive mail on Outlook; I have MSN and CompuServe both set up on my copy of Outlook.

Getting your Internet mail

Here is the fastest way to get your new mail off the Internet:

1. **Choose Tools⇨Check for New Mail (or press F5).**

   The Microsoft Network opening screen appears.

2. **Click Connect.**

   A cute animated dialog box pops up and shows little letters flying back and forth until your mail has been retrieved.

You can save your mail to be read later when you're offline; then disconnect from the network.

Finding addresses on MSN

If you need to send e-mail to someone else who subscribes to MSN, you can find that person's address in the MSN Address Book.

To find an address on The Microsoft Network:

1. **Choose Tools⇨Address Book.**

   The Address Book appears.

2. **Choose Microsoft Network from the Show Names from the Menu list.**

   The Microsoft Network opening screen appears (see Figure 12-2). You have to connect to MSN to check the Address Book.

Figure 12-2:
The MSN
opening
screen.

3. Click Connect.

You'll have to enter your name and password if you didn't check Remember My Password. As MSN connects, it posts progress reports: `Connecting to The Microsoft Network`, `Trying Alternate Number`, or `Cannot Connect to The Microsoft Network`, for example. When MSN connects, the Address Book reappears (see Figure 12-3).

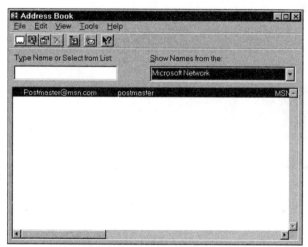

Figure 12-3:
The Address
Book.

4. Choose Tools⇨Find.

The Find dialog box appears (see Figure 12-4).

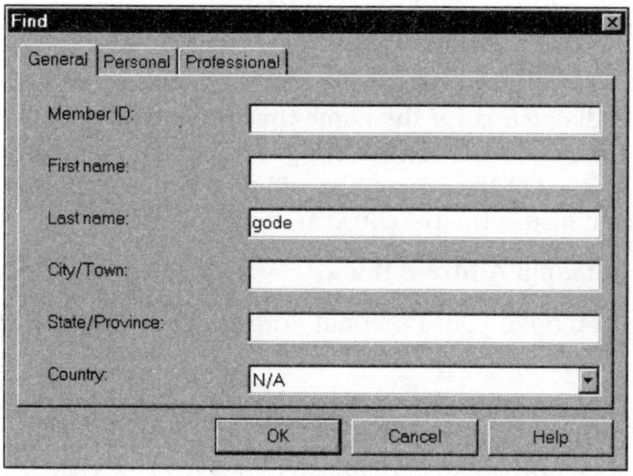

Figure 12-4:
The Find
dialog box.

5. Type the name of the person whose address you're trying to find.

The MSN Address Book allows you to search for as little as one piece of information, so if you know only the last name, you can use that. If the last name is a common one, MSN retrieves a long list of names for you to choose among. If you know more than one of the types of information that the dialog box asks about the person you're searching for, you can enter what you know in the boxes.

6. Click OK.

The list of names, including the text that you entered, appears (see Figure 12-5).

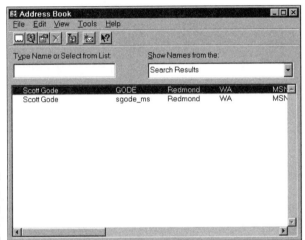

Figure 12-5:
The Name list.

7. If the name that you're looking for appears in the Search Results list, double-click the name.

The Properties dialog box for the name that you chose appears (see Figure 12-6). If more than one MSN subscriber goes by the name that you searched for, looking at the dialog box will give you a clue about whether the person you chose is the person you think you chose.

8. Click Add to Personal Address Book.

The next time you open your Personal Address Book, that person's name will appear.

9. Click OK.

If you're sending mail to someone who doesn't subscribe to MSN (such as someone on the Internet), you need to know that person's Internet e-mail address.

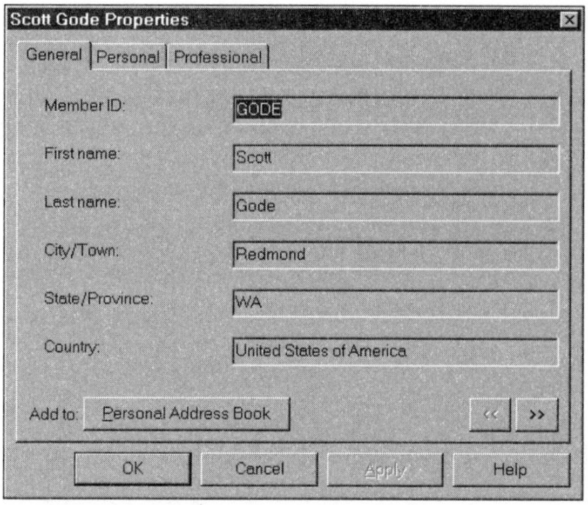

Scott Gode Properties

General | Personal | Professional |

Member ID: GODE

First name: Scott

Last name: Gode

City/Town: Redmond

State/Province: WA

Country: United States of America

Add to: Personal Address Book   << >>

OK   Cancel   Apply   Help

Figure 12-6:
The
Properties
dialog box.

Other Options

Though Microsoft has made joining MSN as easy as shooting fish in a barrel, you do have other choices.

Here are some practical considerations that may cause you to choose a different Internet service provider:

✔ **Is there an access phone number near you?**

If you rack up long-distance phone charges every time you surf the Web, you'll get unhappy fast. MSN doesn't have as many places you can call to access its network as services like CompuServe or some other providers. You may want to check to see which providers can offer you access through a telephone number in your area.

✔ **Do you use the Internet less than five hours per month?**

If you only use the Internet a little bit, the unlimited time deals that MSN and other ISPs offer become less competitive. AT&T has been offering free Internet access to its long-distance telephone customers for up to five hours per month. Free is the best deal you can get, unless you use the Internet a lot more than five hours per month. Because you can manage all your e-mail offline with Outlook, you only incur line charges for the time you send and receive e-mail. If e-mail is the only thing for which you use the Internet, it's possible to stay below five hours per month. If you like to surf the Web, however, you'll use up five hours fast.

✔ **Have prices or conditions changed?**

Prices and conditions for getting access to the Internet change frequently. By the time you read this, some new provider may have popped up or AOL will finally have jumped on the bandwagon and started supporting Outlook.

I'm giving you the most current information available as I write this, but you really need to double-check to be sure that the deals I describe are still available when you're looking for an Internet service provider. New deals may be available as well. Internet access providers seem to change almost daily.

Using CompuServe as your online service

The second biggest online service is CompuServe, the granddaddy of online services. You actually can send and receive CompuServe e-mail with Outlook, although setting up Outlook to use CompuServe mail can be a bit involved. You'll have to check with CompuServe for instructions on setting up Outlook to send and receive your CompuServe mail.

To find out more about configuring Outlook for CompuServe mail, log on to CompuServe and type **GO CISSOFT**. You can't read or write messages to CompuServe forums with Outlook, and you can't retrieve files from CompuServe libraries. To do those things you still have to use CompuServe Information Manager or one of the other programs that are designed to work with CompuServe.

Other Internet service providers

There are literally thousands of Internet service providers throughout the United States that can connect you to the Internet and provide e-mail service. You need to check with the service provider you choose to help you configure Outlook to work with that provider's system to get your Internet e-mail.

Some of the top names include

AT&T WorldNet Service	`www.att.com/worldnet`	1-800-IMAGINE
Concentric Network	`www.concentric.net`	1-800-745-2747
Earthlink Network	`www.earthlink.net`	1-800-395-8410

The Internet, the intranets, what's the difference?

As if all the hoopla about the Internet weren't enough, now the word *intranet* is being bandied about. What's the difference between *the Internet* and *an intranet*? An intranet is the name for an installation of Internet-style Web pages and browsers set up on a company's computer network that's intended for use by the company itself (including the employees and/or customers and suppliers of the company). To people who work at the company, it's like having their own private Internet. Not all intranets are restricted from public view, but they can be if the company that created that particular intranet wants it that way. Using an intranet is exactly like using the Internet. Outlook functions the same way whether you use the Internet or an intranet.

GTE Internet Solutions	`www.gte.net`	1-800-927-3000
IBM Internet Connection Service	`www.ibm.net`	1-800-821-4612
IDT Internet Services	`www.idt.net`	1-201-883-2000
MCI Internet	`www.mci2000.com`	1-800-550-0930
MindSpring	`www.mindspring.com`	1-800-719-4660
Netcom	`www.netcom.com`	1-408-983-5970
SpryNet	`www.sprynet.com`	1-206-957-8998
Whole Earth Networks	`www.wenet.com`	1-415-281-6500

If you're an AOL user, you can't use Outlook to send and receive your AOL e-mail; you'll have to stick with using the mailbox that's part of your AOL software. It's too bad, because Outlook puts the AOL mailbox to shame, but AOL doesn't seem interested in letting you use programs like Outlook to read your AOL mail. I can only guess why this is, but I think it's because Outlook would let you pass up all that flashy advertising that you see when you log on to AOL. Perhaps AOL will change their mind about supporting Outlook in the future, but I don't think that will happen any time soon.

Part III
Taking Care
of Business

The 5th Wave   By Rich Tennant

"BETTER CALL MIS AND TELL THEM ONE OF OUR NETWORKS HAS GONE BAD."

In this part . . .

You know whom to contact and where they are, and you can send them a message almost at warp speed. But what's all the messaging about? Business. Those things that keep you employed and the economy booming. Meetings and deadlines, schedule conflicts, and too many tasks — all crying out for your expert attention. In this part, you see how Outlook makes it easy to keep your business in line.

Chapter 13

Days and Dates: Keeping Your Calendar

All those precious minutes, and where do they go? Outlook makes your computer the perfect place to solve the problem of too little time in the day. Although Outlook can't give you any extra hours, you can use it to get a better grip on the hours you've got, and it can free those precious minutes that can add up to more hours spent in productive work. If only it could solve the problem of having to do productive work in order to earn a living.

I assume you've started up Outlook, although you can easily keep it running all the time. Because you can do nearly everything in Outlook that you can do in Windows, in some ways you're better off using Outlook than using the Windows Desktop. And Outlook is a whole lot easier to use than the Windows Explorer.

No doubt you've been looking at calendars your whole life, so the Outlook Calendar will be pretty simple for you to understand because it looks like a calendar: plain old rows of dates, Monday through Friday plus weekends and so on. You won't have to learn to think like a computer to understand your schedule.

If you want to see more information about something in your calendar, most of the time all you have to do is click the calendar with your mouse. If that doesn't give you enough information, click twice. If that doesn't give you everything you're looking for, read on; I fill you in on the fine points. I suspect that you'll find the Outlook Calendar so easy that you won't need much special training to find it useful.

The Date Navigator: Really Getting Around

The Date Navigator is actually the name of this feature, but don't confuse it with Warren Beatty's chauffeur. The Date Navigator is a trick you can use in Outlook to change the part of the Calendar you're seeing or the time period you want to look at (see Figure 13-1).

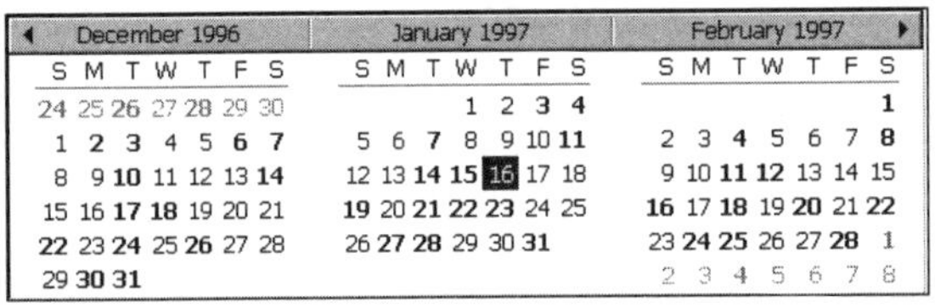

Figure 13-1:
The Outlook
Date
Navigator.

December 1996	January 1997	February 1997
S M T W T F S	S M T W T F S	S M T W T F S
24 25 26 27 28 29 30	1 2 3 4	1
1 2 3 4 5 6 7	5 6 7 8 9 10 11	2 3 4 5 6 7 8
8 9 10 11 12 13 14	12 13 14 15 16 17 18	9 10 11 12 13 14 15
15 16 17 18 19 20 21	19 20 21 22 23 24 25	16 17 18 19 20 21 22
22 23 24 25 26 27 28	26 27 28 29 30 31	23 24 25 26 27 28 1
29 30 31		2 3 4 5 6 7 8

Believe it or not, that unassuming little two- or three-month calendar scrap is probably the quickest way to change how you look at the Calendar and make your way around it. All you have to do is click on the date you want to see and it opens in all its glory; it couldn't be simpler.

To use the Date Navigator:

1. **Choose Go⇨Calendar.**

   The Calendar appears.

2. **Choose View⇨Current View⇨Day/Week/Month.**

   The Date Navigator appears as a small calendar in the upper-right corner.

   - To see details of a single date, click that day in the Date Navigator. You see the appointments and events scheduled for the day you clicked.

   - To see a full-month view, click one of the letters (SMTWTFS) at the top of the months.

   - To see a week's view, move the mouse pointer just to the left of the week you want to see. When the arrow points up and to the right rather than up and to the left, click it.

     As time goes by (so to speak), you'll find that you gravitate to the Calendar view that suits you best. I happen to like the Seven Day view because it includes both Calendar and Task information in a screen that's pretty easy to read. You can leave Outlook running most of the time in order to keep the information you need handy.

Time travel isn't just science fiction. You can zip around the Outlook calendar faster than you can say Buck Rogers. Talk about futuristic, the Outlook calendar can schedule appointments for you well into the year 4500! Think about it:

Between now and then there are more than 130,000 Saturday nights! That's the good news. There are also more than 130,000 Monday mornings. Of course, in our lifetimes, you and I only have to deal with about 5,000 Saturday nights at most, so we have to make good use of them. Better start planning.

So when you need to find a free date fast:

1. **Choose G̲o⇨Go To Date (or press Ctrl+G).**

   A dialog box appears with today's date highlighted.

2. **To go to another date, type the date you want as you normally would, such as** January 15, 1998, **or** 1/15/98.

   A really neat way to change dates is to type in something like **45 days ago** or **93 days from now** (see Figure 13-2). Try it. Outlook understands simple English when it comes to dates. Don't get fancy, though; Outlook doesn't understand **Four score and seven years ago**. Who does?

Figure 13-2:
The Go To
Date dialog
box with a
tall order.

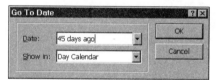

If you want to go to today's date, Choose G̲o⇨Go To Tod̲ay. No matter what date you land on, you can plunge right in and start scheduling. You can double-click on the time and date when you want an appointment to occur and enter the particulars, or you can double check details of an appointment on that date by double-clicking the date and making changes to the appointment if necessary. You can also do something silly like finding out what day of the week your birthday falls on 1,000 years from now. Mine's on Saturday. Don't forget.

Meetings Galore: Scheduling Appointments

Many people live and die by their datebooks. The paper type of datebook is still popular, being the easiest to put stuff in (although once it's in, the stuff can be a pain to find). Outlook makes it easier to add appointments than do most computer calendars, and Outlook makes it a whole lot easier to find things once you've entered something. It also warns you when you've scheduled two dates at once. (Very embarrassing!)

To schedule an appointment:

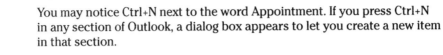

1. **Choose File⇨New from the menu bar. The New Item menu appears (see Figure 13-3).**

   You may notice Ctrl+N next to the word Appointment. If you press Ctrl+N in any section of Outlook, a dialog box appears to let you create a new item in that section.

   Press Ctrl+Shft+A from any section of Outlook to create an appointment. The catch is, you won't see the appointment on the calendar until you switch to the Calendar view.

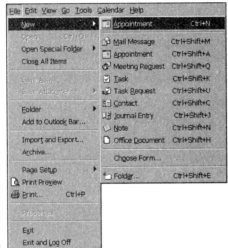

Figure 13-3:
Selecting
a new
appointment.

2. **Choose Appointment.**

   The Appointment form opens (see Figure 13-4).

3. **Click in the Subject box and type something there to help you remember what the appointment's about.**

   Type **Dentist appointment** or **Receive Oscar** or whatever. This text will show up on your calendar.

4. **Click in the Location box and type in the location.**

   Notice the little triangle (scroll bar button) at the right side of the box. If you click on the triangle, you see a list of the last few locations where you scheduled appointments so that you can use the same places over and over without having to retype them. Another advantage to having this recallable list of locations is that it makes it easy to enter locations. That way you can sort your list of appointments according to location to see, for example, if conference rooms are free.

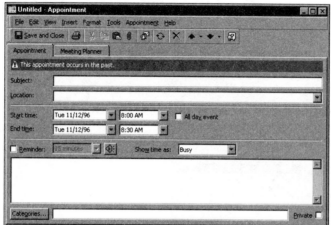

Figure 13-4:
The
Appointment
form.

5. **If you want Outlook to remind you of your appointment, click the Reminder box.**

   Choose how far in advance you want Outlook to notify you of an upcoming appointment. You can set the amount yourself by typing it in, or you can click the scroll-down button and choose a predetermined length from the Reminder box.

   - If you want a sound to play as a reminder, click the sound icon next to the Reminder box to see the Reminder Sound dialog box (see Figure 13-5). (If you don't have a sound card, you won't be able to hear a sound.)

Figure 13-5:
Pick a
sound.

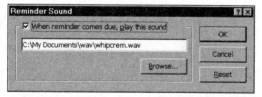

   - If the appointment is tentative, click the scroll-down button to the right of the Show Time As menu and choose Tentative.

   - You can also mark the appointment as Free, Busy, or Out of Office. (Out of Mind is not an option yet.)

   If you're using Outlook on an office network, other people may be able to see your schedule in order to plan meetings with you. Designations like Free, Busy, or Out of Office let co-workers who can view your schedule know whether you're available for a meeting.

• If you need to remember more information about this appointment, type the information in the text box at the bottom of the dialog box. Directions to a new client's office, books for school, the Declaration of Independence, whatever turns you on.

6. Click the Categories button at the bottom left to assign a category to the appointment if you like.

Using the Categories box (see Figure 13-6) is another trick for finding things easily.

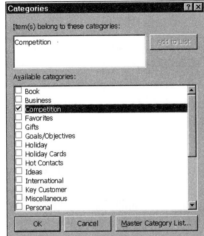

Figure 13-6:
The
Categories
box.

7. Choose an existing category, if one suits you, and then click OK.

8. If none of the existing categories suits you, click the Master Category List button at the bottom right.

The Master Category List box appears (see Figure 13-7).

9. Type a category of your choice in the New category box.

Be sure not to add too many new categories, as you could have a hard time finding things.

10. Click Add and click OK.

You're now back in the Categories box, with the new category added to the list.

11. Choose the new category from the Available Categories list.

You can choose more than one category at a time.

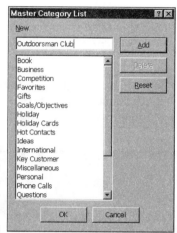

Figure 13-7:
The Master
Category
List.

12. **Click the Private box in the lower-right corner of the New Appointment form if you're on a network and you don't want others to know about your appointments.**

13. **Click Save and then Close.**

The appointment you created appears in the Active Appointments view (see Figure 13-8).

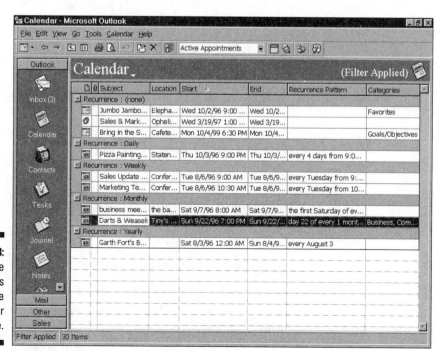

Figure 13-8:
The Active
Appointments
view of the
Calendar
module.

You may have to change your view of the Calendar by clicking the Date Navigator on the date the appointment occurs so that you can see your new appointment.

If you're using reminders for all your important appointments, you must have Outlook running so that the reminder pops up. You can minimize Outlook or keep it running in the background. When the reminder time arrives, you either see a dialog box or a message from the Office Assistant like the one in Figure 13-9.

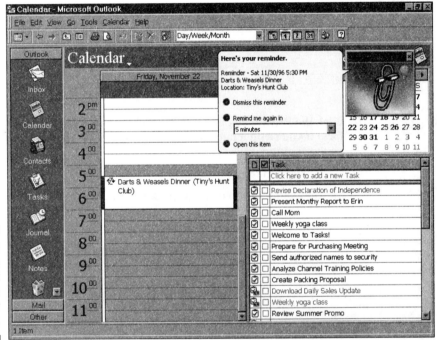

Figure 13-9: The Office Assistant reminds you of your appointment.

Not this time: Changing dates

You can be as fickle as you want with Outlook. In fact, to change the time of a scheduled item, all you do is drag the appointment from where it is to where you want it to be (see Figure 13-10). Or back again . . . Maybe . . . If you feel like it. . . .

To change an appointment:

1. **Click the appointment in the Calendar view.**

   A blue bar appears at the left edge of the appointment.

2. **Place the mouse pointer over the blue bar; the mouse pointer turns into a little four-headed arrow.**

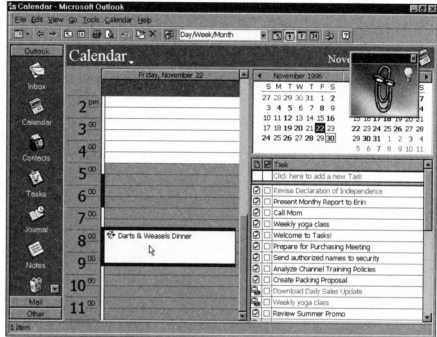

Figure 13-10:
If your
appointment
is a drag,
drop it in a
new spot.

3. **Drag the appointment to the time or date where you want it to be.**

   If you're in the One-Day view, drag an appointment to a different date on one of the small calendars in the upper right.

   If you want to create a copy of an appointment for another time, hold down the Ctrl key while you use the mouse to drag the appointment to another time or date. For example, if you're scheduling a Summer Intern Orientation from 9 to 11 a.m. and 1 to 3 p.m., you can create the 9 a.m. appointment and then copy it to 1 p.m. by holding Ctrl and dragging the appointment. Then you have two appointments with the same subject, location, and date, but different hours.

   If you copy an appointment to a different date by dragging the appointment to a date on the Date Navigator, you retain the hour of the appointment but change the date.

If you want to change an appointment to a date you can't see on the Calendar:

1. **Double-click the appointment.**

   The Appointment dialog box opens.

2. **Click in the Start time block and then click the scroll-down button at the right edge of the Start time block to pull down a calendar (see Figure 13-11).**

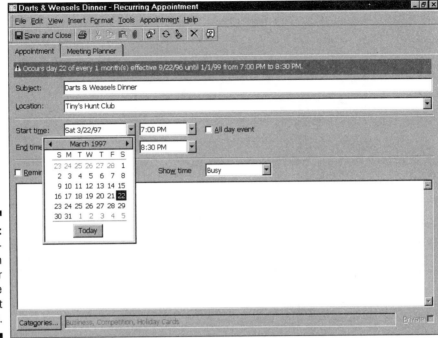

Figure 13-11:
The pull-
down
Calendar
in the
Appointment
form.

3. **Pick the month by clicking on one of the triangles beside the month's name.**

   Clicking the left triangle moves you one month earlier; clicking the right triangle moves you one month later.

4. **Click the day of the month you want.**

5. **Click in the Start Time text box and type in the appointment's new time, if needed.**

6. **Make any other changes you need in the appointment by clicking on the information you want to change and typing the revised information over it.**

7. **Click Save and Close.**

To change the length of an appointment:

1. **Click the appointment.**

2. **Move the mouse pointer over the lines at the top or bottom of the appointment.**

   When it's in the right place, the mouse pointer turns into a two-headed arrow that you can use to drag the lines of the appointment box.

3. **Drag the bottom line down to make the appointment time longer; drag the bottom line up to make the appointment shorter.**

You can only change an appointment's length by dragging in multiples of 30 minutes (see Figure 13-12).

To shorten an appointment to less than 30 minutes:

1. **Double-click the appointment and click the End Time box.**

2. **Type the ending time.**

3. **Click Save and Close.**

You can enter times in Outlook without adding colons and often without using AM or PM. Outlook translates **443** as 4:43 PM. If you plan lots of appointments at 4:43 AM, just type **443A**. Just don't call me at that hour, okay?

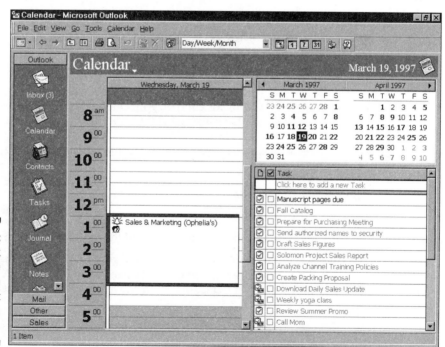

Figure 13-12: The thick dark line shows an appointment being lengthened.

Not ever: Breaking dates

Well, sometimes things just don't work out. Sorry about that. Even if it's hard for you to forget, with the click of a mouse Outlook deletes dates you'd otherwise fondly remember. Okay, two clicks of a mouse. *C'est la Vie, C'est L'Amour, C'est la Guerre.* (Look for my next book, *Tawdry French Cliches*).

To delete an appointment (after you've called to break it, of course):

1. **Right-click the appointment (that is, click with the right mouse button).**

2. **Click _D_elete.**

   Your appointment has been cancelled.

The Ctrl+D combination you see next to the _D_elete command means you can delete the appointment in just one keystroke. How cold.

We've got to keep seeing each other: Recurring dates

Some appointments are like a meal at a Chinese restaurant; as soon as you're done with one, you're ready for another. With Outlook, you can easily create an appointment that comes back like last night's spicy Szechwan noodles.

To create a recurring appointment (that is, an appointment that's regularly scheduled):

1. **Choose _G_o➪Calendar.**

   The Calendar appears.

2. **Click the New tool icon at the left end of the toolbar (see Figure 13-13).**

   The Appointment form appears (refer to Figure 13-4). Yeah, I know. I do it differently earlier in the chapter when I tell you how to create an appointment the first time. This way is the *really* easy way to create a new appointment.

3. **Click the Subject box and type in the subject.**

4. **Click the Location box and type in the location.**

5. **If you want Outlook to remind you, click the Reminder box.**

   • Choose how far in advance you want Outlook to remind you.

   • If you want a sound to play as a reminder, click the sound icon.

6. **Click Appointment Recurrence on the menu bar.**

   The Appointme_n_t menu drops down (see Figure 13-14).

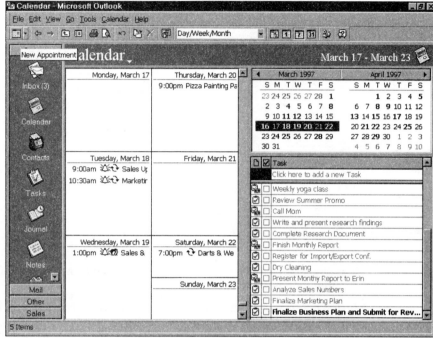

Figure 13-13:
Clicking the
New tool —
the easiest
way to
create
a new
appointment.

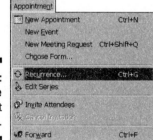

Figure 13-14:
The
Appointment
menu.

7. Select Recurrence.

The letters Ctrl+G next to the Recurrence command mean that you can also create the recurring appointment with just that one keystroke.

The Recurrence dialog box appears (see Figure 13-15).

8. Click the End text box and enter the ending time.

9. In the Recurrence Pattern box, choose the Daily, Weekly, Monthly, or Yearly option button to select how often the appointment recurs.

10. **In the next part of the Recurrence Pattern box, choose how often the appointment occurs.**

11. **In the Range of Recurrence box, enter the first occurrence in the Start box.**

12. **Choose when the appointments will stop.**

    You can select No End Date, End After a certain number of occurrences, or End By a certain date.

13. **Click OK.**

14. **Click Save and Close.**

Even a recurring appointment gets changed once in awhile. To edit a recurring appointment:

1. **Double-click on the appointment you want to edit.**

    The Recurring Appointment dialog box appears (see Figure 13-16).

2. **Choose whether you want to change just the occurrence you clicked or the whole series.**

3. **Edit the details of the appointment.**

    To change the recurrence pattern, click Appointment⇨Recurrence. Then change the recurrence pattern and click OK.

4. **Click Save and Close.**

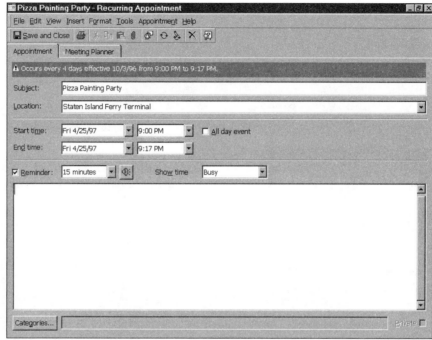

Figure 13-16:
The
Recurring
Appointment
dialog box.

I find it helpful to enter regular appointments, such as classes or regular recreational events, even if I'm sure I won't forget them. Entering all my activities into Outlook prevents me from scheduling conflicting appointments.

Getting a Good View of Your Calendar

Outlook lets you slice and dice the information in every section nearly any way you can imagine, using different views. You could easily fill a cookbook with different views you can create, but I'm going to stick to the standard ways of looking at a calendar that most people are used to. If you want to cook up a calendar arrangement that nobody's ever thought of before, Outlook will probably let you, but you have to live with it. That's okay; if you accidentally create a Calendar view you don't like, you can delete it.

The basic Calendar views are the Daily view, shown in Figure 13-17, the Weekly view, shown in Figure 13-18, and the Monthly view, seen in Figure 13-19.

Other views of the Calendar, such as the Active Appointments view, are big helps when you're trying to figure out when you did something, or when you will do something.

Figure 13-17:
The Daily
view.

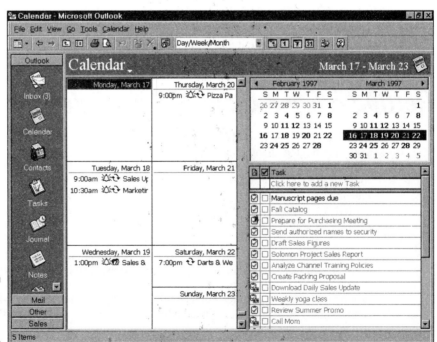

Figure 13-18:
The Weekly
view.

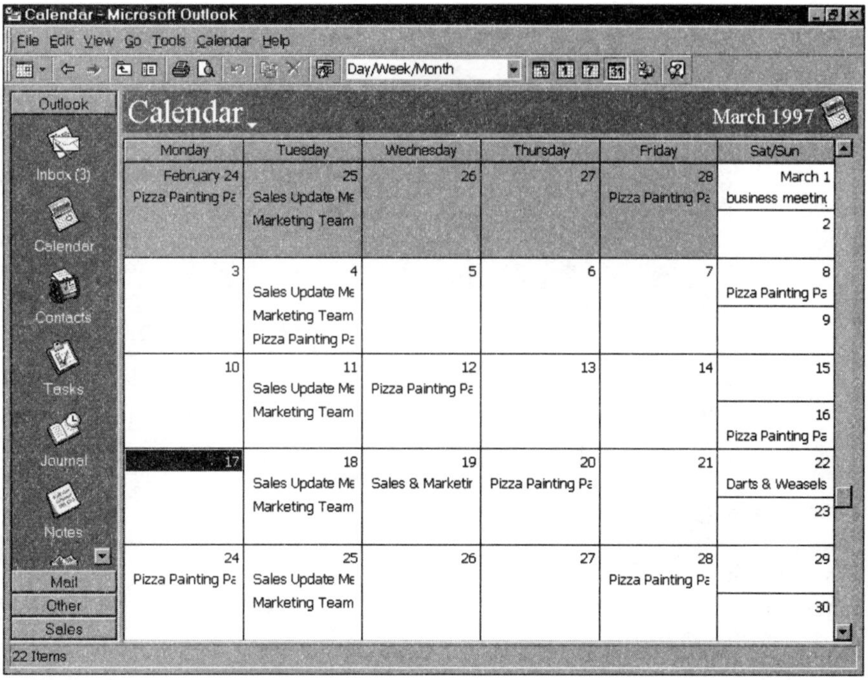

Figure 13-19:
The Monthly
view.

To view Active Appointments:

1. **Choose View⇨Current View.**

   The view menu appears.

2. **Choose Active Appointments.**

   You see a list of appointments yet to come.

In Active Appointments view (see Figure 13-20), you can see details of appointments that you have coming up in a list that's easy to read. You can also sort the view on any column, such as Location, Subject, or Start date by clicking the column's title.

The Active Appointments view is only one of a half-dozen preprogrammed views that come with Outlook. Pull down the menu and try each of the other choices: You've seen the Daily/Weekly/Monthly view, which lets you look at your schedule in the familiar calendar layout; Events view shows you items that last more than a day; Annual Events, shows the list of items that last more than a day and return at the same time each year; Recurring is the view of appointments that you've set up to repeat themselves; and By Category view groups your appointments according to the category you've assigned them.

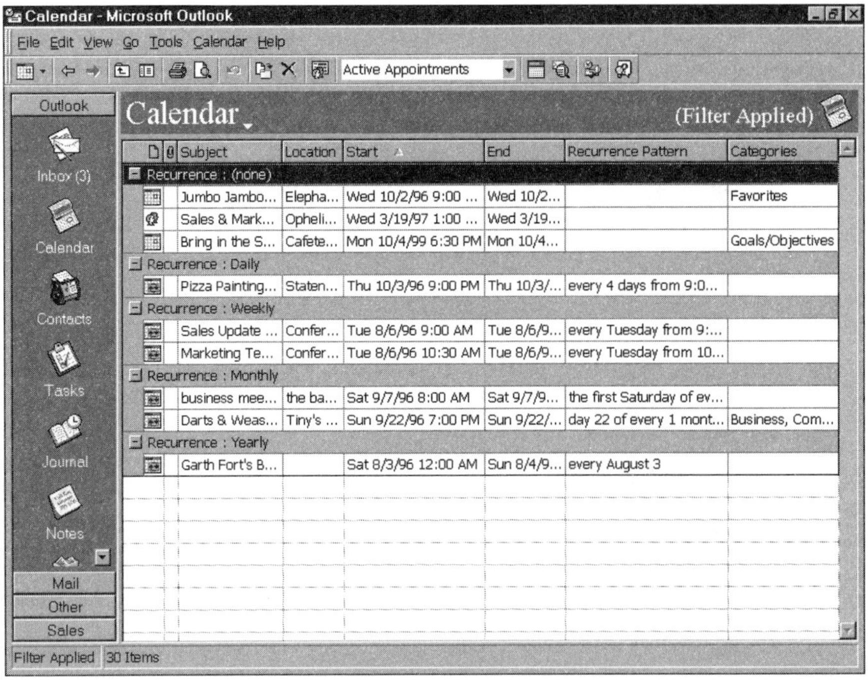

Figure 13-20:
The Active
Appointments
view.

Printing Your Appointments

On plain old paper is still everybody's favorite way to read things. No matter how slick your computer organizer is, you may still need old-fashioned ink-on-paper to make it really useful. You use the same basic steps to print from any module in Outlook. Here's how to print your appointments:

1. **Click on a date within the range of dates you want to print.**

   If you want to print a single day, click just one day (see Figure 13-21). If you want to print a range of dates, click the first date, and then hold the Shift key and click the last date in the range. The whole range is then highlighted to show which dates you've selected.

2. **Choose File⇨Print (or press Ctrl+P).**

   The Print dialog box appears (see Figure 13-22).

3. **In the Print Style group, choose Daily, Weekly, Monthly, Trifold, Memo, or any other style you want that may be available in your Style box.**

   You can define your own print styles in Outlook so you may eventually have quite a collection of choices here.

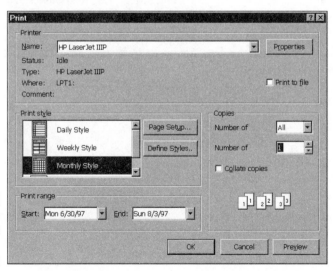

Figure 13-21:
Click a
single day
and press
Ctrl+P
to print
that day's
appointments.

Figure 13-22:
The Print
dialog box.

4. In the Print Range box, set the range of dates you want to print.

Because you began by clicking on a date in that range, it should already be correct. If it's not correct, you can change the range in the Print dialog box to the print range you want.

5. Click OK.

Your dates are sent to the printer.

Clicking the Print icon on the toolbar is another handy way to start the print process. The icon looks like a tiny printer.

Scheduling your main events

You can enter more than just appointments in your calendar. You can also add events by clicking the All day event check box in the Appointment form, or you can begin by choosing Calendar⇨New Event and follow the same steps you use to create an appointment (refer to "Meetings Galore: Scheduling Appointments" earlier in this chapter).

Events allow you to add things to your calendar like business trips or conferences that last longer than an appointment while still letting you quickly enter routine appointments that may take place at the event. For example, you can create an event called "1998 Auto Show" and then add appointments to see General Motors at 9 a.m., Chrysler at noon, and Ford at 3 p.m.

Chapter 14

A Sticky Subject: Using Notes

● ●

In This Chapter

▶ Writing a note

▶ Finding a note

▶ Reading a note

▶ Deleting a note

▶ Changing the size of a note

▶ Changing your colors

▶ Viewing your notes

▶ Assigning a category to your notes

▶ Printing notes

▶ Changing your options for new notes

▶ Forwarding a note

● ●

*T*he simple, dopey features of a program are often my favorites — the features that I end up using all the time, like Outlook Notes. There's really nothing earth-shattering about Notes and certainly nothing difficult. This feature is just there when you need it, ready to allow you to type whatever strange, random thoughts are passing through your head while you're doing your work. (As you can see from my writing, strange, random thoughts are a common occurrence for me. That's why I love using Notes.)

A note is the only type of item you can create in Outlook that doesn't use a normal dialog box with menus and toolbars. Notes are easier to use but somewhat trickier to explain than other Outlook items, because I can only describe the objects you're supposed to click and drag. No name appears on the Note icon and no name for the part of the note that you drag when you want to resize the note (see Figure 14-1).

Note

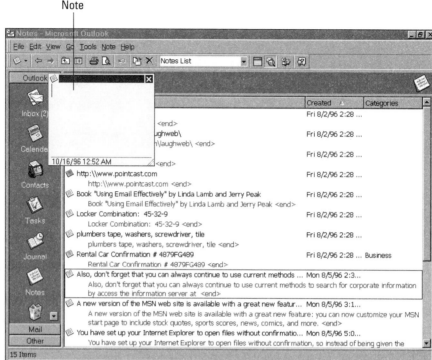

Figure 14-1:
Your note
begins as a
nearly
blank box.

Writing a Note

How did we ever live without those little yellow sticky notes? They're everywhere! The funny thing about sticky notes is that they came from an inventor's
failure. A scientist was trying to invent a new formula for glue, and he came up
with a kind of glue that didn't stick very well. Like the computer scientists who
came later, he said, "That's not a bug, that's a feature!" Then he figured out how
to make a fortune selling little notes that didn't stick too well. It's only natural
that an invention like this would be adapted for computers. Here's how to take
notes while doing your work:

1. **Choose Go⇨Notes (or click the Notes icon in the Outlook Bar).**

   The Notes list appears.

   You don't actually have to go to the Notes module to create a new note;
   you can go right to Step 2. I suggest going to the Notes module first only so
   that you can see your note appear in the list of notes when you finish.
   Otherwise, your note seems to disappear into thin air, but it doesn't;
   Outlook automatically files your note in the Notes module unless you make
   a special effort to send it someplace else.

Tricks with Notes

Each time you start a program, the Windows 95 taskbar at the bottom of the screen adds an icon. That way, you know how many programs you are running. If you click an icon for a program in the taskbar, you switch to that program. If you start Word and Excel, for example, you see two icons in the taskbar. You can have two or more documents open in Word or Excel, but you see only one icon for each program.

When you choose File⇨New to create a new item in Outlook, you see a second icon open in the taskbar for the item you're creating. The icon

remains until you close and save the item. It's like having two or more programs open in Windows 95 at the same time. The advantage of this arrangement is that you can leave something like a note open for a long time and keep switching to it to add comments. The disadvantage is that if you don't look at the taskbar to see how many notes you have open, you may be creating a clutter of notes when you might prefer just one.

Another advantage is that you can have two notes open at the same time, or a note and an e-mail message, and drag text from one to the other.

2. **Choose File⇨New⇨Note (or press Ctrl+N).**

   The blank Note box appears.

3. **Type what you want to say in your note (see Figure 14-2) and click the Note icon in the upper-left corner of the note.**

4. **Click Close (or press Alt+F4).**

   An even quicker way to create a note is to press Ctrl+Shift+N in any Outlook module (except Notes). You won't see your note listed with all the other notes until you switch to the Notes module, but you'll get that thought entered.

Figure 14-2:
You can write a note to remind yourself of something.

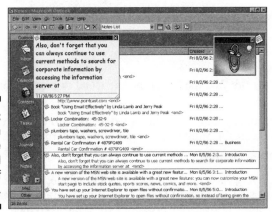

Finding a Note

Unlike paper sticky notes, Outlook Notes always allow you to find the things you write — or at least your computer can find them. As a matter of fact, you can find any item you create in Outlook just by using the Find tool. (I wish I had a Find tool to help me round up all my lost galoshes and umbrellas.)

Here's how to find a misplaced note:

1. **Choose Go⊅Notes (or click the Notes icon in the Outlook Bar).**

   Your list of notes appears.

2. **Choose Tools⊅Find Items (or press Ctrl+Shift+F).**

   The Find dialog box appears (see Figure 14-3). The Look For box should contain the word Notes, which means that Outlook will search only for notes — not tasks, not messages, just notes. You can click the Look For box and choose another type of item to search for, if you like.

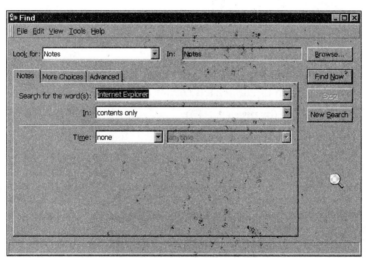

Figure 14-3:
The Find
dialog box.

3. **In the Search for the Word(s) box, type the word or phrase you're looking for.**

   Don't worry about capitalization. Outlook doesn't worry about capitalization unless you click the More Choices tab and check the Match Case box.

4. **Click the Find Now button.**

   The little magnifying glass on the right side of the dialog box circles around for a few seconds; then a list of notes that contain the text you typed appears at the bottom of the dialog box. If the search takes a long time, the list may say There are no items to show in this view. Don't give up. As long as the little magnifying glass is still circling, Outlook is still looking. I think that the list should say Still looking — nothing yet until the search is finished.

5. **If the note you're looking for turns up at the bottom of the dialog box, double-click the Note icon to read what the note says.**

6. **Close the Find dialog box by clicking the Close button in the upper-right corner. The note stays on the screen so you can read it or change it.**

Reading a Note

When you write a note, no doubt you plan to read it sometime. Reading notes is even easier than writing them. To read a note:

1. **Choose Go⇨Notes (or click the Notes icon in the Outlook Bar).**

   Your list of notes appears.

2. **Double-click the title of the note that you want to open.**

   The note appears on your screen (see Figure 14-4). You can close the note when you're done by pressing Esc.

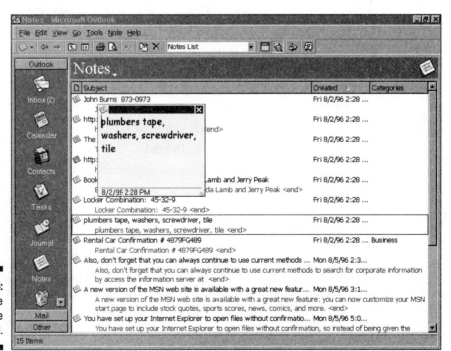

Figure 14-4:
Aha! The missing note is found.

Taking your pick: multiple selections

When you're sorting your notes or assigning them to categories, one way to work a little faster is to select several notes at the same time. If you want to select a group of notes that you can see one right after another in a list, click the first one and then hold down the Shift key while clicking the last one. That action selects both of the notes that you clicked and all the notes in between.

If you're selecting several items that aren't arranged next to one another, hold down the Ctrl key while clicking each item. The notes that you select are highlighted, and the others stay plain. Then you can open, move, delete, or categorize the entire group of notes that you've selected in a single stroke. To view several notes, right-click any notes you've selected and choose Open.

Funny how notes look the same when you're reading them as they do when you're writing them.

Deleting a Note

Notes don't have to be forever. You can write a note this morning and throw it out this afternoon. What could be easier?

Here's how to delete a note:

1. **Choose Go⇨Notes (or click the Notes icon in the Outlook Bar).**

   Your list of notes appears.

2. **Click the title of the note that you want to delete.**

3. **Choose Edit⇨Delete (or press Delete).**

   You can also click the Delete button in the Outlook toolbar.

Changing the Size of a Note

You may be an old hand at moving and resizing boxes in Windows. Notes follow all the rules that other Windows boxes follow, so you'll be okay. If you're new to Windows and dialog boxes, don't worry — Notes are as easy to resize as they are to write and read.

To change the size of a note:

1. **Choose Go⇨Notes (or click the Notes icon in the Outlook Bar).**

   Your list of notes appears.

2. **Double-click the title of the note that you want to open.**

   The note pops up.

3. **Move your mouse pointer to the bottom-left corner of the note until the mouse pointer changes into a two-headed arrow pointed on a diagonal.**

   Use this arrow to drag the edges of the note to resize it. Don't be alarmed. Dragging boxes around is much easier to do than to read about. After you drag one box, you'll have no trouble dragging another.

4. **Drag with your mouse until the note is the size you want it to be.**

   As you drag the mouse pointer around, a gray box appears, showing you what size the note will be when you release the mouse button (see Figure 14-5). Don't worry if the size doesn't come out right the first time; you can change the note size again by dragging the mouse again.

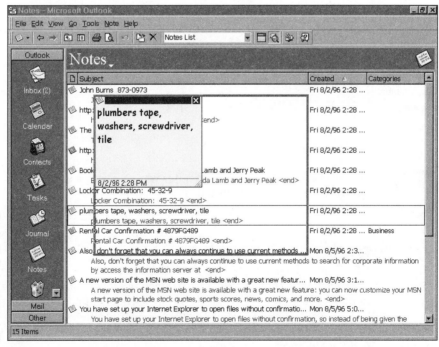

Figure 14-5: A gray box appears around your note when you're resizing it.

Changing Your Colors

Color may seem to be a trifling issue, but it can help you keep track of your notes. You can assign a color to a level of importance, for example, or to a specific task, so you can quickly see the note you want among the many notes in your list. Later in the chapter, you see how you can sort your list of notes according to their color. Sorting is useful, so spending your entire day changing the colors of your notes isn't just aesthetic but also productive.

Here's how to change your note's color:

1. **Open the note and click the Note icon in the top-left corner of the note.**

   I wish there were a better way to describe this icon than "the little thingy up on the left," but that's what it is. The icon is easy to see; it's the only little thingy in the top-left corner of your note.

2. **Choose Color.**

   A menu of colors appears (see Figure 14-6). Currently, the only choices are Blue, Green, Pink, Yellow, and White. I hope you like pastels, because those are your only options at the moment. Perhaps Burgundy and Off-Mauve notes will be in next season for more color-conscious computer users.

Figure 14-6:
The Color
menu.

3. **Pick a color.**

You can also change the colors of notes when viewing a list of notes, just right-click the icon for a note and choose a color.

Viewing Your Notes

Notes are handy enough to be able to stash tidbits of information any way you want, but what makes Notes really useful is what happens when you need to get the stuff back. You can open your notes one by one and see what's in them, but it's even handier for using your notes to arrange, sort, and view your notes in a way that makes sense for you.

Icons view

Some folks like Icons view — just a bunch of notes scattered all over, just as they are on my desk. Because I can already see a mess of notes any time I look at my desk, I prefer organized lists for viewing my notes, but you might like the more free-form Icons view.

To use Icons view:

1. **Choose Go➪Notes (or click the Notes icon in the Outlook Bar).**

   The Notes list appears.

2. **Choose View➪Current View.**

   The Current View menu appears. You can also use the Current View menu in the toolbar.

3. **Choose Icons.**

   The screen fills with a bunch of icons and incredibly long titles for each icon (see Figure 14-7).

Outlook uses the entire text of your message as the title of the icon, so the screen gets cluttered fast. If you prefer creative clutter, this view is for you. If not, keep reading.

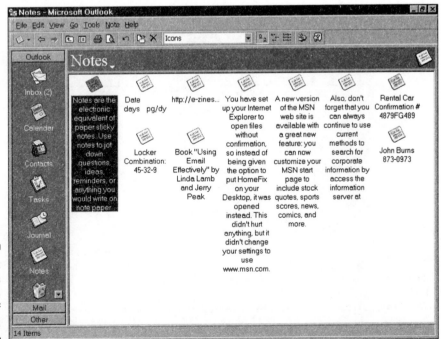

Figure 14-7: The Icons view — a clutter of notes.

Notes List view

The Notes list is as basic as basic gets. Just the facts, ma'am. The Notes list shows the subject and creation date of each note, as well as the first few lines of text.

To use Notes List view:

1. **Choose <u>Go</u>⇨<u>N</u>otes (or click the Notes icon in the Outlook Bar).**

   The Notes list appears.

2. **Choose <u>V</u>iew⇨Current <u>V</u>iew.**

   The Current View menu appears. The Current View menu in the toolbar does the trick, too.

3. **Choose Notes List.**

   A listing of your notes appears (see Figure 14-8).

I usually recommend Notes List view for opening, forwarding, reading, and otherwise dealing with notes because it's the most straightforward. Anything you can do to a note in Notes List view, you can do in the other Notes views as well. The difference is that the other views don't always let you see the note that you want to do things to.

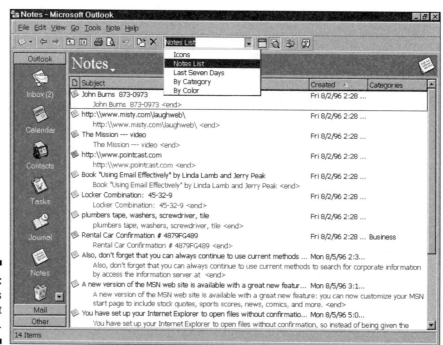

Figure 14-8:
Your notes
in Notes List
view.

Last Seven Days view

The notes that you wrote within the last few days are most likely to be the notes that you'll need. That's why Outlook includes a special view of the notes that you've created in the last seven days; you're more likely to quickly find what you're looking for in the seven-day view.

To see your notes for the last seven days:

1. **Choose Go⇨Notes (or click the Notes icon in the Outlook Bar).**

   The Notes list appears.

2. **Choose View⇨Current View.**

   The Current View menu appears.

3. **Choose Last Seven Days.**

   You see seven days' worth of notes (see Figure 14-9).

If you haven't created any notes in the past seven days, Last Seven Days view will be empty. If having an empty view bothers you, create a note; that'll tide you over for a week.

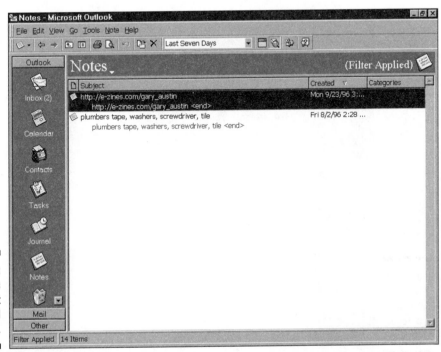

Figure 14-9:
Your notes
for the past
week, in all
their glory.

By Category view

Every item that you create in Outlook can be assigned to a category. You use the same category list for all items, and you can create your own categories. With categories, you have another useful way to organize your views of Outlook items.

To see your notes arranged By Category:

1. **Choose Go⇨Notes (or click the Notes icon in the Outlook Bar).**

   The Notes list appears.

2. **Choose View⇨Current View.**

   The Current View menu appears.

3. **Choose By Category.**

   Your notes are arranged by category (see Figure 14-10).

By Category view is a grouped view, meaning that the notes are collected in bunches, according to the category that you've assigned. You can just look at the category of notes that you're interested in to organize the information that you've collected.

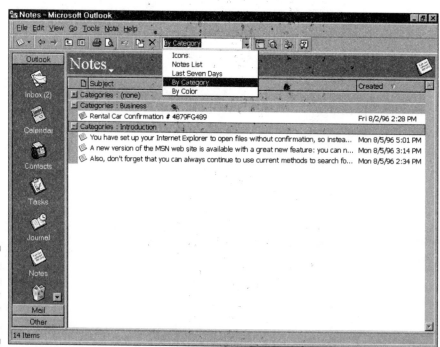

Figure 14-10:
Your notes
in By
Category
view.

By Color

Color coordination means more than making sure your socks match. The fact that you can group notes by color means that you can create a system of organizing your notes that tells you something important about your notes at a glance. If sales representatives call, asking you to buy merchandise, you may want to create and color code a note for each request: green for requests that you're approving, yellow for requests that you're considering, and pink for requests that you're turning down.

To view your notes By Color:

1. **Choose Go⇨Notes (or click the Notes icon in the Outlook Bar).**

   The Notes list appears.

2. **Choose View⇨Current View.**

   The Current View menu appears.

3. **Choose By Color.**

   You see a color-coded list of your notes (see Figure 14-11).

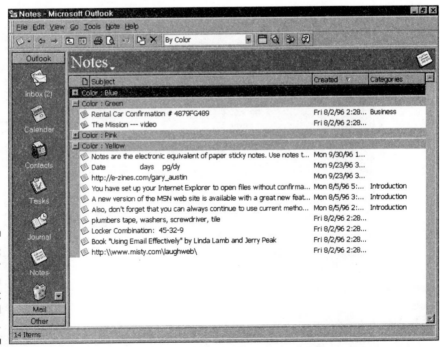

Figure 14-11: By Color view: not a rainbow, but colorful nonetheless.

You can choose among only five colors for an Outlook note, so you can have only that many groups by color.

You can also right-click a note in By Color view and change the color for sorting.

Assigning a Category to Your Notes

If you really want to get yourself organized, you can assign categories to all the items that you create in Outlook. That way, all your items can be sorted, grouped, searched, and even deleted according to the categories you've assigned them to.

To categorize your notes:

1. Click the Note icon in the upper-left corner of the Note.

The Note menu drops down (see Figure 14-12).

2. Choose Categories.

The Categories box appears (see Figure 14-13).

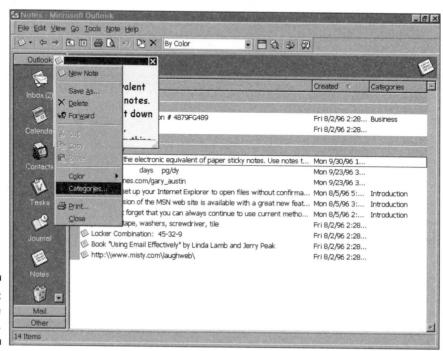

Figure 14-12:
The Note
menu.

3. **Choose one of the existing categories, if one suits you; then click OK.**

   You can also type in your own category in the Item(s) Belong to These Categories box.

4. **If none of the existing categories suits you, click Master Category List.**

   From the Master Category List, you can add or delete categories (see Figure 14-14).

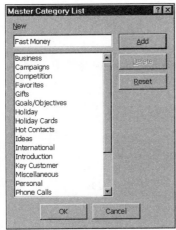

5. **Type a category of your choice in the <u>N</u>ew category box.**

Be sure not to add too many new categories or finding things could get hard.

6. **Click <u>A</u>dd.**

Your new category is part of the Categories list.

7. **Click OK.**

Whenever you see the Categories list, your new category will be among the categories that you can choose.

Printing Your Notes

You can organize and view your notes in so many clever ways that you'll also want to print what you can see, or at least the list of what you can see.

Printing a list of your notes

To print a list of your notes:

1. **Choose <u>G</u>o⇨<u>N</u>otes (or click the Notes icon in the Outlook Bar).**

The Notes list appears.

2. **Choose <u>F</u>ile⇨<u>P</u>rint (or press Ctrl+P).**

The Print dialog box appears (see Figure 14-15).

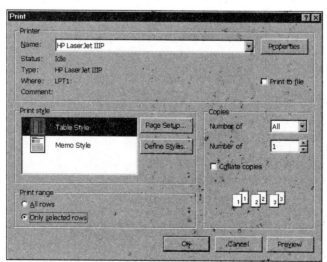

3. **In the Print Style box, choose Table Style.**

   If you choose Memo Style, you print the contents of a note rather than a list of notes.

4. **Click OK.**

If you want to print only a portion of your list of notes, click the first note that you want listed and then hold down the Shift key while clicking the last note that you want in your printout. When the Print dialog box appears, choose Only Selected Rows in the Print Range section.

Printing the contents of a note

Computer screens are pretty, but there's still nothing like ink on paper. Of course you can print a note. Remember, though, that the pretty colors you've given your notes don't show on a black-and-white printer.

To print the contents of a note:

1. **Choose Go➪Notes (or click the Notes icon in the Outlook Bar).**

   The Notes list appears.

2. **Click the title of the note that you want to print.**

3. **Choose File➪Print (or press Ctrl+P).**

   The Print dialog box appears.

4. **In the Print Style box, choose Memo Style (see Figure 14-16).**

   Choosing Memo Style prints the full contents of the note.

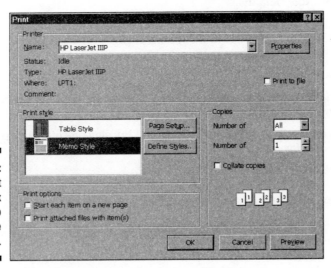

Figure 14-16:
The Print dialog box with Memo Style selected.

5. Click OK.

The full contents of your note are printed.

Changing Your Default Options for New Notes

Plain old notes are fine; you really don't need to change anything. But if you want to make some changes, the Options dialog box in the Tools menu gives you lots of . . . well . . . options. All the adjustments that you make in the Options box change the size, color, and other qualities of your note when you first create the note. You can also change these qualities after you create the note.

Changing size and color

To change the color and size of your notes:

1. **Choose Tools⇨Options.**

   The Options dialog box appears.

2. **Click the Tasks/Notes tab.**

   The Tasks/Notes page is where you change the options for the Tasks and Notes modules of Outlook.

3. **Click the triangle (scroll down button) at the right end of the Color box below Note Defaults.**

   A list of colors (Blue, Green, Pink, Yellow, White) drops down (see Figure 14-17). Choosing one of these options changes the color that all your notes will be when you create them.

4. **Choose a color.**

5. **Click the scroll down button (triangle) at the right end of the Size box below Note Defaults.**

   The list reads Small, Medium, or Large. Choosing one of these options sets the size of your notes when you create them.

6. **Click OK.**

Your notes are in the size and color to which you changed them.

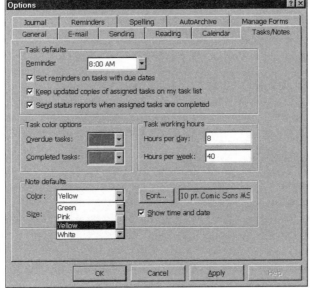

Figure 14-17:
Changing
colors in
the Note
defaults box
of the Tasks/
Notes page.

Turning the date and time display on or off

At the bottom of each note, Outlook displays the date and time when you most recently changed the contents of the note. You may start to notice that you change a lot of notes on Mondays around 9:45 a.m. You may not want to notice that fact, so you can turn this handy little feature off.

To turn off the date and time display:

1. **Choose Tools⟹Options.**

   The Options dialog box appears.

2. **Click the Tasks/Notes tab.**

   The Tasks/Notes page is where you change the options for the Tasks and Notes modules of Outlook (see Figure 14-18).

3. **Click the Show Time and Date check box.**

   Show Time and Date is the little box that looks like a voting block. You can vote for showing the time and date or vote against showing the time and date. The nice part is that what you vote for always wins.

4. **Click OK.**

The time and date will no longer show up on command, unless you follow the same steps you used in turning them off to turn the time and date on again.

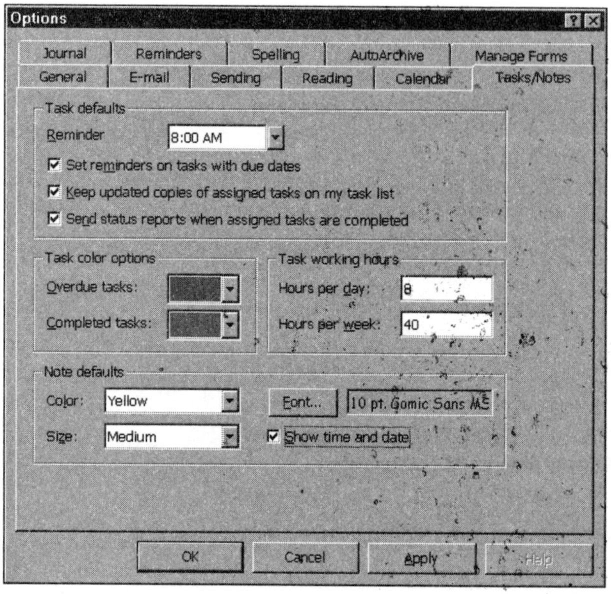

Options

Journal	Reminders	Spelling	AutoArchive	Manage Forms
General	E-mail	Sending	Reading	Calendar	Tasks/Notes

Task defaults

Reminder [8:00 AM ▾]

☑ Set reminders on tasks with due dates
☑ Keep updated copies of assigned tasks on my task list
☑ Send status reports when assigned tasks are completed

Task color options
Overdue tasks: [▾]
Completed tasks: [▾]

Task working hours
Hours per day: [8]
Hours per week: [40]

Note defaults
Color: [Yellow ▾]   Font... [10 pt. Comic Sans MS]
Size: [Medium ▾]   ☑ Show time and date

[OK] [Cancel] [Apply] [Help]

Figure 14-18:
The Tasks/
Notes page
on time.

Forwarding a Note

Forwarding a note really means sending an e-mail message with a note included
as an attachment. It's helpful if the person to whom you're forwarding the note
uses Outlook too.

To forward a note:

1. **Choose Go➪Notes (or click the Notes icon in the Outlook Bar).**

   The Notes list appears.

2. **Click the title of the note that you want to forward.**

3. **Choose Note➪Forward (or press Ctrl+F).**

   The New Message form appears (see Figure 14-19).

4. **Click the To text box and type the e-mail address of the person to whom
   you're sending your note.**

   You can also click the To button to open the e-mail Address Book. Look up
   the name of the person to whom you want to forward your note, click To,
   and then click OK.

5. **Click the Cc text box and type the e-mail addresses of the people to
   whom you want to send a copy of your note.**

   If you're sending your note to several people, separate their addresses
   with a comma or a semicolon.

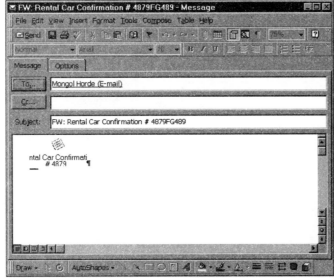

Figure 14-19:
The New
Message
form with
a note
attached.

6. **Type the subject of the note in the Subject box.**

   The subject of your note will already be in the Subject box of the New Message form. You can leave it alone or type something else.

7. **If you wish, type the text of a message in the text box.**

   You don't really have to include a message. Your note may say all that you want to say, but you can also add regular e-mail message text.

8. **Click the Send button (or press Alt+S).**

Your message is off to its intended recipient.

If your note includes the address of a page on the World Wide Web, such as http://www.dummies.com, you can't just click the address to launch your Web browser as you can in all the other Outlook modules. Notes is the one Outlook module that can't launch to the Web.

A Final Note

You can't take Outlook's Notes any more seriously than you take the little sticky notes that you leave all over the fridge; they're just handy tools to help you save silly little scraps of information that you find you'll really need some day. After you've played with Notes a bit, you'll forget how you ever got along without them. When you remember again, make a note of it.

Chapter 15

Journaling

● ●

In This Chapter

▶ Recording items in the Journal

▶ Viewing Journal entries for a contact

▶ Finding a Journal entry

▶ Printing your Journal

▶ Viewing the Journal

▶ Setting up automatic Journal entries

● ●

Stardate 1997: On *Star Trek,* the captain of the starship *Enterprise* faithfully makes daily entries in the star log. The captain records information about the planets the crew has explored, the aliens they've battled, and the bizarre phenomena they've observed out in deep space, where no man (or woman) has gone before!

Now it's your turn. Just like the captain of the *Enterprise,* you can record your daily interactions with strange beings in bizarre environments under stressful circumstances, even if the strange beings are all in your own office. The Outlook Journal is your star log.

No doubt the captain's log is used for terribly important things by the high muck-a-mucks of the galaxy, but your Journal serves you more directly. Sometimes, when you need to find a document or a record of a conversation, you don't remember what you called the document or where you stored it, but you do remember *when* you created or received the item. In this case, you can go to the Journal and check the date when you remember dealing with the item and find what you need to know.

To get good use from the Journal, you need to use it, though. You can set Outlook to make journal entries for nearly everything you do, or you can shut the Journal off entirely and make no entries to it. If you put nothing in the Journal, you get nothing out.

Don't Just Do Something — Stand There!

What's the easiest way to make entries in the Journal? Do nothing. The Journal automatically records any document you create, edit, or print in any Office 97 application. The Journal also automatically tracks e-mail messages, meeting requests and responses, and task requests and responses. In the future, programs other than the Microsoft Office suite may have the capability to make entries in the Journal, but right now, that feature is limited to Office 97 programs.

There's a catch: You have to tell Outlook that you want automatic Journal recording turned on (all right, so you do have to do something besides just standing there).

To turn on the Journal's automatic recording feature:

1. **Choose Tools⇨Options.**

   The Options dialog box appears.

2. **Click the Journal tab.**

   The Journal Options page appears (see Figure 15-1), with check boxes for all the types of activities that you can record automatically and the names of all the people for whom you can automatically record transactions such as e-mail.

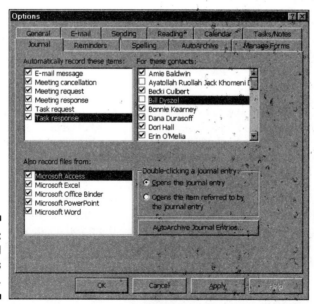

Figure 15-1:
The Journal Options page.

3. **Click to place a check in the check box for those items and files you want to automatically record and for the contacts about whom you want the information recorded.**

   The list of people in the For These Contacts box is the same as the list of people in your Contact list. You can manually create Journal entries for people who are not in your Contact list (see the section "Recording an Outlook item in the Journal manually").

   When you add names to your Contact list in the Contacts module, those names aren't set for automatic recording in the Journal. You either need to check the name in the Journal tab or open the Contact record, click the Journal tab, and check Automatically Record Journal Entries for These Contacts.

4. **Click OK.**

The Journal automatically records those items and files you selected for the contacts you named.

Recording an Outlook item in the Journal manually

If you don't want to clutter your Journal by recording everything automatically, you can enter selected items manually; just drag them to the Journal icon. For example, you may not want to record every transaction with a prospective client until you're certain that you're doing business with that client. You can drag relevant e-mail messages to the Journal and retain a record of serious inquiries. When you actually start doing business with a new client, you can set up automatic recording.

To manually record items in the Journal:

1. **Drag the item that you want to record (such as an e-mail message) to the Journal icon.**

   The Journal Entry form appears (see Figure 15-2). At the bottom of the form there's an icon representing the item you're recording, along with the item's name.

2. **Fill in the information that you want to record.**

   You don't have to record anything, though. The text box at the bottom of the screen gives you space for making a note to yourself, if you want to use it.

3. **Click Save and Close (or press Alt+S).**

   The item that you recorded is entered in the Journal. You can see your new entry when you view your Journal, as I describe later in this chapter in the section "Viewing your Journal."

Figure 15-2:
A Journal
entry with
an e-mail
message
attached in
the text box.

Recording a document in the Journal

If your favorite program, such as a drawing or desktop-publishing program, doesn't show up in the list of programs that can make automatic entries in the Journal, all is not lost — you can drag documents from Outlook's My Computer folder to the Journal folder to create Journal entries for those programs' files, too. Because the Journal can keep track of many types of information about a document other than date and time (such as client, subject, and some notes), you can use the Journal to keep track of files you create in programs that aren't part of Microsoft Office. If you've elected to let Outlook create Journal entries automatically for your Office 97 applications, you don't have to make entries for Office 97 documents.

To record a document in the Journal:

1. **Choose Go⇨My Computer.**

   Your list of drives appears (see Figure 15-3).

2. **Find the document that you want to record.**

   Double-click the drive that contains the document you want to record; then double-click the folder in which you save your documents to find the document that you want to record. Highlight it.

3. **Drag the document to the Journal icon.**

   The Journal Entry form appears, with an icon in the text box representing the file that you're recording.

4. **Click Save and Close (or press Alt+S).**

   Your document is recorded in the Journal.

Figure 15-3:
The list of
drives
in My
Computer.

The big benefit of recording documents in the Journal is the fact that Journal entries are really shortcuts to the documents themselves. When you enter a document in the Journal, you have quick access to information you've saved about the document, and you're only one click away from the document itself. So if you use a non-Office 97 program that creates files that don't keep track of much information about themselves, the Journal is a great central location for keeping track of document information. For example, if you're saving pictures from a drawing program on your computer, you may want to save more information about each picture than just the filename. If you create Journal entries for each file, you can keep notes about each picture in the Journal. When you find the Journal entry for the picture you want, just double-click the icon for the picture; the program you use to see the picture then opens.

Viewing Journal Entries for a Contact

My friend Vinnie in Brooklyn says, "You gotta know who you dealt wit' and when you dealt wit' 'em." You can use the Contact list together with the Journal to keep track of whom you dealt with when. Just look in the person's Contact record of a person to see when you made Journal entries:

1. **Choose Go⇨Contacts.**

   The Contact list appears.

2. **Double-click the name of the contact that you want to view.**

   The Contact record opens.

3. **Click the Journal tab in the Contact form.**

   A list of every Journal entry you've made for that person appears (see Figure 15-4), including the automatic entries that Outlook made if you chose that option.

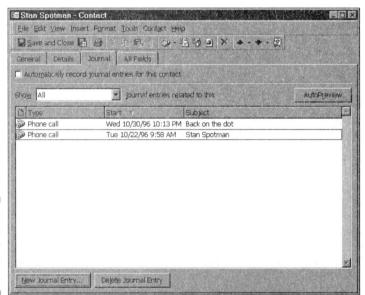

Figure 15-4:
Journal
entries for
Stan
Spotman.

Finding a Journal Entry

When you don't remember exactly when you did something or dealt with somebody, you can look it up by searching for words in the Journal item.

To find a Journal entry when you don't know the when:

1. **Choose Go⇨Journal (or click the Journal icon).**

   The list of Journal items appears.

2. **Choose Tools⇨Find Items.**

   The Find dialog box appears (see Figure 15-5) with a magnifying glass on the right side.

Magnifying Glass

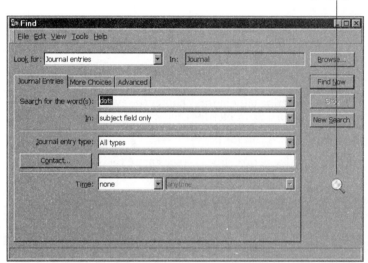

Figure 15-5:
The Find
dialog box.

3. Type a word or phrase that you can find in your Contact record.

If you're looking for information about an upcoming meeting on inventory liquidation, type **inventory**, **liquidation**, or both.

4. Click the Find Now button.

On the right side of the Find dialog box, a magnifying glass circles until items that include your text are found. When items are found that match the description you've entered, a list of matching items appears at the bottom of the Find dialog box.

5. Double-click the icon next to your item in the list at the bottom of the Find box.

The Journal item item that you clicked appears. An icon in the text box at the bottom is a shortcut to any other Outlook item or document that the Journal entry represents. If you want to see the Calendar item that has details about the Inventory Liquidation meeting, double-click the icon at the bottom of the Journal entry; the Calendar item pops up.

Printing Your Journal

I can't explain why, but I just don't get a complete picture from information on a screen; I still like to print out my work on paper to really see what I've done. Printing your Journal (or segments of it) allows you to see a printed list of recent or upcoming activities and stick it on the wall where you can look at it often.

To print your Journal:

1. **Choose Go⇨Journal.**

   The list of Journal items appears.

2. **Select the entries that you want to print.**

   If you select nothing, you print the entire list. Also, if you use one of the views I describe later in this chapter (or even create your own view by grouping, sorting, or filtering), what you see is what you print.

3. **Choose File⇨Print (or press Ctrl+P).**

   The Print dialog box appears (see Figure 15-6).

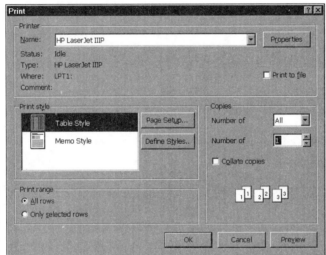

Figure 15-6:
The Print
dialog box.

4. **Choose Table or Memo style.**

   Table style prints only a list of your Journal entries, not the contents of each entry. Memo style prints the contents of your Journal entries, with each item appearing as a separate memo.

5. **Choose All Rows or Only Selected Rows.**

   If you want to print only certain rows, you have to select the rows that you want to print before you choose File⇨Print; then click the Only Selected Rows button to limit what you print to those rows.

6. **Click OK.**

   The list of Journal entries you selected prints.

The printed list won't go up on the wall for you, however, unless you put it there.

Viewing the Journal

As with other Outlook modules, the Journal comes with multiple views that show your entries in different ways, depending on what you need to see. You may just want to see your record of phone calls or a list organized by the names of the people you've dealt with. The Current View menu allows you to change from one view to the next quickly.

The Entry List

The Entry List is the whole tomato — all your Journal entries, regardless of whom, what, or when. To call up the Entry List, simply choose View⇨Current View⇨Entry List (see Figure 15-7).

You can click the heading at the top of any column to sort the list according to the information in that column. If you want to arrange your list of Journal entries by the type of entry, for example, click the header that says Entry Type. Your list is sorted alphabetically by type of entry, with conversations before e-mail before faxes and so on.

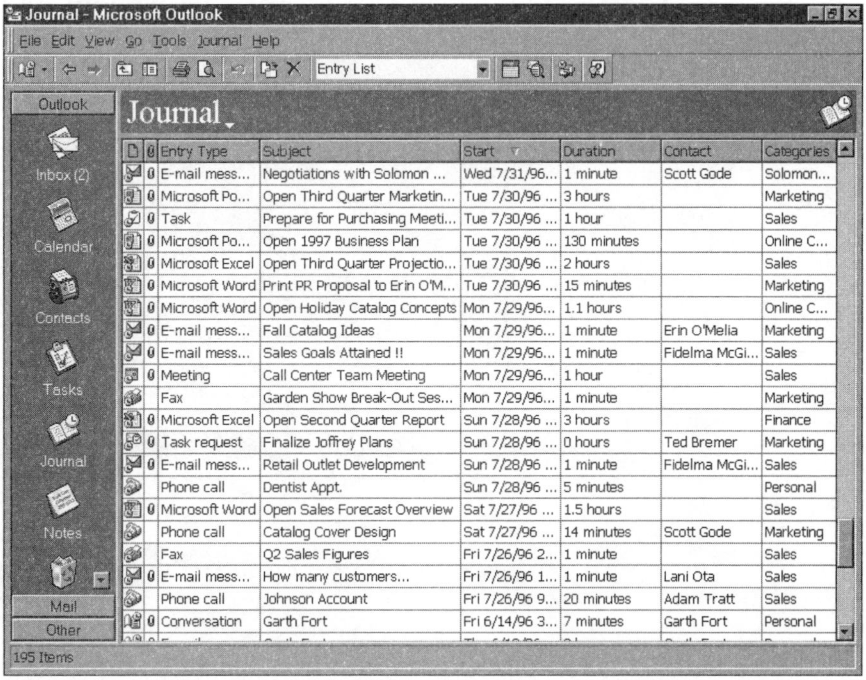

Figure 15-7: Viewing the Entry List — everything you've ever entered.

By Type

By Type view takes sorting one step further by grouping items according to their type. To view your entries by type, choose View⇨Current View⇨By Type (see Figure 15-8). You can click the plus sign next to the name of the type to view your entire list of items of that type. Click the icon next to the name of the Entry Type again to close the list of that type. Then you can click to open another list of entries by type.

By Contact

By Contact view shows your Journal items grouped by the name of the person associated with the item. To see your entries in By Contact view, choose View⇨Current View⇨By Contact (see Figure 15-9).

You can click the plus sign next to the name of the person whose entries you want to see. You can see entries for more than one person at a time.

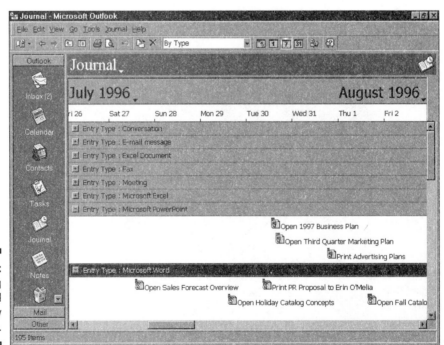

Figure 15-8:
Grouping your Journal items in By Type view.

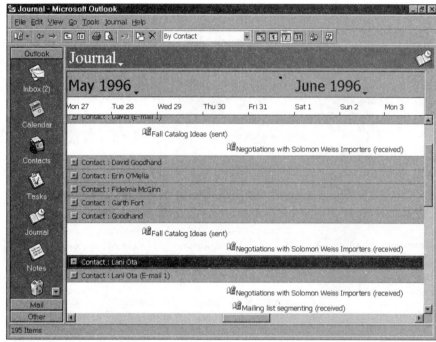

Figure 15-9:
Seeing your
entries in By
Contact
view.

By Category

If you've been assigning categories to your Journal items, By Category view collects all your entries into bunches of items of the same category. To see your entries by category, choose View⇨Current View⇨By Category (see Figure 15-10).

If you've assigned more than one category to an item, the item shows up under both categories you've assigned.

Last Seven Days

The items that you're most likely to need first are the ones you used last. Last Seven Days view is a quick way to see your most recent activities at a glance. To see a week's worth of Journal entries, choose View⇨Current View⇨Last Seven Days (see Figure 15-11).

Documents that you've created, phone calls, e-mail — anything you've done in the last seven days — you can see them all in Last Seven Days view.

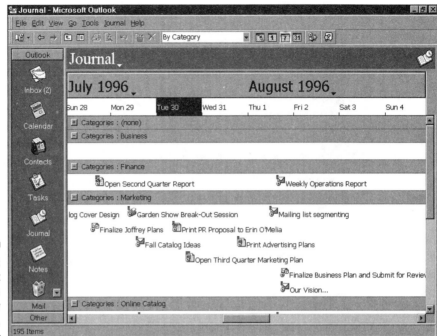

Figure 15-10:
Looking at
your list in
By Category
view.

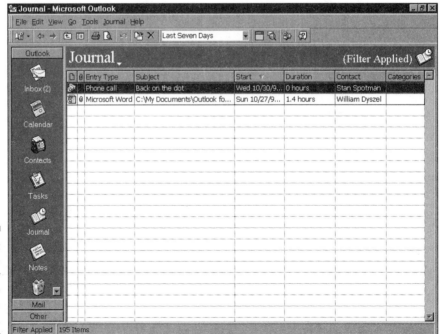

Figure 15-11:
Some
seven-day
periods are
busier than
others.

Phone Calls

Because you can keep track of your phone calls in the Journal, the Journal lets you see a list of the calls you've kept track of. Simply choose View⇨Current View⇨Phone Calls (see Figure 15-12).

To print a list of your phone calls, switch to Phone Calls view and press Ctrl+P.

It's All in the Journal

The Journal can be enormously helpful whether you choose to use it regularly or rarely. You don't have to limit yourself to recording documents or Outlook items; you can keep track of conversations or customer inquiries or any other transaction in which chronology matters. If you set the Journal for automatic entries, you can ignore it completely until you need to see what was recorded. You can also play starship captain and record everything that you do — I haven't tried Outlook in outer space yet, but I know I would enjoy the views.

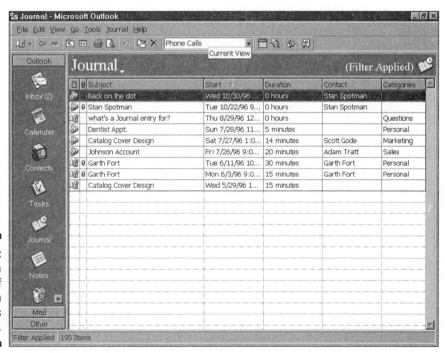

Figure 15-12: Keep a record of your calls in Phone Calls view.

Chapter 16

Do It Yourself — Scheduling Your Own Tasks

*Y*ou can store and manage more information about your daily tasks in Outlook than you may have wanted to know, but you'll certainly find that Outlook makes it easy to remember and monitor your daily work. Organizing your tasks doesn't have to be a task in itself.

Some people say that work expands to fill the available time, and chances are that your boss is one of them. Who else would keep expanding your work all the time? One way of saving time is to keep a list of the tasks that are filling your time. That way, you can avoid getting too many more tasks to do.

I used to scrawl a to-do list on paper and hope I'd find the list in time to do the things I wrote down. Now Outlook pops up and reminds me of the things I'm trying to forget to do just before I forget to do them. It also keeps track of when I'm supposed to have done my daily tasks and when I actually did them. That way, I can use all the things I was supposed to do yesterday as an excuse not to do the things I'm supposed to do today. (Outlook still won't do the stuff for me — it just tells me how far I'm falling behind. Be forewarned.)

Using the Outlook Tasks List

The Outlook Tasks list is easy to recognize as an electronic version of the good old plain-paper-scribbled to-do list. It's every bit as simple as it looks: a list of tasks and a list of dates for doing the tasks (see Figure 16-1).

The Tasks list actually turns up in more than one section of Outlook. Of course, it's in the Tasks module, but it also turns up in certain views of the Calendar. Seeing your Tasks list in Calendar view is very handy for figuring out when you need to do things, as well as what you need to do (see Figure 16-2).

Entering New Tasks

I don't mean for you to add work to your busy schedule; you already have plenty of that. But adding a task to your Tasks list in Outlook isn't such a task. Even though you can store gobs of information about your tasks in Outlook, you have both a quick way and a really quick way to enter a new task.

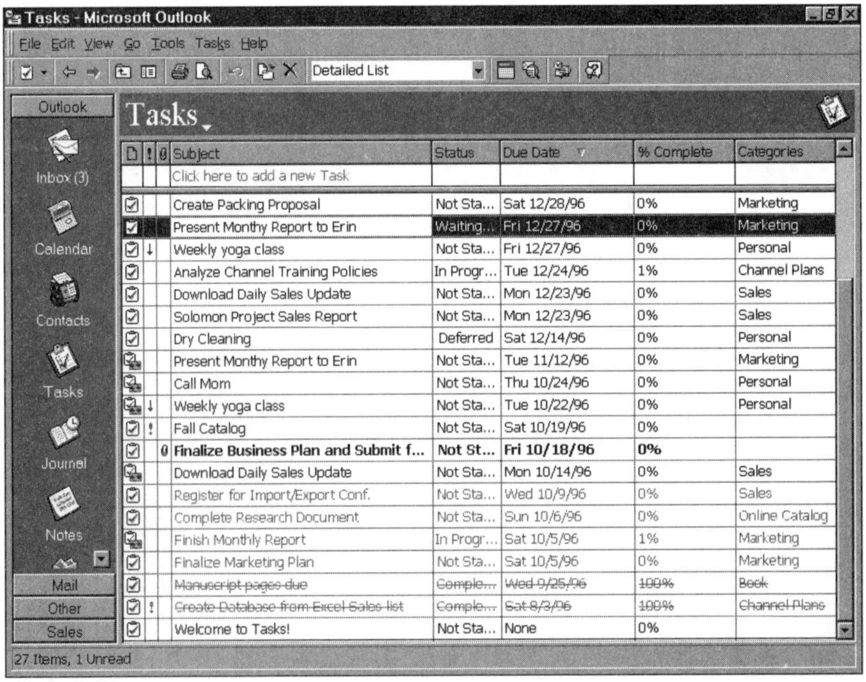

Figure 16-1:
Your Tasks list — more than you ever want to do.

Figure 16-2:
A list of your
tasks in
Calendar
view.

The quick-and-dirty way to enter a task

If you're in one of the views that appear in Figure 16-1 and Figure 16-2, a little box at the top of the list says Click here to add a new Task. Do what the box says. (If you can't see the box, go on to the following section to learn the regular, slightly slower way to enter the task.)

To enter a task using the quick-and-dirty way:

1. **Click the text that says** Click here to add a new task.

   The words disappear, and you see the Insertion Point (a blinking line).

2. **Type the name of your task.**

   Your task appears in the block under the Subject line on the Tasks list. (See Figure 16-3.)

3. **Press the Enter key.**

Your new task moves down to the Tasks list with your other tasks.

Isn't that easy! If only the tasks themselves were that easy to do. Maybe in the next version of Outlook, the tasks will get easier, too (in my dreams).

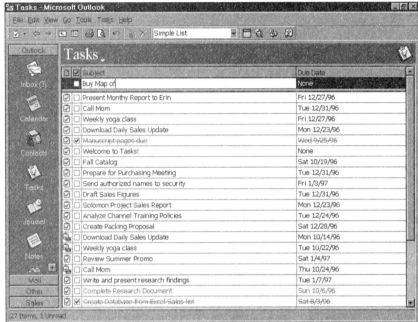

Figure 16-3:
Entering
your task
in the
Tasks list.

Of course, all you have is the name of the task — no due dates, reminders, or any of the cool stuff. If you want that information, you have to enter the task the regular way. (See the next section, "The regular way to enter a task.")

The regular way to enter a task

The regular way to enter a task is through the Task dialog box, which looks like more work, but it's really not. As long as you enter a name for the task, you've done all that you really must. If you want to go hog-wild and enter all sorts of due dates or have Outlook remind you to actually *complete* the tasks that you've entered (heaven forbid!), you just need to put information in a few more boxes.

To add a task to your Tasks list, follow these steps:

1. Choose Go⇨Tasks.

Your Tasks list appears.

2. Choose File⇨New⇨Task.

The Task form appears (see Figure 16-4).

3. Type the name of the task in the Subject box.

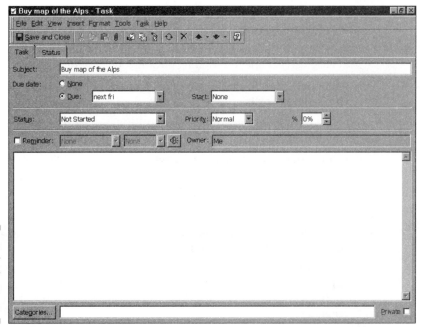

Figure 16-4:
You enter
your new
task in the
Task form.

Use a subject that will help you remember what the task is. The main reason to create a task is to help you remember to do the task.

You can finish at this point by jumping to Step 21 (choose <u>S</u>ave and Close or press Alt+S) if you only want to add the name of the task to your list. If you want to note a due date, start date, reminders, and so on, there's more to do. All the rest of the steps are optional; you can skip the ones that don't interest you.

4. (Optional) To assign a due date to the task, click the <u>D</u>ue Date button.

5. (Optional) Click the <u>D</u>ue Date box and enter the due date.

You can enter a date in Outlook in several ways. You can type **7/4/97, the first Friday of July**, or **Three weeks from Friday**. You can also click the scroll down button (triangle) at the right end of the <u>D</u>ue Date text box and choose the date you want from the drop-down calendar.

6. (Optional) To assign a start date to the task, click the Sta<u>r</u>t box and enter the start date.

If you haven't started the task, you can skip this step. You can use the same tricks to enter the start date that you use to enter the due date.

When you're entering information in a dialog box such as the Task dialog box, you can press the Tab key to move from one text box to the next. You can use the mouse to click each text box before you type, but pressing the Tab key is a bit faster. I've written the directions in the order that you follow if you use the Tab key to move through the dialog box.

7. **(Optional) Click the triangle at the right end of the Status box to choose the status of the task.**

   If you haven't begun, leave Status set to Not Started. You can also choose In Progress, Completed, Waiting on Someone Else, or Deferred.

8. **(Optional) Click the triangle at the right end of the Priority box to choose the priority.**

   If you don't change anything, the priority stays Normal. You can also choose High or Low.

9. **(Optional) Click the Reminder check box if you want to be reminded before the task is due.**

   If you'd rather forget the task, forget the reminder. But then, why enter the task at all?

10. **(Optional) Click the date box next to the Reminder check box and enter the date when you want to be reminded.**

    If you entered a due date, Outlook has already entered that date in the Reminder box. You can enter any date you want (see Figure 16-5). If you choose a date in the past, Outlook lets you know that it won't be setting a reminder.

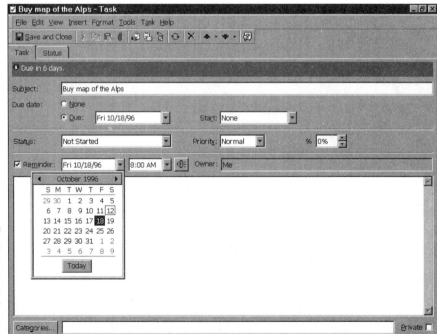

Figure 16-5:
A calendar drops down to show the date your task is due.

If you open the scroll down menu by clicking the triangle on the right of the date box, a calendar appears. You can click on the date you desire in the calendar.

11. **(Optional) Enter the time you want to activate the reminder in the time box.**

The easiest way to set a time is to type the numbers for the time. You don't need colons or anything special. If you want to finish by 2:35 p.m., just type **235**. Outlook assumes that you're not a vampire, and it schedules your tasks and appointments during daylight hours unless you say otherwise. If you are a vampire, type **235a**; Outlook translates that to 2:35 a.m. If you simply *must* use correct punctuation, Outlook translates it.

12. **(Optional) In the text box, enter miscellaneous notes and information about this task.**

If you need to keep directions to the appointment, a list of supplies, or whatever, it all fits here.

13. **(Optional) Click the Categories button to assign a category to the appointment, if you want.**

(Using the categories setting is another trick for finding things easily.) The Categories dialog box appears (see Figure 16-6).

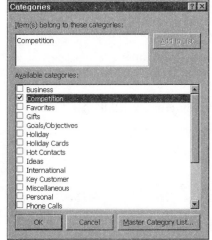

Figure 16-6:
The
Categories
dialog box.

14. **(Optional) Choose one of the existing categories, if one suits you; then click OK.**

15. **(Optional) If none of the existing categories suits you, click Master Category List.**

The Master Category List dialog box appears (see Figure 16-7).

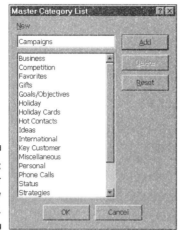

Figure 16-7:
The Master
Category
List.

16. **(Optional) Type a category of your choice in the New box.**

    Be sure not to add too many new categories; if you do, finding things could get hard.

17. **(Optional) Click Add.**

18. **(Optional) Click OK.**

19. **(Optional) Choose the new category from the categories list.**

    You can choose more than one category at a time.

20. **(Optional) Click the Private box, in the lower-right corner of the Task dialog box, if you're on a network and you don't want other users to know about your appointments.**

21. **Click the Save and Close button (or press Alt+S) to finish.**

    Your new task is now standing at the top of your task list, waiting to be done.

Adding an Internet link to a Task

If you type the name of a Web page, such as http//www.pcstudio.com, in the text box at the bottom of the Task form, Outlook changes the text color to blue and underlines the address, making it look just like the hypertext you click to jump between different pages on the World Wide Web. That makes it easy to save information about an exciting Web site; just type or copy the address into your task. To view the page you entered, just click the text to make your Web browser pop up and open the page.

Editing Your Tasks

No sooner do you enter a new task than it seems that you need to change it. Sometimes, I enter a task the quick-and-dirty way and change some of the particulars later — add a due date, a reminder, an added step, or whatever. Editing tasks is easy.

The quick-and-dirty way to change a task

For lazy people like me, there's a quick-and-dirty way to change a task, just as there's a quick-and-dirty way to enter a task. There's a limit to how many details you can change, but the process is quick.

If you can see the name of a task, and if you want to change something about the task you can see, follow the steps below; if you can't see the task or the part that you want to change, use the regular method, described in the next section.

1. Click the thing that you want to change.

You see a blinking line at the end of the text, a triangle at the right end of the box, or a menu with a list of choices.

2. Select the old information.

The old text is highlighted to show you that it's selected (see Figure 16-8).

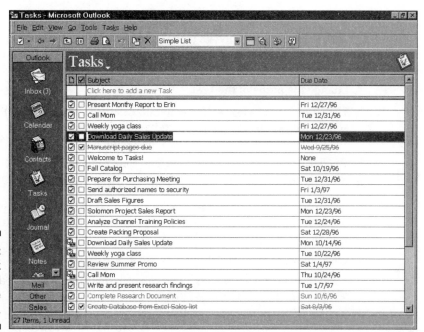

Figure 16-8:
A task highlighted in the Tasks list.

	Subject	Due Date
	Click here to add a new Task	
☑ ☐	Present Monthy Report to Erin	Fri 12/27/96
☑ ☐	Call Mom	Tue 12/31/96
☑ ☐	Weekly yoga class	Fri 12/27/96
☑ ■	Download Daily Sales Update	Mon 12/23/96
☑ ☑	Manuscript pages due	Wed 9/25/96
☑ ☐	Welcome to Tasks!	None
☑ ☐	Fall Catalog	Sat 10/19/96
☑ ☐	Prepare for Purchasing Meeting	Tue 12/31/96
☑ ☐	Send authorized names to security	Fri 1/3/97
☑ ☐	Draft Sales Figures	Tue 12/31/96
☑ ☐	Solomon Project Sales Report	Mon 12/23/96
☑ ☐	Analyze Channel Training Policies	Tue 12/24/96
☑ ☐	Create Packing Proposal	Sat 12/28/96
☑ ☐	Download Daily Sales Update	Mon 10/14/96
☑ ☐	Weekly yoga class	Tue 10/22/96
☑ ☐	Review Summer Promo	Sat 1/4/97
☑ ☐	Call Mom	Thu 10/24/96
☑ ☐	Write and present research findings	Tue 1/7/97
☑ ☐	Complete Research Document	Sun 10/6/96
☑ ☑	Create Database from Excel Sales list	Sat 8/3/96

Tasks - Microsoft Outlook

File Edit View Go Tools Tasks Help

Simple List

Tasks

Outlook
Inbox (3)
Calendar
Contacts
Tasks
Journal
Notes
Mail
Other
Sales

27 Items, 1 Unread

3. **Type the new information.**

   The new information replaces the old. If you click the Status box, a menu drops down and you can choose from the list.

4. **Press the Enter key.**

Isn't that easy? If all you want to change is the name, status, or due date, the quick-and-dirty way will get you there.

The regular way to change a task

If you don't want to be quick and dirty, or if the information that you want to change about a task isn't on the list you're looking at, you'll have to take a slightly longer route. The regular way is a little more work, but not much.

To make changes to a task the clean-and-long way (a.k.a. the regular way), follow these steps:

1. **Choose Go➪Tasks.**

   The Tasks module opens.

2. **Choose View➪Current View➪Simple List.**

   You can choose a different Current View if you know that the view includes the task you want to change. The Simple List is the most basic view of your tasks; it's sure to include the task you're looking for.

3. **Double-click the name of the task that you want to change.**

   The New Task form appears (see Figure 16-9). Now you can change anything you can see in the box. Just click the information you want to change, type the new information, and click Save and Close (or Alt+S).

4. **Change the name of the task.**

   The name is your choice. Remember to call the task something that helps you remember the task. There's nothing worse than a computer reminding you to do something that you can't understand.

5. **To change the due date, click the Due Date button.**

6. **Click the Due Date box and enter the new due date.**

   Plenty of date styles work here — **7/4/97**, **the first Friday in July**, **Six weeks from now**, whatever. Unfortunately, **the 12th of Never** isn't an option. Sorry.

7. **Click the Start Date box and enter the new start date.**

   If you haven't started the task, you can skip this step. You don't absolutely need a start date; it's just for your own use.

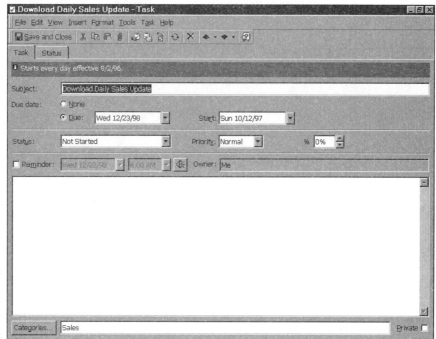

Figure 16-9:
The New
Task form.

8. **Click the scroll down button (triangle) at the right end of the Status box to see a menu that lets you change the status of the task.**

If you're using Outlook at work and you're hooked up to a network, the Status box entry is one way of keeping your boss informed of your progress. You'll need to check with your boss or system administrator if this is the case.

If you're using Outlook at home, chances are that nobody else will care, but you may feel better if you know how well you're doing. You can't add your own choices to the Status box. I'd like to add "Waiting, hoping the task will go away." No such luck. Figure 16-10 shows the Task box with the Status line highlighted.

9. **Click the scroll-down button (triangle) at the right end of the Priority box to change the priority.**

Switch the priority to High or Low, if the situation changes (see Figure 16-11).

10. **Click the Reminder check box if you want to turn the reminder on or off.**

Reminders are easy and harmless, so why not? If you didn't ask for one the first time, do it now.

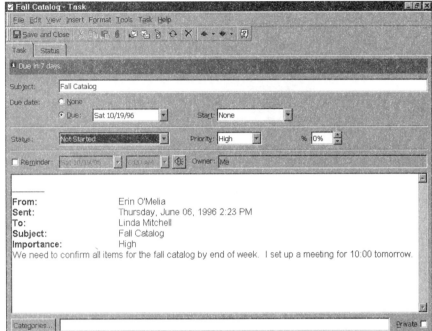

Figure 16-10:
This Task
dialog box
shows a
nonstarter in
the Status
box.

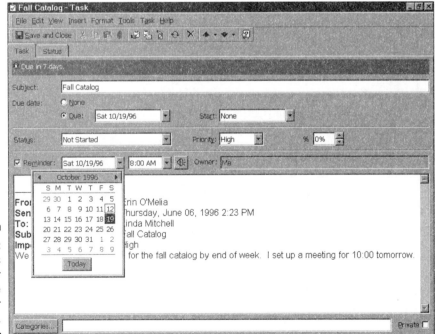

Figure 16-11:
Maybe this
nonstarter
should have
a lower
priority.

11. Click the date box next to the Reminder check box to enter or change the date when you want to be reminded.

You can enter any date you want. Your entry doesn't have to be the due date; it can be much earlier, reminding you to get started. You can even set a reminder after the task is due, which isn't very useful. You should make sure that the reminder is before the due date. The default date for a reminder is the date the task is due.

12. Change the time you want to activate the reminder in the time box.

When entering times, keep it simple. **230** does the trick when you want to enter 2:30 p.m. If you make appointments at 2:30 a.m. (I'd rather not know what kind of appointments you make at that hour), you can type **230a**.

13. Click the text box to add or change miscellaneous notes and information about this task.

You can add detailed information here that doesn't really belong anywhere else in the Task dialog box (see Figure 16-12). You see these details only when you open the Task dialog box again; they don't normally show up in your Tasks list.

14. Click the Save and Close button (or press Alt+S) to finish.

There! You've changed your task.

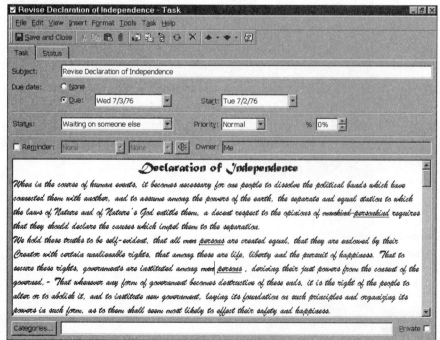

Figure 16-12:
Details,
details. Add
'em in the
text box.

Copying a task

By now, you're probably saying, "I had so much fun setting up a task for myself; I'd like to set up another one." If it's the same task, different day, the easiest approach is to copy the task.

To copy a task, follow these steps:

1. **Select the task that you want to copy.**

   The selected task is highlighted in blue (see Figure 16-13).

2. **Choose Edit⊅Copy (or Ctrl+C).**

3. **Choose Edit⊅Paste (or Ctrl+V).**

   A new, identical copy of your task appears just below the old one. The problem is that it's exactly the same task. You don't need Siamese-twin tasks, so you probably want to change the date of the new task. Double-click the new task and change the date.

For creating tasks that recur every day, copying the task is pretty laborious, that's why you can set up a task as a recurring task the way I describe in "Managing Recurring Tasks" later in this chapter.

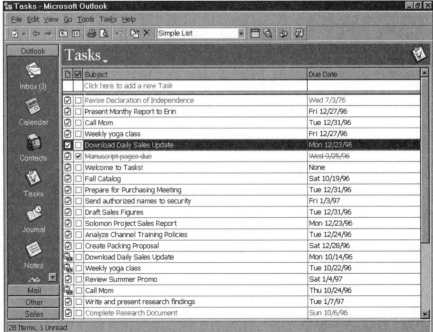

Figure 16-13:
Your
selected
task is
highlighted.

		Subject	Due Date
		Click here to add a new Task	
☑	☐	Revise Declaration of Independence	Wed 7/3/76
☑	☐	Present Monthy Report to Erin	Fri 12/27/96
☑	☐	Call Mom	Tue 12/31/96
☑	☐	Weekly yoga class	Fri 12/27/96
☑	☐	Download Daily Sales Update	Mon 12/23/96
☑	☑	Manuscript pages due	Wed 9/25/96
☑	☐	Welcome to Tasks!	None
☑	☐	Fall Catalog	Sat 10/19/96
☑	☐	Prepare for Purchasing Meeting	Tue 12/31/96
☑	☐	Send authorized names to security	Fri 1/3/97
☑	☐	Draft Sales Figures	Tue 12/31/96
☑	☐	Solomon Project Sales Report	Mon 12/23/96
☑	☐	Analyze Channel Training Policies	Tue 12/24/96
☑	☐	Create Packing Proposal	Sat 12/28/96
	☐	Download Daily Sales Update	Mon 10/14/96
	☐	Weekly yoga class	Tue 10/22/96
☑	☐	Review Summer Promo	Sat 1/4/97
	☐	Call Mom	Thu 10/24/96
☑	☐	Write and present research findings	Tue 1/7/97
☑	☐	Complete Research Document	Sun 10/6/96

28 Items, 1 Unread

Deleting a task

The really gratifying part about tasks is getting rid of them, preferably by completing the tasks you've entered. You may also delete a task you changed your mind about. Of course, there's nothing to stop you from deleting tasks you just don't want to bother with; this version of Outlook can't really tell if you've actually completed your tasks. Rumor has it that the next version of Outlook will know if you've finished your tasks and report to Santa. Don't be naughty!

To delete a task, follow these steps:

1. **Select the task.**

2. **Choose Edit⇨Delete (or press Ctrl+D, or click the Delete button in the toolbar).**

Poof! Your task is gone.

Assigning a Task to Someone Else

As Tom Sawyer could tell you, anything worth doing is worth getting someone else to do. Outlook provides a simple way to assign a task to somebody else. The catch is, the person you assign a task to must also be using Outlook and you must both be using a network that supports assigning tasks to others. Check with your network administrator to see if this feature is available to you. Even if you're not fully equipped to send tasks to other people, you can try to send a task, but what the other person will get is an e-mail message describing the task.

To assign a task to someone else:

1. **Double-click the task you want to assign to someone else.**

   The form for the task you want to assign opens.

2. **Choose Task⇨Assign Task.**

   A banner appears on the form saying `This message has not been sent` and a new To button and text field appear.

3. **Type the name of the person to whom you wish to assign the task in the To box.**

   If Outlook recognizes the person from your Contact list, the name appears in the To box with an underline. You can also click the To button, double-click the person's name in the Address Book, and click OK.

4. **Click Send.**

   The form closes and your task is sent by e-mail to the person you've assigned it to.

Once you've assigned tasks to others, the tasks remain listed on your Tasks list, but a different icon appears alongside assigned tasks to indicate that someone else is responsible. To see which tasks you've assigned to whom, see the description of the Assignment view or the By Person Responsible view later in this chapter.

Managing Recurring Tasks

Lots of tasks crop up on a regular basis. You know how it goes, same stuff, new day. To save you the effort of entering a task like a monthly sales report or a quarterly tax payment over and over again, just set it up as a recurring task. Outlook can then remind you whenever it's that time again.

To create a recurring task, follow these steps:

1. **Open the task by double-clicking it.**

   The Task form appears (see Figure 16-14).

2. **Click the Recurrence button in the Task form toolbar (or press Ctrl+G).**

   The Task Recurrence dialog box appears (see Figure 16-15).

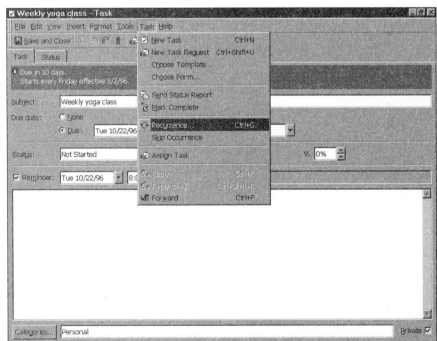

Figure 16-14:
Getting a
handle on
recurring
tasks.

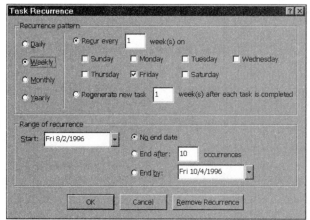

Figure 16-15:
How often
should this
task be
done?

3. **Choose the Daily, Weekly, Monthly, or Yearly option to specify how often the appointment occurs.**

   Each choice you make, Daily, Weekly, or Monthly, changes the types of exact choices available for when the task recurs. For example, a daily recurring task can be set to recur every day or every five days or whatever. A monthly recurring task can be set to recur on a certain day of the month, such as the 15th of each month, or on the second Friday of every month.

4. **In the next box to the right, specify how often the appointment occurs, such as every third day or the first Monday of each month.**

   If you choose to create a monthly task, for example, you can click the scroll down buttons (triangles) to choose "First" then "Monday" to schedule a task on the first Monday of each month.

5. **In the Range of Recurrence box, enter the first occurrence in the Start box.**

6. **Choose when you want the appointments to stop (no end date, after a certain number of occurrences, or at a certain date).**

7. **Click OK.**

   A banner appears at the top of the Task form describing the recurrence pattern of the task.

8. **Click Save and Close.**

Your task appears in the list of tasks once, but it has a different type of icon than nonrecurring tasks so that you can tell at a glance that it's a recurring task.

Creating a regenerating task

A *regenerating task* is like a recurring task except that it only recurs when a certain amount of time passes after the last time you completed the task. Say that you mow the lawn every two weeks. If it rains for a week and one mowing happens a week late, you still want to wait two weeks for the next one. If you schedule your mowings in Outlook, you'd use the Regenerating Task feature to enter your lawn-mowing schedule.

To create a regenerating task:

1. **Open the task by double-clicking it.**

   The Task dialog box appears.

2. **Click the Recur button in the toolbar in the Task dialog box (or press Ctrl+G).**

   The Task Recurrence dialog box appears.

3. **Click the Regenerate New Task button (see Figure 16-16).**

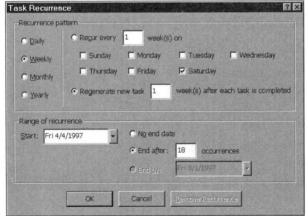

Figure 16-16: You can regenerate a task in the Task Recurrence dialog box.

4. **Enter the number of weeks between regenerating each task.**

5. **Click OK.**

   A banner appears in the Task form describing the regeneration pattern you've set for the task.

6. **Click Save and Close.**

Your task appears in the list of tasks once, but it has a different type of icon than nonrecurring tasks so that you can tell at a glance that it's a regenerating task.

Skipping a recurring task once

When you need to skip a single occurrence of a recurring task, you don't have to change the recurrence pattern of the task forever; just skip the occurrence you want to skip and leave the rest alone.

To skip a recurring task:

1. **Choose Go⇨Tasks.**

   Your list of tasks appears.

2. **Choose View⇨Current View⇨Simple List.**

   It doesn't matter what view you use, as long as you can see the name of the task that you want to skip. I suggest the Simple List because it's . . . well, simple.

3. **Double-click the name of the task that you want to change.**

   The Task form appears.

4. **Choose Task⇨Skip Occurrence.**

   The due date changes to the date of the next scheduled occurrence.

5. **Click Save and Close.**

Your task remains in the list with the new scheduled occurrence date showing.

Marking Tasks Complete

Marking off those completed tasks is even more fun than entering them and much easier. If you can see the task that you want to mark complete in your Tasks list, just click the check box next to the name of the task. Nothing could be simpler.

To mark a task complete, follow these steps:

1. **Choose Go⇨Tasks.**

   The Tasks module opens.

2. **Choose View⇨Current View⇨Simple List.**

   Actually, you can choose any view you want, as long as the task that you're looking for shows up there. If the task that you want to mark complete isn't in the view you chose, try the simple list, which contains everything.

3. **Click the box next to the name of the task that you want to mark complete.**

   The box in the second column from the left is the one that you want to check (see Figure 16-17).

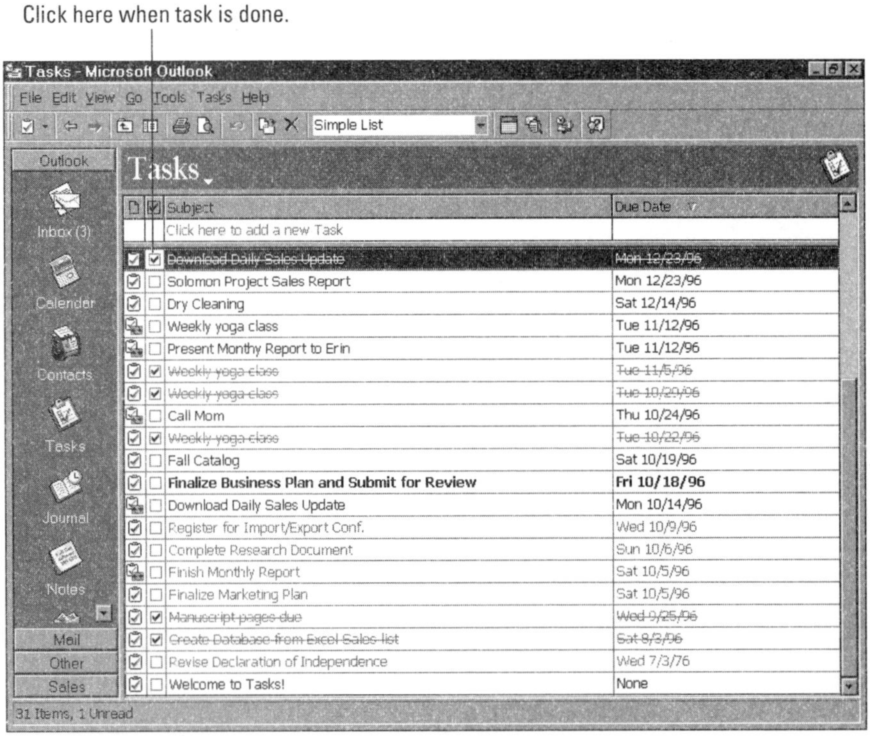

Click here when task is done.

Figure 16-17:
A check
marks the
task
complete.

When you check the box, the name of the task changes color and gets a line through it. You're finished.

Marking several tasks complete

Perhaps you don't race to your computer every time you complete a task. Marking off your completed tasks in a bunch is faster than marking them one by one. Outlook allows you to do that by making a multiple selection.

To mark several tasks complete, follow these steps:

1. Choose Go⇨Tasks.

The Tasks module opens.

2. Choose View⇨Current View⇨Simple List.

Again, I'm just suggesting Simple List view because it's most likely to show you all your tasks. You can pick any view that allows you to see the tasks that you want to mark.

3. **Click the first task that you want to mark.**

4. **Hold down the Ctrl key and click each of the other tasks that you want to mark.**

   All the tasks you clicked are highlighted, showing that you've selected them.

5. **Right-click one of the tasks that you've highlighted.**

   A menu appears (see Figure 16-18).

Figure 16-18:
A shortcut menu in the Tasks module.

6. **Choose Mark Complete.**

The tasks you selected are marked complete.

Picking a color for completed or overdue tasks

When you complete a task or when it becomes overdue, Outlook changes the color of the text for the completed tasks to gray and the overdue tasks to red, which makes it easy for you to tell at a glance which tasks are done and which tasks remain to be done. If you don't like Outlook's color choices, you can pick different colors.

Here's how to change the color of completed and overdue tasks:

1. **Choose Tools⇨Options.**

   The Options dialog box appears.

2. **Click the Tasks/Notes tab.**

   The Tasks/Notes page appears (see Figure 16-19).

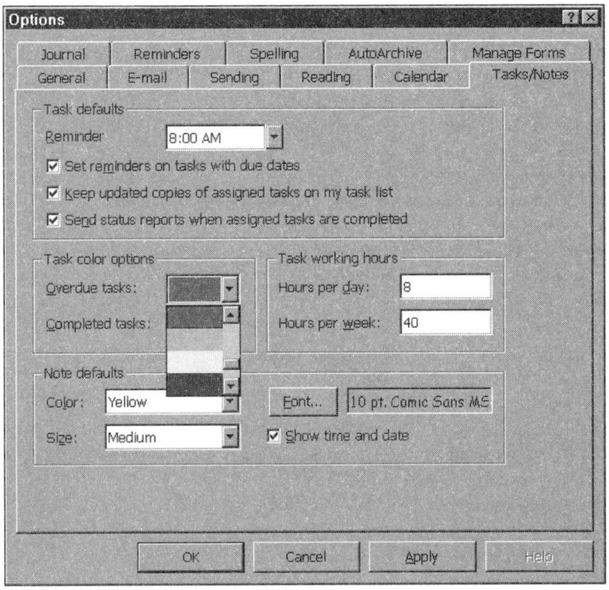

Figure 16-19:
The Tasks/
Notes page.

3. **Click the scroll down button (triangle) at the right end of the Overdue Tasks box.**

   A list of colors drops down.

4. **Choose a color for overdue tasks.**

5. **Click the scroll down button (triangle) at the right end of the Completed Tasks box.**

   A list of colors drops down.

6. **Choose a color for completed tasks.**

7. **Click OK.**

Your completed and overdue tasks will appear on your list in the colors you chose.

Viewing Your Tasks

Outlook comes with ten ways to view your Tasks list and allows you to invent and save as many custom views as you like. The views that come with Outlook take you a long way when you know how to use them.

I tell you how to use the menus to select each view of your Tasks list because the menus are consistent and reliable, although not always the fastest way to change views. The quickest way is to choose the name of the view from the Current View menu. Because you can turn off the toolbar but not the menu bar, I stick with describing the menu-bar method, because you know that the menu bar will always be there.

Simple List

As its name implies, the Simple List shows you basic information about your tasks. Most of the time, all you need to know about your tasks is the name and due date of each task, so that's all the Simple List shows.

To see the Simple List of tasks:

1. **Choose View⇨Current View.**

   The list of current views appears.

2. **Choose Simple List.**

   You simply see a list of your tasks (see Figure 16-20).

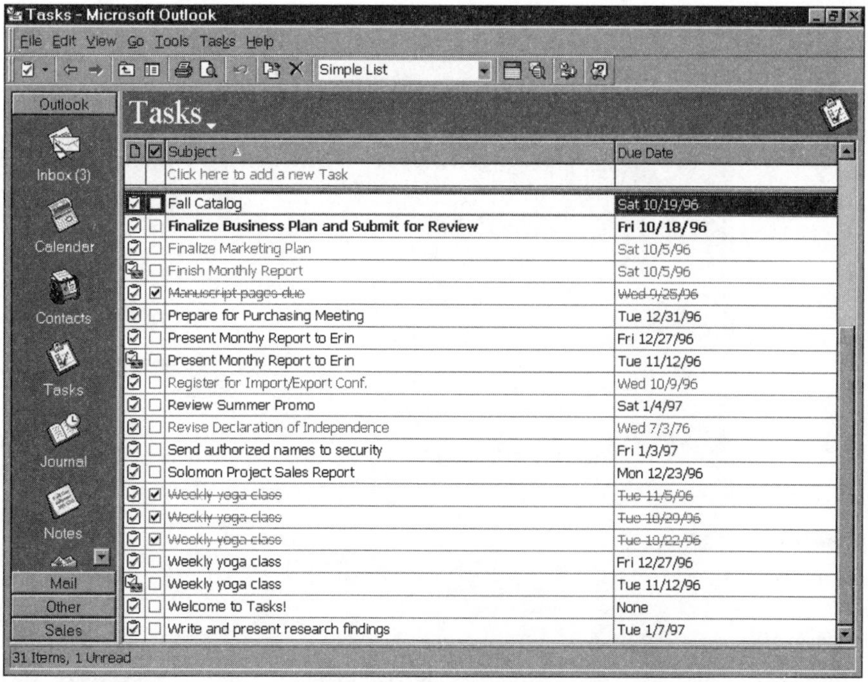

Figure 16-20:
Your tasks in
a Simple
List.

A bar at the top of list displays the names of the columns: Subject and Due Date. If you need to see more information, you can open the task by double-clicking its name in the list or by switching to a more detailed view.

Detailed List

If you need to keep track of more information than the Simple List contains, the Detailed List adds priority, status, completion, and category information. Considering how many items of information you can include in a task, it's not all that detailed, but you can always customize the Detailed List or create a new one to suit your taste. For more about customizing views, see Chapter 5.

Here's how you view your Detailed List of tasks:

1. **Choose View⊷Current View.**

   The list of current views appears.

2. **Choose Detailed List.**

   You see your tasks in more detail (see Figure 16-21).

Priority column

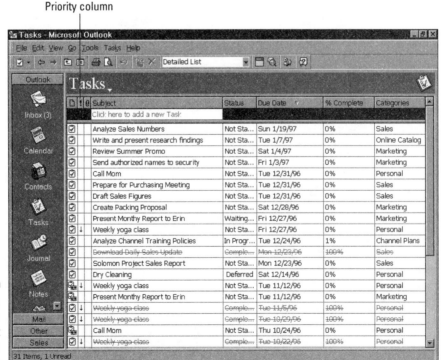

Figure 16-21: Your tasks in Detailed List view.

The column at the left with the exclamation point at the top is the Priority column. If you click the Priority box for any task, Outlook allows you to choose High, Normal, or Low. The paper clip thingy represents an attachment — you can attach any kind of file, such as a spreadsheet or word-processing document, to any Outlook item. You might want to attach a document to a task that reminds you to complete the document. If your task is "Revise Monthly Sales Report," for example, you can attach the report to the task. Then when you open the task, you can just double-click the icon in the Task form and the report itself opens, ready for your revision.

Active Tasks

Of course you're proud of all the tasks that you've completed, but you don't have to keep looking at them. The Active Tasks list shows you only the tasks that you still have to do.

Here's how to see your Active Tasks:

1. **Choose View⇨Current View.**

   The list of current views appears. You can also click the Current View scroll down menu on the toolbar.

2. **Choose Active Tasks.**

   Your list includes only those tasks that you've still to complete.

This list looks a lot like the Detailed List, without the completed tasks and the space at the top that says `Click here to add a new task.` That's just what it is. The Active Tasks view leaves out the completed tasks in order to give you a shorter list that only includes the tasks you still need to complete. You can choose File⇨New or press Ctrl+N to open the Task dialog box and create a new task.

Next Seven Days

There's no time like the present, so you can use Next Seven Days view to focus on the work that you need to do this week.

Here's how to call see your next seven days at a glance:

1. **Choose View⇨Current View.**

   The list of current views appears. You can also click the Current View scroll down menu on the toolbar.

2. **Choose Next Seven Days.**

   You see a list of the tasks you have due in the next week.

As you can in all the other Tasks list views, you can edit the information that you see about a task directly in Next Seven Days view. For example, you can change the name of a task by clicking on the name itself and typing in a new name. You may also want to change the status and completion percentage as you get within seven days of a task's due date.

Overdue Tasks

Now and then, stuff happens, and you don't finish your tasks on time. Even if you forget, Outlook remembers and shows your overdue tasks in red to alert you.

Here's how to view the bad news about your dropped deadlines:

1. **Choose View➪Current View.**

   The list of current views appears.

2. **Choose Overdue Tasks.**

   You see a list of the tasks you're behind on (see Figure 16-22).

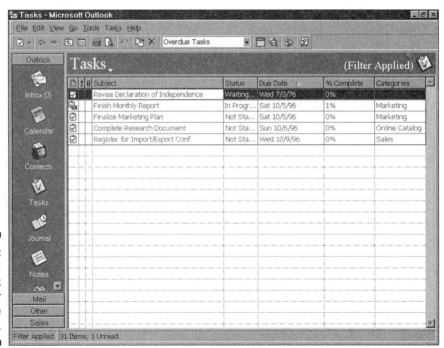

Figure 16-22:
You're late!
Outlook
groups your
Overdue
Tasks.

If you want to sort your Overdue Tasks according to the information in one of the columns of the list, just click the title of that list. If you want your Overdue Tasks sorted in order of how overdue each item is, for example, click the words Due Date at the top of the column.

By Category

The By Category view looks quite different than the other views I describe. By Category view is a grouped view, rather than a Table view, which means that tasks are clumped together according to the categories you've assigned them instead of being presented in a continuous list. You may only see the name of the category with a plus sign next to it, which means that a clump of tasks listed under it will show up if you click the plus sign. Then the plus sign turns into a minus sign, and the tasks in that category are revealed.

Here's how to view your tasks By Category:

1. **Choose View⊏>Current View.**

   The list of current views appears.

2. **Choose By Category.**

   Your tasks are grouped by category (see Figure 16-23).

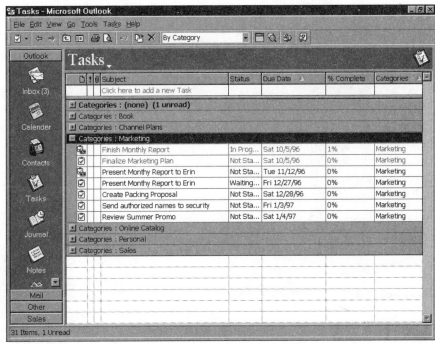

Figure 16-23: How many categories? Let me count the types.

The other big difference in the By Category view is that a single task may turn up more than once if you've assigned it to more than one category. You might create a task to send holiday cards to your key customers, for example. You could assign the categories Holiday Cards and Key Customer to the task, and the task would show up in both groups in By Category view.

Assignment

If you've assigned tasks to other people (see "Assigning a Task to Someone Else" earlier in the chapter), Assignment view shows you what you've assigned to whom and how the task is progressing.

To use the Assignment view:

1. **Choose View⇨Current View.**

   The list of current views appears.

2. **Choose Assignment.**

   You see the tasks that you've assigned to others (see Figure 16-24).

Figure 16-24:
Delegating is the mark of a good leader. Assignment view lets you see how you measure up.

You can delete a task from your list in Assignment view, but if you've assigned the task to someone else, that person will still have it. You'll have to let him or her know that you no longer need the task to be done.

By Person Responsible

The By Person Responsible view contains the same information as Assignment view, but it groups the tasks according to the name of the person you've assigned to finish each task. It works like the By Category view that I describe in a previous section.

To see your tasks By Person Responsible:

1. Choose View➪Current View.

The list of current views appears.

2. Choose By Person Responsible.

You see the names of the people to whom you've assigned tasks, with plus or minus signs next to the names (see Figure 16-25). A plus sign means that you can see a group of tasks under that name when you click the plus sign.

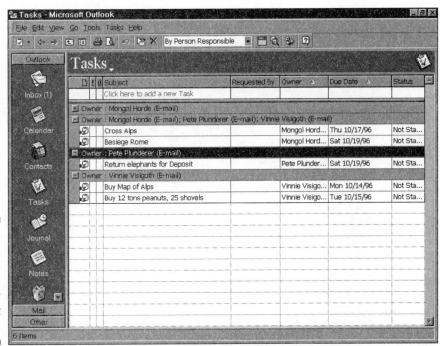

Figure 16-25: By Person Responsible view lets you know who's most responsible.

3. To view the tasks that you've assigned to a person, click the plus sign next to that person's name.

If there's a minus sign, you're seeing all the tasks there are to see for that person. If there's a minus sign next to the person's name and you see no tasks under their name, no tasks are assigned to that person.

Completed Tasks

"What have you been doing all this time?" Funny you should ask. The Completed Tasks list gives you a quick view of everything you've done and when you did it. So there!

To see how much you've done and take a well-earned breath:

1. Choose View⇨Current View.

The list of current views appears.

2. Choose Completed Tasks.

You see how much you've accomplished (see Figure 16-26).

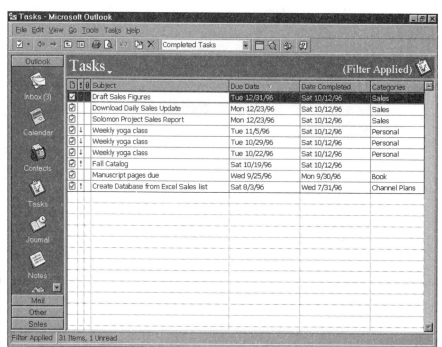

Figure 16-26:
A Completed
Tasks list.

If you want to sort the Completed Tasks list in order of when you finished each task or when each task was due, just click the title at the top of the appropriate column.

Task Timeline

Task Timeline is one of the more interesting views in the Tasks list. This view draws you a picture of what tasks are due when. If you've assigned start dates and due dates, Task Timeline view draws a graph, with lines representing the length of each task.

Here's how to set up a Task Timeline:

1. **Choose View⇨Current View.**

   The list of current views appears.

2. **Choose Task Timeline.**

   You see a graph with a timeline for your tasks (see Figure 16-27).

The little icons in the Task Timeline are actually shortcuts to the Task form where all the task data is stored. You can see details of a task by right-clicking the icon next to the task and choosing Open.

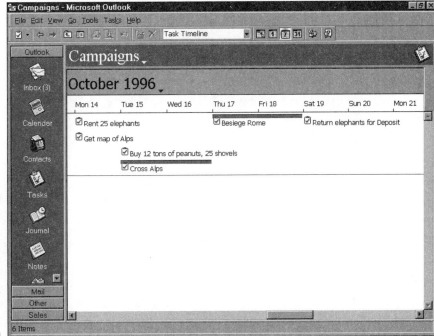

Figure 16-27:
You see the ebb and flow of your tasks in Task Timeline view.

Chapter 17

Going Public with Discussion Folders

. . . .

In This Chapter

▶ Adding new items to a public folder

▶ Replying to items in an existing public folder

▶ Copying items to a public folder

▶ Understanding the Microsoft Exchange server and other
messaging and groupware technologies

. . . .

*P*eople who use Outlook at work, on their company's network, may have
some features that computer users at home don't have. One of them is the
ability to use public folders. *Public folders* are places that a whole group of
people can look at and add items. You can have a public folder for tasks or
contacts. You can also create a public folder which contains messages, a lot like
your Inbox, except that everybody can add messages and read the same set of
messages. This kind of arrangement is often called a *bulletin board;* you post a
message, someone replies to it, a third party then replies to both of you, and so
on. It's a method of conducting a group conversation without having all the
parties to the conversation available at the same time.

The capability to use public folders is one of the convenient features of Outlook
that is more available to a corporate computer user than to a person using a
stand-alone machine. If you're using a stand-alone machine you don't generally
need public folders, since you're the only one on the machine.

It's possible to use a set of public folders by connecting over the Internet to a
computer running Microsoft Exchange Server, but making that kind of connection is beyond the scope of this book. If you do find yourself using public
folders on the Internet, the process you follow to do so is no different than what
I describe here.

In Outlook, public folders look just like any other folders. A public folder may
contain a Contact list that the entire company shares or a Tasks list used by an
entire department. You can set up a public discussion folder for an ongoing
group conference about topics of interest to everyone sharing the folder, such

as current company news. You can also use a public discussion folder to collect opinions about decisions that have to be made or as an intra-company classified ad system. Any kind of information that you'd like to exchange among groups of people on your network can be organized as a public folder.

When you click a public folder, you see a list of items that looks like a list of e-mail messages, except that all the messages are addressed to the folder instead of to a person. In a public folder, you can change your view of the items, add items, or reply to items that someone else entered.

Viewing a Public Folder

Your company may maintain a public folder for an ongoing online discussion about important issues in your business or as a company bulletin board for announcements about activities, benefits, and other news.

To view a public folder:

1. **Choose <u>V</u>iew⇨Fold<u>e</u>r List or click the Folder List button in the toolbar.**

   The Folder List appears (see Figure 17-1).

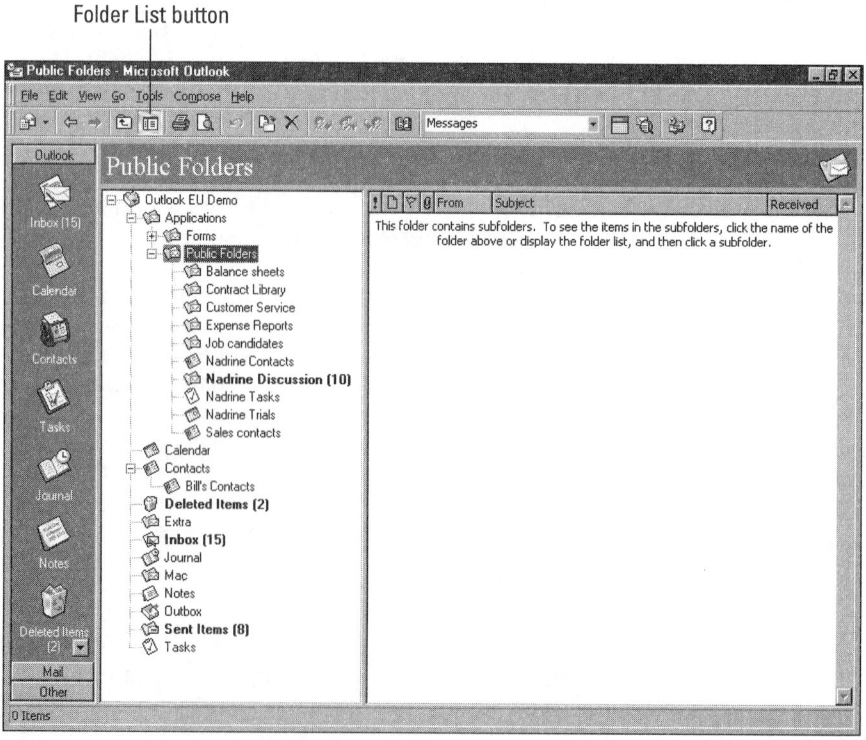

Folder List button

Figure 17-1:
The Folder
List with
public
folders.

2. Click the name of the folder you want to see.

The list of items in the folder appears.

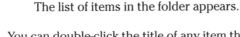

You can double-click the title of any item that you see to view the contents of that item.

Adding New Items

Many public folders are organized as open discussions in which anyone can put in his or her two cents' worth. All the messages can be read by anybody, so everybody reads and replies to everybody else. If you view a folder and find it's full of messages from different people all replying to one another, you're looking at a discussion folder.

To add new items to a public folder:

1. Choose View⇨Folder List or click the Folder List button in the toolbar.

The Folder List appears.

2. Click the name of the folder.

The list of messages in the folder appears.

3. Choose File⇨New⇨Post in This Folder.

The New Item form appears (see Figure 17-2).

4. Type a subject and your message.

5. Click Post.

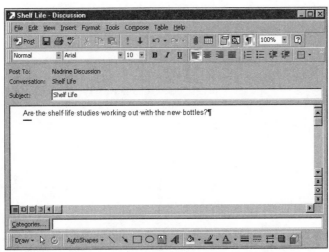

Figure 17-2:
The New
Item form.

Now your message is part of the list of items in the folder.

Replying to Items in an Existing Public Discussion Folder

Good manners and good sense say that if you want to join a discussion, the best thing to do is respond to what the other members of the discussion are saying. But be nice — posting nasty responses to people in an online discussion group is called *flaming*. Flaming is not well regarded but not uncommon. Flaming creates online conversations that most people don't want to participate in. What good is a discussion when nobody talks? Besides, flaming in the workplace can get you fired. So cool down.

When you're participating in public folder discussions at work, assume that everything you write will be read by everyone in the company, from the top executives to the newest temp. Check your spelling, DON'T WRITE IN CAPITAL

Are you being served?

A great deal goes on behind the scenes in Outlook. Any number of products may be feeding messages and other information to Outlook if you're on an office network. Some of those other products are Lotus Notes, Novell GroupWise, and Microsoft Exchange Server. All three products are usually categorized as groupware, which means that they have features that enable groups of people to collaborate by sharing files, folders, and discussion forums.

New features could turn up on your computer in the future, thanks to these other programs, including receiving fax messages and voice mail in your Inbox and sending messages to pagers. If you're using Outlook, it may look as though Outlook is providing all the fancy new services, but looks can deceive.

Microsoft Exchange Server is one of the products that may be working silently in the background and adding features to Outlook without your ever knowing it. You never need to know,

really, except that if Microsoft Exchange Server is in the background, you'll be able to share folders with other people and create collaborative collections of information that all of you can use at the same time. If you're using Outlook on an office network, check with your system administrator to see what features are available to you.

Exchange Server will never call attention to itself, so you won't know from looking whether you're using it. The possibilities are striking, though. Beyond allowing you to use public folders, Exchange Server allows you and your coworkers to share your schedules, so that you can plan meetings without having to play phone tag.

If you're on a stand-alone system and don't have Exchange Server installed, you can still benefit from Exchange Server through an Internet connection. You can log on to a site on the Internet and view public folders.

LETTERS (IT LOOKS LIKE YOU'RE SHOUTING), and use discretion in what you say and how you say it. The same rule applies to interoffice e-mail; you don't know who reads what you send.

To reply to items in a public discussion folder:

1. **Double-click the item that you want to reply to.**

   The item opens so that you can read it.

2. **Click the Post Reply button in the toolbar.**

   The Discussion Reply form appears. The text of the message to which you're replying is already posted in the form (see Figure 17-3).

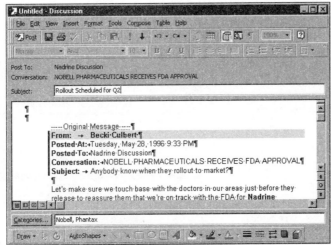

Figure 17-3:
Use the Discussion Reply form to add your comments to a public discussion.

3. **Type your subject and reply.**

4. **Click Post.**

Your item joins the list of discussion items.

Moving Items to a Public Folder

Not all public folders are discussion folders. Public folders can be designed to hold any type of item. You can share lists of tasks, calendars, or files of other types. You don't have to create a public folder item in the folder where you want the item to end up; you can create a task in your own Tasks list, for example, and then move it to a public task folder.

To move items to a public folder:

1. **Right-click the item that you want to move.**

   A menu appears (see Figure 17-4).

2. **Click Move to Folder.**

   A dialog box that includes the Folder List appears.

3. **Click the folder to which you want to send the item.**

   The name of the folder you clicked is highlighted.

4. **Click OK.**

   Your item moves to its new folder.

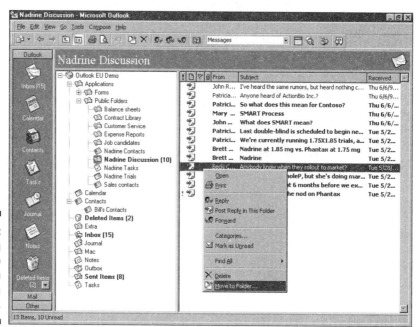

Figure 17-4: Getting ready to move an item to a folder.

For the Public Record

You may be using public folders without even knowing it. In Outlook, all folders look the same, whether you create them yourself on your own PC or whether they're on a corporate network or the Internet. All you really need to know about public folders is that they're public, so whatever you post to a public folder can be seen by anybody who has access to that folder. You can also create your own public folders; check with your system administrator to see if you have the rights to create public folders and a place to put them.

Chapter 18

Mail Merge from Outlook to Microsoft Word

. . . .

In This Chapter

▶ Creating mailing labels

▶ Addressing envelopes

▶ Compiling form letters

▶ Merging from selected contacts

. . . .

*O*utlook and Word 97 were made to work as a team. Word adds its services as your e-mail editor in Outlook, and the Contact list in Outlook is on-call for mail-merge duty. Any information in the Address Book can be plugged into Word so that you can create a Mail Merge, or a repetitive letter which is printed many times with the same contents but each letter is addressed to a different person. You'll use Mail Merge to plug addresses into a form letter most often, but you can include other information as well.

If you already use the Mail Merge feature of Word, you'll enjoy how Outlook manages your address lists and makes using your address lists simple. If you're new to Word or the Mail Merge feature, take a look at *Word 97 For Windows For Dummies*.

Creating Mailing Labels

You can create a set of mailing labels for everybody in your Address Book lickety-split. The Outlook Contact list turns up right in Word's mail-merge dialog boxes, so you won't have to mess around with exporting files and figuring out where they went when you want to merge to them. All you have to do is pick Outlook as the source of your addresses.

To create a set of mailing labels:

1. **Choose Tools⇨Mail Merge.**

   The Mail Merge Helper appears.

2. **Click Create.**

   A drop-down list appears (see Figure 18-1).

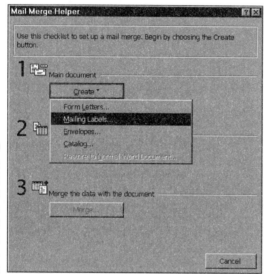

Figure 18-1:
The Mail
Merge
Helper with
the Create
drop-down
list showing.

3. **Choose Mailing Labels.**

   A dialog box appears, asking whether you want to turn the active document window into your mail-merge document or create a new document.

4. **Click the Active Window button.**

   If your active document window contains text that you don't want to use in the mail merge, click the New Main Document button instead. When the dialog box disappears, the choice you make appears in the Mail Merge Helper dialog box.

5. **Click the Get Data button in the Mail Merge Helper.**

   A drop-down menu appears, giving you a choice about where to get the data for your labels.

6. **Choose Use Address Book.**

   A dialog box appears (see Figure 18-2), offering you another choice about which address book to use for your label data.

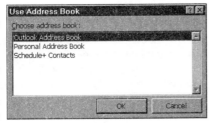

Figure 18-2:
The Use
Address
Book dialog
box.

7. **Click the Outlook Address Book.**

If you have more than one folder designated as your Outlook Address Book, another dialog box appears, asking you to choose which Address Book to use. If in doubt, choose the default by clicking OK; otherwise, pick the one that you know is right.

8. **Click OK.**

A dialog box appears. It has only one button, which says Set Up Main Document.

9. **Click the Set Up Main Document button.**

The Label Options dialog box appears (see Figure 18-3).

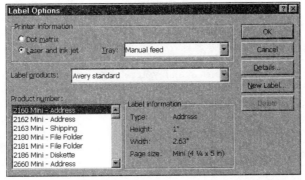

Figure 18-3:
The Label
Options
dialog box.

10. **Choose the label type you want; then click OK to return to the Mail Merge Helper.**

Check the stock number on your label, and make sure it's the same as the one you're choosing. If the stock number isn't available, you can look at the label dimensions in the Label Information section of the Label Options dialog box.

11. **In the Mail Merge Helper, click Insert Merge Field.**

A list of field names appears. The collection of names in the list bears a striking resemblance to the kinds of data that you can enter in the Outlook Contact list. Funny.

12. **Click each piece of data that you want to include in your label.**

For example, on a typical address label, you'd click Insert Merge Field, First_Name, press the spacebar, click Insert Merge Field, Last_Name, press Enter, click Insert Merge Field, and Postal_Address. You don't have to mess with City, State, and Zip, because Outlook deals with the entire mailing address as a single unit.

13. **Click OK.**

The Mail Merge Helper dialog box reappears.

14. **Click the Merge button.**

The Mail Merge dialog box opens.

15. **Click Merge again.**

Again? Yes, there are two Merge buttons. The first button was the Mail Merge Helper; the second one is the actual Merge command.

I like to test a Mail Merge in mailing-label format before doing an actual merge, just to be sure that everything works out. You can print labels on regular paper to see what they look like. If you make a mistake setting up the merge, it's faster to find out by printing ten pages of messed-up "labels" on plain paper than by printing 300 messed-up letters.

Printing Envelopes

You don't have to print to labels at all if you're planning a mass mailing; you can print directly onto the envelopes that you're sending. Make sure that your printer has an envelope feeder. Feeding envelopes one at a time gets old fast.

To print addresses directly onto your envelopes:

1. **Choose Tools⇨Mail Merge.**

The Mail Merge Helper appears.

2. **Click Create.**

A drop-down list appears.

3. **Choose Envelopes.**

A dialog box appears (see Figure 18-4), giving you a choice between adding the envelope to the document that you currently have open on the screen (Active Window) or creating a new main document for the envelope.

4. **Click the New Main Document button.**

A new document is created as your main mail-merge document and you return to the Mail Merge Helper form.

Figure 18-4:
Does your
document
need an
envelope?

5. **Click the Get Data button on the Mail Merge Helper form.**

   A menu drops down, giving you a choice of where to get the names and addresses.

6. **Choose Use Address Book.**

   Another menu appears listing several Address Books, including the Outlook Address Book.

7. **Double-click the Outlook Address Book.**

   If you have more than one Outlook Address Book available, a dialog box appears, asking you to choose the Address Book you want to use.

8. **Click OK to return to the Mail Merge Helper.**

9. **Click the Set Up Main Document button.**

   The Envelope Options dialog box appears, with a choice of envelope sizes (see Figure 18-5).

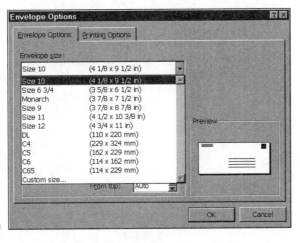

Figure 18-5:
The
Envelope
Options
dialog box
with the
Envelope
Size menu
showing.

10. **Choose the size and type you want to use; then click OK to open the Envelope Address form.**

    Normal business envelopes are number 10; pull down the menu to choose a different size.

11. **Click Insert Merge Field on the Envelope Address form.**

    The list of fields from the Outlook Contact list drops down (see Figure 18-6).

12. **Click each piece of data that you want to include in your envelope.**

    The simplest entry is to click Insert Merge Field, choose Company, press Enter, click Insert Merge Field, and choose Postal_Address. You can add as many fields as will fit on the envelope.

13. **Click OK.**

14. **Click the Merge button.**

    The Merge dialog box appears.

15. **Click Merge again.**

    The merge begins.

If you've never printed multiple envelopes on your printer before, start small. Try printing four or five, just to make sure that your printer feeds envelopes properly. Word and Outlook happily sends your printer a command to print hundreds of envelopes in a flash. If your printer chokes on the fourth envelope, however, fixing the problem can take a long time.

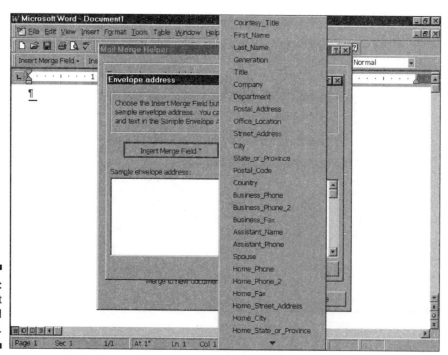

Figure 18-6:
The Insert
Merge Field
list.

Creating a Form Letter from the Contact List

Today I received a personalized invitation to enter a $250,000 sweepstakes that had my name plastered all over the front of the envelope. How thoughtful and personal! Whenever you get a sweepstakes letter with your name already entered, you're getting a form letter. A form letter is a letter with standard text that's printed over and over but with a different name and address printed on each copy. You can send form letters, too, even if you're not holding a sweepstakes. An annual newsletter to family and friends is one form letter you may want to create.

To create a form letter:

1. **Choose Tools⇨Mail Merge.**

   The Mail Merge Helper appears.

2. **Click Create.**

   A drop-down list appears.

3. **Choose Form Letters.**

   A dialog box appears.

4. **Click the Active Window button in the dialog box.**

   You return to the Mail Merge Helper form.

5. **Click the Get Data button.**

   A drop-down menu appears, giving you a choice about where to get the data for your labels (see Figure 18-7).

6. **Choose Use Address Book.**

   Another menu appears, with choices including the Outlook Address Book.

7. **Double-click the Outlook Address Book.**

   If you have more than one Address Book running in Outlook, a dialog box asks you to choose just one as the source of names and addresses for your letters.

8. **Click OK.**

   A dialog box appears, offering you only one choice: Edit Main Document. Go figure.

9. **Click the Edit Main Document button.**

   You return to the Microsoft Word main editing screen, which now has one more toolbar. The new toolbar includes buttons that say Insert Merge Field and Insert Word Field.

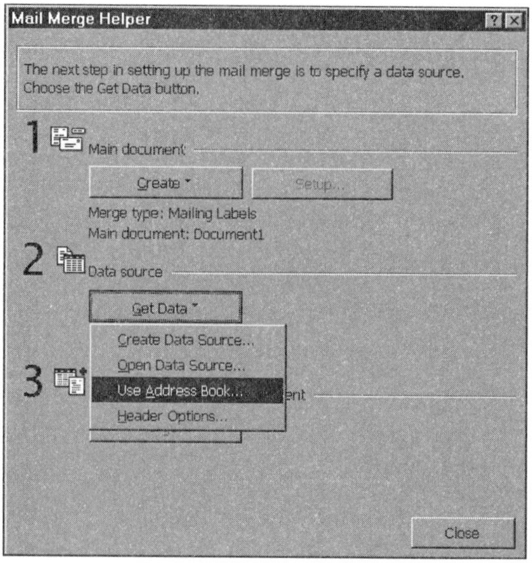

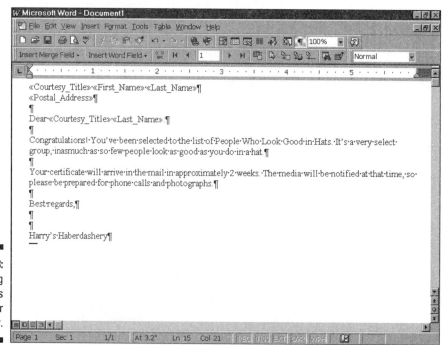

Figure 18-7:
Getting data
for your mail
merge.

10. **Type your form letter and click the Insert Merge Field button to insert merge fields everywhere you want data from your Outlook Address Book to appear in your form letter (see Figure 18-8).**

Figure 18-8:
Adding
merge fields
to your
letter.

Now you don't have to settle for sending impersonal, annoying form letters to dozens of people; you can send a personal, annoying form letter to hundreds of people. If you're planning to send an annoying form letter to me, my address is 1600 Pennsylvania Avenue, Washington, D.C.

Merging Selected Records

You can assemble a large Contact list in Outlook. Chances are that you don't want to send a merge letter to everybody in a 5,000-name Contact list every day. You really should have a way to select a few records in an Outlook Contact list and send a letter to those people.

You don't — at least, not in Outlook.

In this section, I spell out Microsoft's prescribed way of dealing with a selective merge from Outlook, but I think it's a lame method. So if the process doesn't seem to make sense, it's because it doesn't make sense. Sorry. But I'll try my best to make some sense of it for you.

I start with the bottom line. You can merge only an entire Outlook Contact list to Word. You can have more than one Contact list, however, and you can copy names from one list to another. So here's what you do:

1. **Click the Contact icon.**

   The Contact list appears.

2. **Choose File➪New➪Folder.**

   The Create New Folder dialog box appears (see Figure 18-9).

3. **Type a name for your new folder.**

   I like to use something like **Merge Items**. Be sure there's a check mark next to Create a shortcut to this folder in the Outlook Bar. (If there's no check mark, click the check box to enter one.)

4. **Click OK.**

   The new folder appears in the Outlook Bar.

5. **While holding down the Ctrl key, drag the contact items that you want to use in your Mail Merge to the new icon in the Outlook Bar.**

   You now have a new Contact list to use as a merge file.

When you create your main merge document, as I describe earlier, you need to specify Merge Items (or whatever you named the new folder) when Word asks for the name of the Address Book you want to use.

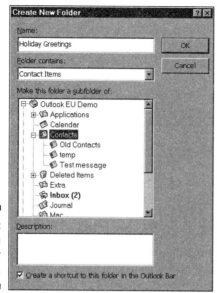

Several things can go wrong when you're merging from a list made of copies of contacts:

✔ If you fail to hold down the Ctrl key when you're dragging the contacts, the contacts will be moved, not copied, so you have to make sure to move the contacts back when you're done by dragging them with your mouse again.

✔ If you have two copies of each contact in your merge list, it's easy to change the wrong one accidentally. The "real" contact and the "temporary" contact don't synchronize automatically. If a contact's phone number or other information has changed, you could easily change the wrong set of information, so don't keep more than one copy of each of your contacts hanging around for too long.

I wish I could find a more sensible way to merge from selected records in Outlook. You have a couple of other ways to get around the problem, such as exporting a file (which defeats the purpose of merging from Outlook) or using some of the advanced features in Word, but those methods are limited. I'm sure that a better selective merge method will be developed in the future, but for now, this is what Microsoft recommends.

Part IV
The Part of Tens

The 5th Wave

By Rich Tennant

"THIS IS YOUR GROUPWARE?! THIS IS WHAT YOU'RE RUNNING?! WELL HECK—I THINK THIS COULD BE YOUR PROBLEM!"

In this part . . .

Top Ten lists are everybody's favorite. They're short. They're easy to read. And they're a perfect spot for writers like me to toss useful stuff that defies fitting easily into the main chapters of the book. Flip through my top ten lists for tips you'll want to use, including a time-saving look at things you can't do with Outlook, so you won't waste your time trying.

Chapter 19

Ten Shortcuts Worth Taking

. . . .

In This Chapter

▶ Using the New Item tool

▶ Adding your floppy drive to the Outlook Bar

▶ Sending a file to e-mail recipient

▶ Sending a file from an Office 97 application

▶ Clicking open the Folder List

▶ Undo-ing

▶ Go To Date

▶ Adding items to list views

▶ Keeping a note open

▶ Navigating with browser buttons

. . . .

*E*ven though computers are said to save you time, you may not think that's true when you're in a hurry and juggling menus, keys, and buttons seems to take all day. Here are some shortcuts that can really save you time and tension as you work.

Use the New Item Tool

To create a new item in whatever module you're in, just click the New Item tool at the far left end of the toolbar. The icon changes when you change modules, so it becomes a New Task icon in the Tasks module, a New Contact icon in the Contacts module, and so on. You can also click the arrow next to the New Item tool to pull down the New Item menu (see Figure 19-1).

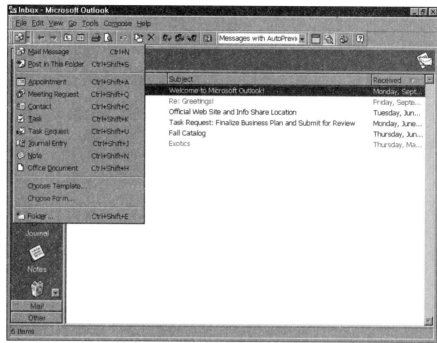

Figure 19-1:
The New
Item tool
with the
New Item
menu pulled
down.

When you choose an item from the New Item menu, you can create a new item in an Outlook module other than the one you're in without changing modules. If you're answering e-mail, for example, and you want to create a note, pull down the New Item menu, choose Note, create your note, and then go on working with your e-mail.

Add Your Floppy Drive to the Outlook Bar

I find adding an icon for my floppy drive to the Outlook Bar to be a great time-saver. I normally run Outlook along with whatever other program I'm running, so I can always switch to it easily.

To add your floppy drive to your Outlook Bar, follow these steps:

1. **Click the Other group separator bar in the Outlook Bar.**

   The Other group is where you go to manage files and folders.

2. **Click the My Computer icon.**

   Your list of drives appears.

3. Right-click the floppy-drive icon.

A shortcut menu appears.

4. Choose Add to Outlook Bar.

An icon for your floppy drive appears in the Outlook Bar.

Now you can just click the floppy-drive icon in the Outlook Bar to move or copy files from your floppy drive to other drives on your system.

Send a File to an E-Mail Recipient

You can send a file by Outlook E-mail with only a few mouse clicks. Here's how:

1. Right-click the file that you want to send after choosing Go⇨My Computer.

A menu appears.

2. Choose Send To.

Another menu appears.

3. Choose Mail Recipient.

A New Message form appears, displaying an icon that represents the file in the text box to indicate that the file is attached to the message.

4. Type the subject of the file and the name of the person to whom you're sending the file.

If you want to add comments to your message, type them in the text box, where the icon for the file is.

5. Click Send.

Your message goes to the Outbox. Then press F5 to send it on its way. If you send your files by modem, you also have to press F5 to dial your e-mail service.

Send a File from an Office 97 Application

You can e-mail any Office 97 document from the Office application itself, without using Outlook's E-Mail module.

1. Open an Office 97 document that you want to send in the application that created it.

2. **Choose File⇨Send.**

A New Message form appears, displaying an icon for the file in the text box to indicate that the file is attached to the message.

3. **Type the subject of the file and the name of the person to whom you're sending the file.**

If you want to add comments to your message, type them in the text box where the icon for the file is.

4. **Click Send.**

Your message goes to the Outbox. If you send your files by modem, you also have to switch to Outlook and press F5 to dial your e-mail service.

Click Open the Folder List

If you need to open the Folder List for only a second to open a folder, just click the name of the Outlook module that you're using (Calendar, Tasks, and so on) where it appears in large type just above the Information Viewer. A small triangle next to the name of the module indicates that you can click there to drop the Folder List for one operation. The Folder List drops down until you click it, or click something else; then it disappears.

Undo

If you don't know about the Undo command, it's time that you heard the good news. When you make a mistake, you can undo it by pressing Ctrl+Z or choosing Edit⇨Undo. So feel free to experiment; the worst that you'll have to do is undo! (Of course, you must undo it right away, before you do too many things to undo at one time.)

Go To Date

You can use the Go To Date command in all Calendar and Timeline views (see Figure 19-2). If you're looking at the Calendar, for example, and you want to skip ahead 60 days, press Ctrl+G and type **60 days from now**. The Calendar advances 60 days from the current date.

Figure 19-2:
The Go To
Date dialog
box.

Add Items to List Views

Many Outlook lists have a blank line at the top where you can type an entry and create a new item for that list. When you see the words Click here to add a new task, that's exactly what they mean. Just click in that line and type your new item.

Keep a Note Open

If you like to keep random notes throughout the day, open a note and leave it open. When a note is open, an icon appears in the Windows 95 taskbar at the bottom of the screen. To edit today's note, click the note's icon at the bottom of the screen; the note pops up again. When you see a note, you can click in it and edit what you see. Click any part of any other application screen that you can see and you'll return to that application. If you want to close the note, right-click the note's icon on the taskbar and choose Close.

Navigate with Browser Buttons

The toolbar has two buttons with blue arrows that point away from each other. These buttons serve as *browser buttons*. When you change from one Outlook module to another and then want to change back, click the button with the arrow that points to the left. To change to the second module again, click the button with the arrow that points to the right.

If you're accustomed to using Web browsers such as Netscape or Microsoft Internet Explorer, you'll find that the Outlook browser buttons work exactly the same way as the navigation buttons in your Web browser.

Chapter 20

Ten Office 97 Tricks for Creating Snappier E-Mail

* *

In This Chapter

▶ Animated text

▶ New table tools

▶ Office Art

▶ Hyperlinks

▶ Document Map

▶ Versions

▶ Browsing

▶ Automatic grammar checking

▶ Excel conditional formatting

▶ Merged Excel cells

▶ Angled Excel text

* *

*O*utlook can use Word 97 as an e-mail editor, which means that you can create extremely cool e-mail like you've never seen before — graphics, special effects, you name it. E-mail was never this much fun.

If you're an old hand at Microsoft Office and feel confident that you know what you need to know to get around Office 97, you're probably right. Everything that you knew from before still works; Outlook is the only new part of Microsoft Office. If you're not familiar with Microsoft Office, pick up a copy of *Microsoft Office 97 For Windows For Dummies* from IDG Books Worldwide, Inc. (Okay, another plug, but have I steered you wrong so far?) The other parts of Office have acquired some really cool new features that can help you create attractive, impressive documents to send by e-mail. This chapter describes some of my favorites.

Tricks that Work in Word

When you want to dream up snazzy-looking e-mail text, Word is your tool. These tricks help customize your e-mail text to give it punch and pizzazz.

Animated text

Now you can put your message in blinking lights (in your e-mail, anyway). Blinking, flashing, or sparkling text is easy to create. Just follow these steps:

1. **Select the text that you want to animate.**

2. **Choose Format➪Font (or right-click the selected text and choose Font).**

   The Font dialog box appears.

3. **Click the Animation tab.**

   The Animations page of the Font dialog box appears, including a list of animation effects (see Figure 20-1).

4. **Choose an animation effect, such as Sparkle Text.**

   A sample of the animation effect appears at the bottom of the dialog box.

5. **Click OK.**

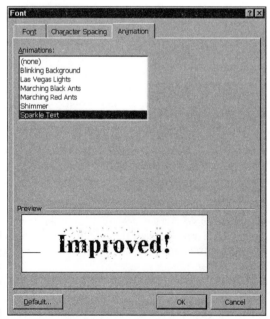

Figure 20-1: The Animations page.

Animated text, of course, is not useful for a document that you plan to print or for e-mail that goes to someone who is not set up to read animated text, but it's great for calling attention to text in your interoffice e-mail.

Table tools

The new Table tools are wild! Just grab a pencil tool and start drawing boxes; then draw lines in the boxes and erase some of the lines. You just have to try these tools. Tables will never be the same.

To use the Table tools:

1. **Choose T̲able⇨Draw Table.**

   A special Table toolbar appears.

2. **Click the Draw Table button in the Table toolbar.**

   This button is the little pencil at the left end of the toolbar.

3. **Drag a diagonal line to draw a box where you want the table to be.**

   You've got to see this to appreciate it (see Figure 20-2).

Figure 20-2:
Use these
neat tools to
create a
table.

Table Tools

4. Draw lines where you want to divide the table.

You can create the strangest tables you ever imagined just by dragging that pencil around. It's as much fun to create tables in Word 97 as it is to create strange drawings in the Paint accessory that comes with Windows. (If you haven't tried making strange drawings with Paint, give it a try. There's no better way to get comfortable with using a mouse.)

Office Art

Office Art is so cool that I could easily write an entire chapter — if not an entire book — on it. I think Office Art is nearly as cool as Outlook. Nearly, I said. Here's how to use Office Art:

1. Click the Drawing button in the toolbar.

The Drawing toolbar appears.

2. Click one of the drawing buttons to create drawn objects in your document.

The toolbar includes a great collection of predefined shapes, as well as tools for rotating, aligning, and editing the graphics that you've drawn (see Figure 20-3).

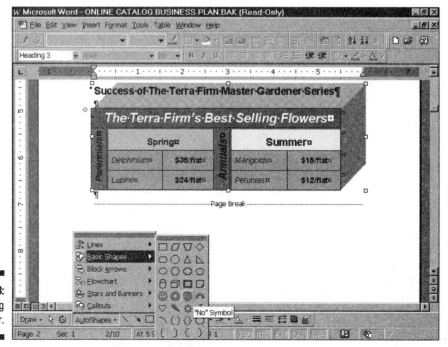

Figure 20-3:
The Drawing toolbar.

3. Click any text to return to text-entry mode.

You can also place graphics on top of your text or wrap text around a drawing.

Hyperlinks

The Internet-hyperlink mania has struck Office 97 like a tidal wave. You can create links from any Office document to a Web page as well as to another Office document. Linking is a method of letting you move from one document to another by using your mouse to click on a picture or specially formatted text (usually underlined blue text) that makes the document you're looking at disappear and another appear. You create your own web of links between Office documents that acts like the World Wide Web, but better; it's quicker and more versatile, and you can create it yourself.

To create a hyperlink:

1. Click the Insert Hyperlink button in the toolbar.

The Insert Hyperlink dialog box appears (see Figure 20-4).

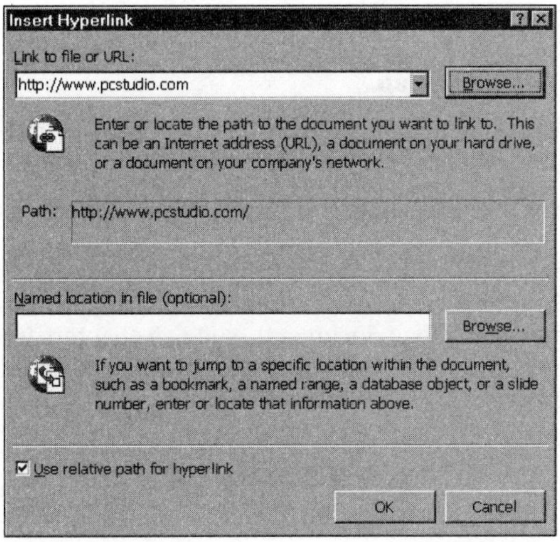

Figure 20-4:
The Insert
Hyperlink
dialog box.

2. Enter the Internet address (URL) of the Web page or the file name of the Office document that you want to link to.

You can also click the Browse button and select the file that you want to link.

3. **If you're creating a link to another Office document, enter the cell address (for an Excel spreadsheet) or the bookmark name (for a Word document) in the Named Location in File box.**

Including a link in an e-mail message is a handy way to refer to information without creating an enormous message. To call your reader's attention to a file on the Internet or on your local network (as long as you're both on the same network), just include a link in your document to the file that you want your reader to see.

4. **Click OK.**

Your link appears in the document in blue underlined text, just like it would on the World Wide Web.

Document Map

To get where you're going quickly, use a map. Word 97 can show you a map of your document right alongside the document itself. The Document Map is an outline of your document that sits to the right of the free-text version on-screen. You can move between widely separated sections of your document with a single click of the heading.

To use a Document Map:

1. **Choose View⇨Document Map.**

Any text to which you've assigned a Heading style appears in the Document Map, becoming the mileposts of your Document Map (see Figure 20-5).

2. **Click the name of the heading to the text that you'd like to read.**

It's easy to click among the headings and swiftly navigate your document, just like having a table of contents alongside it. I find it especially handy to use the Document Map when creating long documents, such as chapters for this book. I can jump back and forth between headings to get a quick look at different parts of my document without having to scroll up and down.

Versions

I confess: I'm a compulsive reviser. I revise documents over and over. I revise some things so much, I can't remember what they were supposed to be about in the first place. I'll get help; I promise. But first, I've got to show you the repeat reviser's dream: versions. You can keep a separate version of each revision of a document that you make. Then you can go back to an earlier version after you've revised the first version beyond recognition. You can also revise some-one else's revisions and not lose either set of revisions.

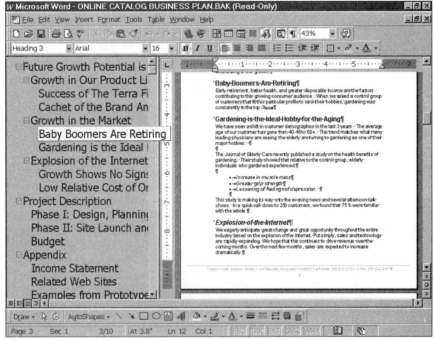

Figure 20-5:
Traverse
your
document
with a
Document
Map.

Here's how to keep different versions:

1. **Choose File⇨Versions.**

   The Versions dialog box appears (see Figure 20-6).

2. **Click the Save Now button.**

   The Comments dialog box appears. You can enter a brief description of the current version and say what you think of it.

3. **Type your comments, if any, about the version that you're currently saving.**

Remember that other people can see your comments, so entering a comment like "A great improvement on the boss's illiterate version" is not advisable. The boss might suggest that you use the Version feature to create a new version of your résumé.

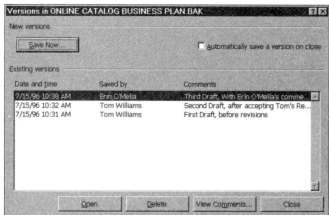

Figure 20-6:
Have as
many
versions as
you want,
complete
with
comments.

Browsing

There's more to Word than just words; you can find tables, fields, graphics, and good old-fashioned pages in a Word 97 document. You can use the Object browser to skip from one table to the next or to move from field to field, or even from edit to edit.

To use the Object browser:

1. **Click the Select Browse object in the scroll bar.**

    The Browse Object flyout menu shows you the tools you can use for browsing (see Figure 20-7).

2. **Choose the type of object that you'd like to browse on.**

    A nice round dozen choices should suffice. A ToolTip tells you the function of each object.

3. **Click the Next button to move to the following object of the type that you selected or click Previous to move to the preceding object of that type.**

I particularly like the tool that moves you from one edit to the next; it works only on edits for the current session of Word, but even that's a big help. A reviseaholic like me needs to know where the next revision is.

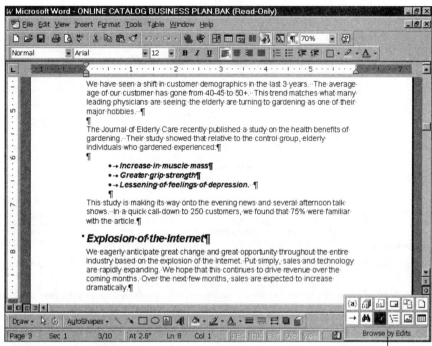

Figure 20-7: Ready to browse?

Browser flyout menu

Check grammar as you type

I have another confession: I slept through the classes where they taught sentence diagramming. I'm never sure when who is what to whom, grammaticallywise. You may have seen the wavy red underlines that Word puts below misspelled words; now there's a wavy green line that Word uses to show that your grammar ain't what it ought to be. As you can tell from this paragraph, you can turn off automatic grammar checking.

To use the grammar checker:

1. **Right-click text that has a green underline.**

   A little flyout menu appears (see Figure 20-8), displaying a list of suggested revisions and a little grammar lecture (just what I wanted).

2. **Choose the option that you prefer.**

   Throwing a spitball is no longer a choice (not that you could ever get away with it in grammar school).

3. **Click OK.**

Now you ain't got no more excuse for no bad grammar.

Grammar menu ⌐

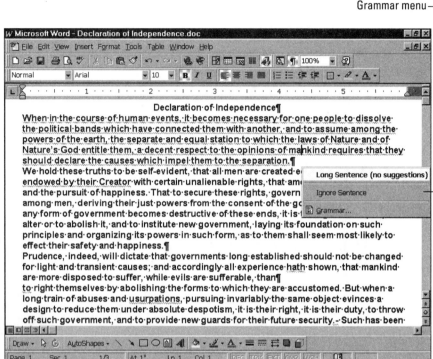

Figure 20-8:
Click on the wavy green lines to see the Grammar menu.

Tricks You Can Do in Excel

You can send Excel spreadsheets by e-mail or include portions of spreadsheets in the Word documents that make up your e-mail messages. So the new features of Excel should be part of your palette if you want to create impressive e-mail.

Apply conditional formatting

Spreadsheets full of numbers don't have much visual pizzazz. Excel has a new way to make a list of numbers mean something at first glance; it's called conditional formatting.

Imagine a chart of average daily temperatures for a year. You could create conditional formatting that would make any cell that contains a temperature below 32 degrees chilly blue and any cell with a temperature above 72 degrees hot red. That way, you can tell the warmer days from the cooler ones at first glance, without having to study the numbers and without making a chart.

To apply conditional formatting:

1. **Select the range of cells to which you want to apply conditional formatting.**

2. **Choose F̲ormat⇨Conditional Formatting.**

   The Conditional Formatting dialog box appears (see Figure 20-9).

3. **Set rules for formatting, such as** `If Value Is Greater Than 50.`

   Choose the conditions from the Condition box.

4. **Set formatting that will apply if the condition is met.**

   You can set more than one condition. In my high–low temperature example, you need to set two conditions. Set one condition for temperatures below 32 degrees; then click the Add button and add a second condition for temperatures above 72 degrees.

5. **Click OK.**

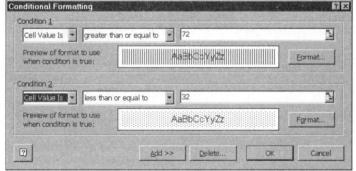

Figure 20-9:
The
Conditional
Formatting
dialog box.

After you create conditional formatting, it stays there until you remove it, even if the formatting isn't showing. In the example, temperatures between 32 degrees and 72 degrees had conditional formatting, but the formatting didn't show unless the temperature listed in the cell crossed the threshhold for conditional formatting (in this case, below 32 or above 72). If you entered a number below 32 or above 72, you'd see the cell change to blue or red.

Merge Excel cells

Spreadsheets used to be nothing but rows and columns — nothing fancy; just rows and columns. Now you can merge cells vertically and horizontally to your heart's content.

To merge cells in Excel:

1. Select the cells that you want to merge.

2. Click the Merge Cells button in the toolbar.

All the cells that you highlighted are now one cell (see Figure 20-10).

If you still worry about things like cell names, the new one takes the name of the upper-leftmost cell that you selected. You can put a formula, a number, or plain text in the merged cell.

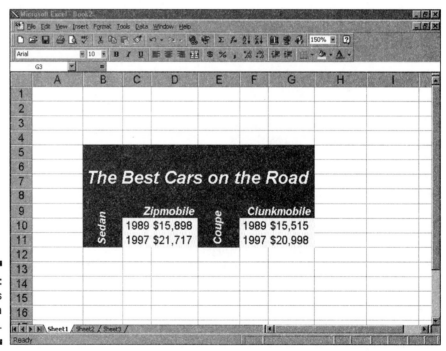

Figure 20-10:
Outlook has completed a merger.

Angle Excel text

Those true-blue, pencil-necked number crunchers don't need cute text effects like rotated text, but to the rest of us, rotated text looks better. That's enough for me. The ability to angle text by rotating it also gives you some options for creating more professional layouts.

Here's how to reorient your boring old cells:

1. **Select the cells that contain the text you want to rotate.**

2. **Choose Format⇨Cells (or press Ctrl+1).**

   The Format Cells dialog box appears (see Figure 20-11).

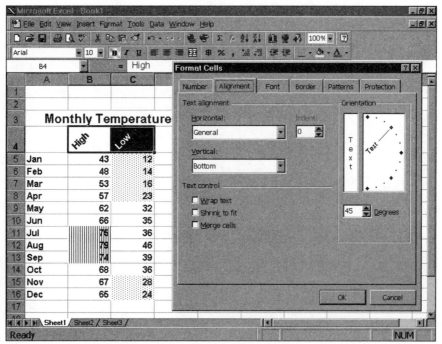

Figure 20-11:
The Format
Cells
dialog box.

3. **Click the Alignment tab.**

   The Orientation box shows the current angle of the selected text.

4. **Drag the angle indicator to the angle that you desire.**

   You can also set the angle by typing a number in the Degrees box.

5. **Click OK.**

   The cells that you selected resize to accommodate the angled text.

Now for This Message

Use the creative tools in Office 97 to make your e-mail messages jump off the screen and grab your reader's attention.

Be aware, however, that not everybody to whom you can send e-mail can get the special effects you create. Many Internet e-mail recipients still get by on plain text, so your creativity may be lost on them until everybody in the world uses nothing but the latest Microsoft products (that sounds a little scary to me).

But when you're creating messages for people who have what you have, such as people in your own office, go ahead and knock 'em dead with your snazzy e-mail tricks.

Chapter 21

Ten Things Outlook Can Do That Windows Explorer Can't

● ●

In This Chapter

▶ Print a list of files

▶ Rearrange columns

▶ Format columns

▶ Group views

▶ Display Office 97 document comments

▶ Create custom views of each folder

▶ Save different views of each folder

▶ Create views based on document properties

▶ Sort, group, and view by predefined criteria

▶ Show files on Document Timeline

● ●

*F*or copying, moving, and organizing your files, Outlook file-management skills blow those of the Windows Explorer away. When you get the hang of creating and customizing views in Tasks, Calendar, or any of Outlook's other modules, you find that using the same features in the Outlook Folder view gives you abilities that you never thought of. You'll be able to do things that you didn't know you wanted to do until you started doing them; then you won't know how you did without.

Print a List of Files

The capability to print a list of files is way overdue. MS-DOS has been around for more than 15 years, piling up files like there's no tomorrow, but it never gave you a decent way to print a list of your files. Yeah, you could use some half-baked method like PrintScreen or some really geeky workaround, but you couldn't just click Print anywhere and print a list of files.

Why would you want a list? Suppose that you're doing something weird, like writing a book. (Okay, I told you it's weird, but bear with me.) You keep each chapter in a separate file, and you want to print a list of how many chapters are done. Keep all the finished chapters in one folder, open the folder in Outlook, and just click Print. Hooray! (I'm so easy to entertain.)

To print a list of files:

1. Select a file or group of files that you want to print a list of.

You don't have to select anything. If you do nothing, Outlook prints the entire list.

2. Choose File⇨Print (or press Ctrl+P).

The Print dialog box appears (see Figure 21-1).

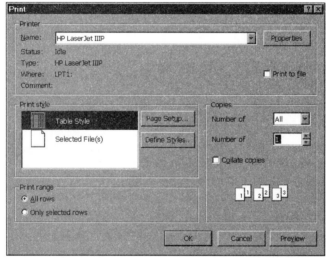

Figure 21-1:
The Print
dialog box.

3. Choose Table Style from the Print Style list.

Outlook prints a list.

We're talking about printing a list of files here. The other choice in the Print Style list (Memo Style) prints the *actual files*. That printing could take a long time if you've selected several files or, worse, if you've selected nothing and plan to print everything in the list. I have more than a thousand documents in my main document folder, which wouldn't finish printing until I'm on Social Security. Be sure that you pick Table Style unless you've chosen only a few documents or you have a great deal of time on your hands (and a great deal of paper).

4. **If you want to print a list of only the files that you select, choose Only Selected Rows in the Print Range section.**

If you want to print the entire list of files visible in the Folder view that you've chosen, choose All Rows.

5. **Click OK.**

Your list of files is printed.

Your printed list of files looks quite a bit like the list that was displayed on-screen, so you may want to format your list carefully before printing it by clicking the Page Setup button in the Print dialog box. You can choose a different font and layout of the page from the choices in the dialog box.

Rearrange Columns

You can move a column to a new location simply by dragging its heading. Doing this is handy when you're looking to clear some disk space, so you want to find the largest, oldest files that you have and see which ones you can delete (see Figure 21-2).

If you're looking for files created by a certain author before a certain date, dragging the Author and Date fields together and sorting by Author gives you an idea.

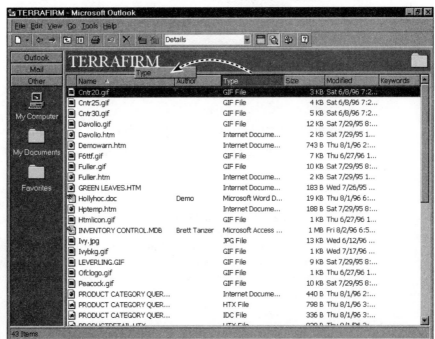

Figure 21-2: Rearranging columns makes it easier for you to organize your files.

Format Columns

You have always been able to format columns in a spreadsheet program such as Excel; now you can do the same thing when you view any of your files with Outlook. The most useful reason to format columns is to change the Date format to take up less space or to choose your size styles (such as 1,000KB, 1MB, or 1,000,000 bytes). Another reason is to control how you list of files looks when you print it (see "Print a List of Files" earlier in this chapter).

To format columns:

1. **Right-click the title of the column that you want to format.**

   A menu appears.

2. **Choose Format Columns.**

   The Format Columns dialog box appears (see Figure 21-3). The name of the column that you right-clicked appears in the Format text box.

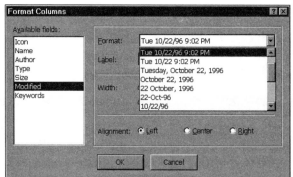

Figure 21-3:
The Format
Columns
dialog box.

3. **From the Format menu, choose the format that you want to use.**

   You have to choose a format from the list; you can't make up your own format.

4. **Click OK.**

After you format a column in an Outlook Folder view, the format remains until you change views. Even if you switch to another folder, the next time you look at the folder that you formatted, it will have the formatting that you selected. When you change views, Outlook asks whether you want to save the view the way that you formatted it (see Chapter 5 for more on views).

Create Grouped Views

You can group items in all Outlook modules; Folder views are no exception. The principles are the same throughout Outlook. A grouped view is really a collapsing outline of the items that you're looking at. You choose which column in the list you want to group everything by. After you create a grouped view, the items in the view are bunched up with other items of the same type. It's useful to group files by author, for example, or by the name of the program that created them, or both.

To group views:

1. **Click the Group By Box button in the toolbar.**

   This button in the toolbar makes the Group By box appear (see Figure 21-4). The Group By box is the spot where you drag a column heading to group the list by the information in the heading.

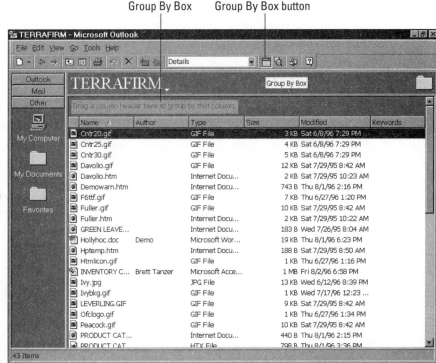

Figure 21-4: Drag column headings to the Group By box to create grouped views of your files.

2. **Drag to the Group By Box the header of the column that contains the data you want to group by.**

   The name of the field that you're grouping by will be in the Group By Box rather than in the heading row, where it began. You can group by more than one field, if you want — just drag a second field up to the right of the Group By box (see Figure 21-5). Outlook won't let you group certain fields, such as Date Modified. If you try to group by a field that Outlook won't group a dialog box appears saying "You cannot group items by this field."

Some fields have to be filled in when you create the document. The Category and Author fields in a Word document, for example, are created by choosing File⇨Properties from the Word menu when you're creating or editing the document.

Display Office 97 Document Comments

Microsoft Office documents have a Properties command that allows you to assign comments to your documents. You can display your comments about each document within your list of files, making it easier to remember details about each document.

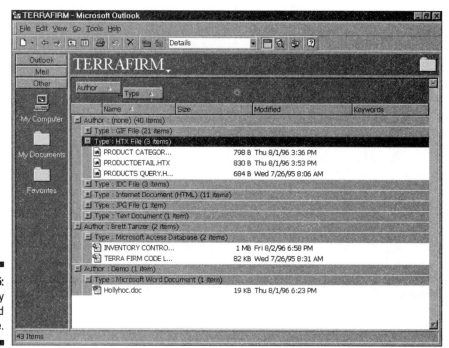

Figure 21-5:
Grouping by
Author and
Type.

1. **Choose View➪Field Chooser.**

   The Field Chooser dialog box appears (see Figure 21-6). You can also right-click the heading of any column and choose Field Chooser from the menu.

2. **Choose All File Fields in Folder from the Field Chooser menu.**

   If you created custom fields when you created the documents, the fields appear in the Fields box; if not, the box is empty.

3. **Drag the field that you want to display up to the header area next to the other headers.**

   A pair of red arrows appears above and below the borders between headings to show where your custom field will appear when you drop it off.

4. **Click the Close button in the top-right corner of the Field Chooser dialog box.**

   Your list appears, with a file containing your custom fields (see Figure 21-7).

As you can do with all the other fields on-screen, you can use the information in the comments field to group or sort the view. You can also display the name of the author, keywords, and any other document properties in the file list.

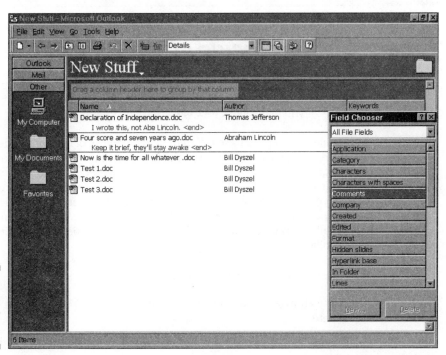

Figure 21-6:
The Field
Chooser
dialog box.

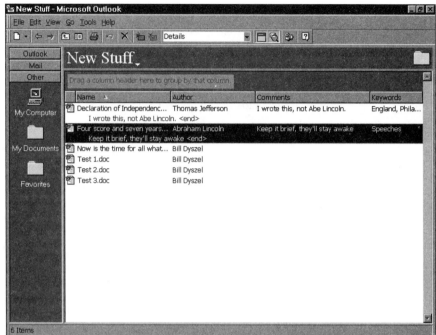

Figure 21-7:
Your list in
Folder view.

Create Custom Views of Each Folder

When you customize your view of a folder in Outlook, the changes apply only to that folder. Each view applies to a single folder. You can copy a view to apply to all folders, if you really like a new view that you create.

Why would you want to have different kinds of views of different folders? You may need to organize different types of files different ways. A list of invoices, for example, is more useful if you organize it by client and date, so you know who owes you what and how long they've owed it. A list of expense reports is more useful if you organize it according to what department created it and what project the expenses are related to. The number of ways that you can organize files in Outlook is great; mathematicians say that it's more than a zillion. I think it's two zillion.

To create custom views of each folder:

1. Make changes in the view of a folder by rearranging any item or adding a field.

Any of the changes that I describe in the preceding paragraph will fill the bill.

2. Choose any other view from the Current View menu in the toolbar.

The Save View Settings dialog box appears (see Figure 21-8).

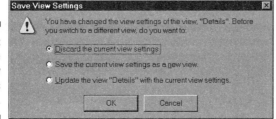

3. Choose Save the Current View Settings As a New View and click OK.

The Copy View dialog box appears.

4. Type a name for the new view in the Copy View dialog box.

Choose a name that will help you remember what kind of view it is, such as By Zodiac.

5. Choose This Folder, Visible Only to Me.

If you want this view to apply to other folders, choose All File Folders.

6. Click OK.

Now the view that you created will be available any time you view this folder. You can choose the view from the Current View menu in the toolbar, or you can choose View⇨Current View⇨*Name of View*.

Save Different Views of Each Folder

As mentioned previously, the views that you use for one folder don't have to be the views that you use for another. You may want to look at different collections of files in completely different ways. The folder in Figure 21-9 is grouped by author.

The folder in Figure 21-10 is sorted by date. If I switch between the two folders, I'll see each in its own type of view.

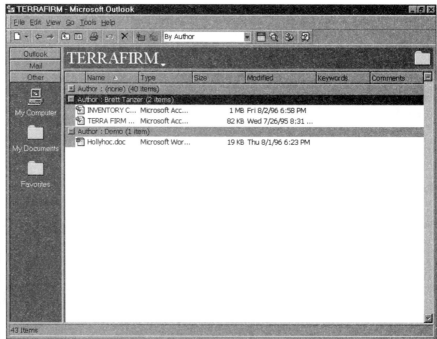

Figure 21-9:
Looking at a
folder in By
Author view.

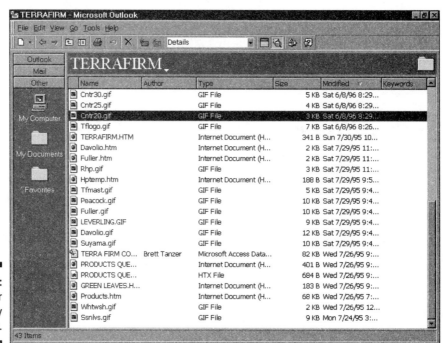

Figure 21-10:
A folder
sorted By
Date.

Create Views Based on Document Properties

As noted previously, Office property fields such as Comments or Keywords work just like other fields. You can group or sort on a document property, provided that the program you used to create the type of file that you're looking at can also use property fields. Some programs can't; Office 97 programs can. Figure 21-11 shows a folder sorted by two property fields, By Category By Author. (See Chapter 5 for more about views.)

To add or change what shows in the Comments, Keywords, or other document property fields, open your document in the Office application that you used to create it, choose File⇨Properties, then fill in the blanks.

Sort, Group, and View by Predefined Criteria

You can see many kinds of information about a file in an Outlook File view. You can see the names of the fields that are available by scrolling through the Field Chooser dialog box (see Figure 21-12).

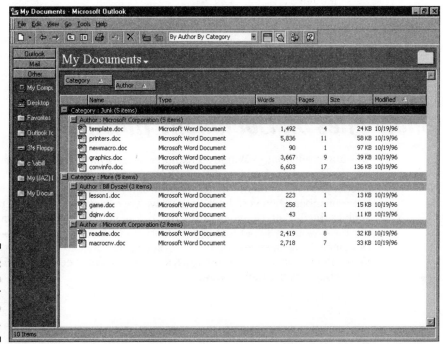

Figure 21-11:
You can
create your
own fields to
sort by.

Figure 21-12:
Choose from
all available
fields in the
Field
Chooser.

The criteria include:

Name	Template
Author	Words
Type	Lines
Size	Paragraphs
Modified	Pages
Keywords	Last Date Printed
Subject	Notes
Title	Comments

Show Files on Document Timeline

Talk about different — Windows Explorer doesn't have anything that even looks like the Document Timeline view in Outlook. It's useful to be able to see your documents in Document Timeline view when you can't remember what you did but remember when you did it. Some days are easier than others to remember, such as the day after payday or the day before you leave on vacation. If you're like me — you get 80 percent of your work done on those two days — the Document Timeline view will help you keep track. Just choose View⇨Current View⇨Document Timeline and you'll see what I mean. See Chapter 5 for more on the Document Timeline view.

Chapter 22

Let's Go Surfin' Now: Ten Ways to Use Outlook with the Internet

● ●

In This Chapter

▶ Use the Favorites folder

▶ Store a contact's Web pages

▶ Send Internet e-mail

▶ Receive Internet e-mail

▶ Include Internet hotlinks in e-mail messages

▶ Save Internet e-mail addresses in your Address Book

▶ Drag scraps of text and graphics from a Web page to an Outlook item

▶ Download new Outlook forms from the Internet

▶ Get help on the Web

● ●

*E*veryone wants to surf the Net these days, or pull the strands on the Web. Outlook and the Internet work together just fine. Following are just some of the ways Outlook and the Internet can interact.

Use the Favorites Folder

When you install Outlook, the Favorites folder automatically turns up in the Other group in the Outlook Bar. The Favorites folder is full of shortcuts to all the Web pages that you added to your favorite places section of Microsoft Internet Explorer.

To see a Web page that's listed in your Favorites folder (assuming you've entered some favorites there), all you have to do is double-click the name of the page. Your Web browser automatically opens, dials, and finds that page. If you run across any other pages that you want to keep track of while you're surfing the Web, choose Favorites⇨Add to Favorites in Internet Explorer. If you don't use Internet Explorer, this feature won't be very useful, but if you do use Internet Explorer you can get to your favorite Web pages a bit faster through Outlook.

Store a Contact's Web Pages

Every Contact record has a field in which you can store the address of the person's Web page, along with all other vital information about that person. That way, you don't have to remember that Jack's Web page is called `http://www.wherever.net/wiseguys/jackwalters.htm`.

Just look up Jack in your Contact list and choose Contact⇨Explore Web Page.

Send Internet E-Mail

To send e-mail to someone on the Internet, just type that person's Internet e-mail address in the To box of your message. If the person is already entered in your Contact list, just drag his or her Address Card to the Inbox icon.

Receive Internet E-Mail

You don't have to do anything to receive Internet e-mail; it comes to you. If you use an online service such as CompuServe or The Microsoft Network for your e-mail, you need to check for mail periodically by pressing the F5 key.

Include Internet Hotlinks in E-Mail Messages

You can use Word 97 as your e-mail editor. If you do, you can create links between one Word document and any other Office 97 document by clicking the Insert Hyperlink button in the toolbar and filling in the Insert Hyperlink dialog box. If you want to create a link to a particular bookmark in a Word document, choose the name of the bookmark in the Insert Hyperlink dialog box.

Include Internet Hotlinks in Any Outlook Item (Except Notes)

As soon as you type **http://**, any Office 97 application — including Outlook — recognizes that text as the beginning of an address for a Web page. If you type the address of a Web page in the text box of any Outlook item, the address immediately changes to blue underlined text. If you click that text, your Web browser launches and shows you the corresponding page.

Save Internet E-Mail Addresses in Your Address Book

A great deal of mail is flying around the Internet, some of it useful and lots of it junk. You'll want to ignore the junk, but now and then, you'll want to save an address for future use. The easiest way is to drag the message to the Contacts icon and have Outlook create a new contact.

Sometimes, though, you don't want to clutter your Contact list with addresses that you got from Internet junk mail. If you open the message and right-click the From line, a menu appears. To save just the address, choose Enter in Personal Address Book. That way, the address of the person who sent you the message is saved without adding anything to your Contact list.

Drag Scraps of Text from a Web Page

I often cull through hundreds of pages of junk on the Web, only to find a single sentence that I want to save. I don't want to save the entire page, and I surely don't want to try to surf my way back to the same place in the same page again; I probably won't remember how I got there in the first place.

I like to save small scraps of text from the Web by selecting the text with my mouse and then dragging the text to the Notes icon in Outlook. I end up saving exactly the text that I want — no more.

Download New Outlook Forms from the Internet

Microsoft has many extra goodies for Office 97 applications available on the World Wide Web. All you have to do is choose Help⇨Microsoft on the Web⇨Free Stuff and cruise around until you find what you want.

Get Help on the Web

You can also find a great deal of free support for all Office 97 applications on the Web. Just choose Help⇨Microsoft on the Web⇨Online Support.

Chapter 23

Ten Things You Can't Do with Outlook

*M*aybe I sound crabby listing the things that Outlook can't do, considering all the things that it *can* do. But it takes only a few minutes to find out something that a program can do, and you can spend all day trying to figure out something that a program can't do. There are easily more than ten things that Outlook can't do; this chapter lists just the first big ones that I've run into.

The Top Ten List

Bear in mind that Outlook doesn't do these ten things when you take it out of the box. Because Outlook can be reprogrammed with the Visual Basic programming language, a clever programmer could make Outlook do many of these things. But Outlook doesn't do these things when you first get it.

Customize the toolbar

You can customize the toolbar in all the other Office 97 applications, but not in Outlook. That toolbar is fixed; you can only turn it on or off. I prefer to leave it on, because the tools in the Outlook toolbar make the program so much easier to use and get around in.

Use Outlook categories in a Word 97 Mail Merge

You can use any of several dozen of the fields from your Outlook Contacts module, but not the Categories field — a very unfortunate oversight. If you have a 1,500-name Contact list, and you want to send different mailings to different groups of a few hundred people each, you have to copy the Contact records to separate folders and tell Word to merge from them, rather than use the Word Query feature to address different mailings to people in different categories. Maybe Microsoft will fix that situation in the next version.

Use Outlook custom fields in a Word 97 Mail Merge

An even better idea than being able to use the Categories field would have been to allow you to use your own custom fields as merge fields in Word. No dice.

Use Word custom fields in Outlook views

When I'm looking at a list of documents in the My Computer section of Outlook, I can set up a view to include all kinds of items about the documents if they were created in Office, such as the number of pages in the document, name of client, and so on (if I've entered that information in the Properties section of Word or another Office program). If I create a custom field in the Properties section, though, that custom field doesn't show up in the Outlook Field Chooser, so I can't add it to the view.

Make Outlook start other programs

I wish that I could make Outlook start my checkbook program once a month to remind me to pay the bills or balance the checkbook or automatically open the Excel spreadsheet that I use every day. Sorry — no can do.

Display parts of different modules in the same view

I'm glad that I can see the Calendar and the Tasks list at the same time, but sometimes, I'd like to see the Calendar and the Phone Book side by side and save that as a view. No luck.

Save the Folder List in a custom view

Sometimes the Folder List is essential, such as when you're using Outlook to move or copy files. Sometimes the Folder List is useless, such as when you're viewing the Calendar. I wish that I could save certain views that include the Folder List and save other views that exclude it. I'll have to keep waiting.

Embed pictures in notes

You can copy and paste a picture, file, or other item into the text box at the bottom of any item when you open the item's form. You can paste a photo of a person in the text box of the person's Contact record, for example. But those little yellow sticky notes don't let you do that; they accept only text.

Automatically Journal all contact stuff

You can open the Options dialog box and check off all the names of contacts you want to record, but you can't click a single button that checks 'em all. When you add new contacts, you have to be sure to check the Journal page box titled Automatically Record Journal Entries for This Contact. Otherwise, that contact's transactions won't be recorded.

Calculate expenses with Journal Phone Call entries

You can keep track of how much time you spend talking to any person, but you can't calculate the total call time or total call cost for billing purposes.

Cross-reference items to jump to different modules

You can include a Contact record in a Journal Entry, for example, but when you double-click the icon for the record in the Journal, Outlook only opens that person's record; it doesn't jump to the Contacts module. If someone from XYX Co. called, and you want to look at the names of your other contacts from that company, you have to switch from the Journal module to the Contacts module and search for the names you want.

Ten More Things Outlook Can't Do for You

Outlook is also deficient in some other ways, though you may prefer to do these things for yourself, anyway.

Outlook can't

- Give you washboard abs
- Dance the Macarena
- Shout out stains
- Make you as rich as Bill Gates
- Buy you a Mercedes-Benz
- Sing like Janis Joplin
- Blame it on the bossa nova
- Play the accordion (thank heavens!)
- Give you a tattoo
- Fly you to the moon

Oh, well. At least you can save time and work more smoothly with all the things Outlook *can* do for you.

Chapter 24

Ten Things You Can Do Once You're Comfy

In This Chapter

▶ Add a group to the Outlook Bar

▶ Rename a group in the Outlook Bar

▶ Delete a group from the Outlook Bar

▶ Rename an icon in the Outlook Bar

▶ Select merge records by Outlook fields

▶ Add a photo to a contact item

▶ Select dates as a group

▶ Sign out with Auto Signature

▶ Change your Office Assistant

▶ Create your own type of Outlook field

I show you only the tip of the iceberg in this book in terms of the things you can do with Outlook. It's hard to say how much more you'll be able to do with Outlook, Exchange Server, and all the other powerful technology that will be associated with Outlook as time goes by.

You can't do much to really mess up Outlook, so feel free to experiment. Add new fields, new views, new icons — go wild. This chapter describes a few things to try.

Add a Group to the Outlook Bar

The Outlook Bar starts with three groups, but it doesn't have to stay that way. You can add groups, rename groups, or delete the existing groups.

To add a group to the Outlook Bar, follow these steps:

1. **Right-click any of the group dividers.**

   A menu appears.

2. **Choose Add New Group.**

   A New Group divider appears at the bottom of the Outlook Bar. The name (New Group) is highlighted.

3. **Type a new name for the group.**

   You can leave the name New Group, if you want. You can even have several groups of the same name in the Outlook Bar.

Rename a Group in the Outlook Bar

You can name Outlook groups anything you want. You can change the names at the drop of a hat (well, actually at the click of a mouse).

To rename a group:

1. **Right-click the divider of the group that you want to rename.**

   The old name is highlighted.

2. **Type the new name.**

3. **Press Enter.**

   Your group has a new name.

Delete a Group from the Outlook Bar

Enough is enough, already! I think that the three groups that the Outlook Bar starts with are enough. You can delete any extra groups in a snap. Or is that a click?

To delete a group from the Outlook Bar:

1. **Right-click the divider of the group that you want to delete.**

   A menu appears.

2. **Choose Remove Group.**

   A dialog box appears, asking whether you're sure that you want to delete this fine group.

3. Click Yes.

Your excess group is gone for good. You can't undo this one.

Rename an Icon in the Outlook Bar

The names of the icons in the Outlook Bar are descriptive, but not personal. If you want to name the icons after movie stars or chemical elements, Outlook does nothing to stop you. I suggest that you leave the names of the original icons alone, however, to make running the program easy. But when you add icons, anything goes.

To rename an icon:

1. Right-click the icon that you want to rename.

A menu appears.

2. Choose Rename Shortcut.

The name of the icon is highlighted. (By the way, *Shortcut* is not a politically correct name. *The vertically challenged cut* is more palatable but harder to spell.)

3. Type a new name.

4. Press Enter.

Now your icon has a new stage name. Name your folder Norma Jean, but name the icon Marilyn.

Using Outlook Fields to Create Special Mailings

Suppose that you want to mail invitations to a party. If your Contact list includes people who live in another part of the country, you probably won't want to invite them, and they probably won't want to come (unless they're *very* good friends). To prevent hurt feelings, you may want to mail invitations only to the people who live in your state.

To select only those records you want from a merge list:

1. Choose Tools⇨Mail Merge after you set up your document in Word 97.

The Mail Merge Helper appears. (For more about setting up your Mail Merge document, see Chapter 18.)

2. Choose Query Options.

The Query Options dialog box appears.

3. Click the first field box and choose the field Home_State from the menu.

The Home_State field appears in the field box, and the words Equal to appear in the Comparison box.

4. Type the abbreviation for your state in the Compare To box.

You've now told Word to address invitations only to people in your state.

5. Click OK.

Now when you click the Merge button, the only names that appear in your form letter are those of people in your state. None of the other names will appear in this document. Each time you want to create a new Mail Merge document, you need to reset any query options you want.

Add a Photo to a Contact Item

Wouldn't it be great to see the face of the person you're looking up, as well as his or her name? It's easy.

To add a photo to a Contact item:

1. If you have the picture scanned into your computer already, open the picture in the program that you use to view it.

2. Select the picture.

3. Choose Edit⇨Copy and open the Contact record.

4. Click the text area at the bottom of the form and choose Edit⇨Paste.

The picture appears in the text area at the bottom of the record every time you open the item.

Select Dates as a Group

When you're viewing a range of dates, you don't have to limit yourself to fixed days, weeks, or months. Suppose that you need to look at a range of dates from September 25 to October 5. Click September 5; then hold down the Shift key and click October 5. All the dates in between are selected, and the dates appear in the Information Viewer.

Sign Out with Auto Signature

Many people like to end their messages with a tag that includes the name of their business, their address, their phone numbers, and even a little quote. The Auto Signature feature adds the text of your choice to the end of all your messages.

To use the Auto Signature feature:

1. **Choose Go⇨Inbox.**

   Your Message list appears.

2. **Choose Tools⇨Auto Signature.**

   The Auto Signature dialog box appears.

3. **Type the text that want to append to all your messages.**

   You can also click the Font and Paragraph buttons to format the text attractively.

4. **Click the check box titled Add This Signature to the End of New Messages.**

5. **Click OK.**

Now all your messages will end with your fabulous slogan.

Change Your Office Assistant

After seeing one those little Office Assistant critters for a while, you may want to switch to another one. Some folks like the Clipit character that Office 97 begins with, others prefer another character like Shakespeare or Einstein. There's no functional difference between the Office Assistant characters; you can choose whatever character you like.

Here's how to change your Office Assistant:

1. **Right-click the Office Assistant.**

   A menu appears.

2. **Select Choose Assistant.**

   The Office Assistant Gallery appears.

3. **Click Back or Next until the Office Assistant that you want to use appears.**

   Sorry, I'm not available in this version. Kind of you to ask, though.

4. **Click OK.**

In some cases, the Office Assistant complains that it can't find the files unless you insert the Office 97 CD-ROM. Put the CD-ROM in the drive and try again.

Create Your Own Type of Outlook Field

You can create your own fields in any Outlook module, form, or view. You can even define what type the field will be and how it will look.

To create your own type of Outlook field:

1. **Choose View⇨Field Chooser.**

   The Field Chooser appears. You can also open the Field Chooser by right-clicking the heading of a Table view or by choosing Field Chooser from the Form Design menu.

2. **Click New.**

   The New Field dialog box appears.

3. **Type the name of your new field in the Name box.**

4. **In the Type box, choose the type of field from which you want to make your new field.**

   The type box allows you to choose what kind of information will go in the field — text, time, or percentage. Feel free to experiment; it's easy to change the type later by using the Format⇨Fields command.

5. **In the Format list, choose the format of the information that you want to put in the field.**

   Some types of information have several possible formats. Dates, for example, could have the format 7/4/97, July 4, 1997, or Fri 7/4/97. Some types of information, such as plain text, have only one format.

6. **Click OK.**

   Your new field appears in the Field Chooser.

7. **Drag your new field to the position where you want it to appear.**

You have so many different ways to customize and use Outlook; I've only begun to scratch the surface. Feel free to experiment; there's really nothing you can break, and most features of Outlook are easiest to understand when you see them in action.

Index